THE ULTIMATE TRADING GUIDE

WILEY TRADING ADVANTAGE

The New Options Market, Fourth Edition / Max Ansbacher
Trading without Fear / Richard W. Arms, Jr.
Neural Network Time Series Forecasting of Financial Markets / E. Michael Azoff
Option Market Making / Alan J. Baird
Genetic Algorithms and Investment Strategies / Richard J. Bauer, Jr.
Technical Market Indicators / Richard J. Bauer, Jr. and Julie R. Dahlquist
Seasonality / Jake Bernstein
The Hedge Fund Edge / Mark Boucher
Encyclopedia of Chart Patterns / Thomas Bulkowski
Macro Trading and Investment Strategies / Gabriel Burstein
Beyond Technical Analysis / Tushar Chande
The New Technical Trader / Tushar Chande and Stanley S. Kroll
Trading the Plan / Robert Deel
New Market Timing Techniques / Thomas R. DeMark
The New Science of Technical Analysis / Thomas R. DeMark
Point and Figure Charting / Thomas J. Dorsey
Trading for a Living / Dr. Alexander Elder
Study Guide for Trading for a Living / Dr. Alexander Elder
The Day Trader's Manual / William F. Eng
The Options Course / George A. Fontanills
The Options Course Workbook / George A. Fontanills
Stock Index Futures & Options / Susan Abbott Gidel
Contrary Opinion / R. Earl Hadady
Technical Analysis of the Options Markets / Richard Hexton
Pattern, Price & Time / James A. Hyerczyk
Profits from Natural Resources / Roland A. Jansen
The Trading Game / Ryan Jones
Trading Systems & Methods, Third Edition / Perry Kaufman
Trading to Win / Ari Kiev, M.D.
The Intuitive Trader / Robert Koppel
Nonlinear Pricing / Christopher T. May
McMillan on Options / Lawrence G. McMillan
Trading on Expectations / Brendan Moynihan
Intermarket Technical Analysis / John J. Murphy
The Visual Investor / John J. Murphy
Beyond Candlesticks / Steve Nison
Cybernetic Trading Strategies / Murray A. Ruggiero, Jr.
The Option Advisor / Bernie G. Schaeffer
Fundamental Analysis / Jack Schwager
Study Guide to Accompany Fundamental Analysis / Jack Schwager
Managed Trading / Jack Schwager
The New Market Wizards / Jack Schwager
Technical Analysis / Jack Schwager
Study Guide to Accompany Technical Analysis / Jack Schwager
Schwager on Futures / Jack Schwager
Gaming the Market / Ronald B. Shelton
The Dynamic Option Selection System / Howard L. Simons
Option Strategies, 2nd Edition / Courtney Smith
Trader Vic II / Victor Sperandeo
Campaign Trading / John Sweeney
The Trader's Tax Survival Guide, Revised Edition / Ted Tesser
The Trader's Tax Solution / Ted Tesser
The Mathematics of Money Management / Ralph Vince
The New Money Management / Ralph Vince
Trading Applications of Japanese Candlestick Charting / Gary Wagner and Brad Matheny
Trading Chaos / Bill Williams
New Trading Dimensions / Bill Williams
Long-Term Secrets to Short-Term Trading / Larry Williams
Expert Trading Systems / John R. Wolberg
The Ultimate Trading Guide / John Hill, George Pruitt, Lundy Hill

THE ULTIMATE TRADING GUIDE

JOHN R. HILL
GEORGE PRUITT
LUNDY HILL

JOHN WILEY & SONS, INC.

New York • Chichester • Weinheim • Brisbane • Singapore • Toronto

This book is printed on acid-free paper. ∞

Charts by Q Charts and Omega Research

Published by John Wiley & Sons, Inc.

Published simultaneously in Canada.

This publication is designed to provide accurate and authoritative information in regard to the subject matter covered. It is sold with the understanding that the publisher is not engaged in rendering professional services. If professional advice or other expert assistance is required, the services of a competent professional person should be sought.

Library of Congress Cataloging-in-Publication Data:
Hill, John, 1926–
   The ultimate trading guide / John Hill, George Pruitt, Lundy Hill.
     p.   cm.—(Wiley trading advantage)
   Includes index.
   ISBN 0-471-38135-7 (cloth : alk. paper)
   1. Speculation. 2. Electronic trading of securities. 3. Options (Finance).
4. Futures. I.
Pruitt, George, 1967– II. Hill, Lundy, 1964– III. Title. IV. Series.
HG6015.H58 2000
332.64′2′0285—dc21

00-021217

Printed in the United States of America

10 9 8 7 6 5 4 3 2 1

This book is dedicated to Carol, my sweet wife and partner for these many years. She gave us three beautiful children and has stood by a trader with an addiction to trading. It is also dedicated to Dylan, Waverly, Emily, and Chelsea, our grand-children. May your spiritual and other journeys through life be as enjoyable and rewarding as mine have been and a sincere thank you for helping make it so.

J.H.

I would like to dedicate this book to my lovely wife, Leslie and our beautiful children Brandon and Emily.

G.P.

This book is dedicated to my mother and father who have taught me so much about life and the markets.

L.S.H.

CONTENTS

Preface   xi
Acknowledgments   xv
Introduction: The Search for Truth   1

Chapter 1
The Set-Ups or the Big Picture   8

Trading versus Investing   8
The Ultimate Timing Tool for All Markets   9
Technology Revolution   9
Stages of Market Action   10
How to Make Money with This Theory   19
Case Study of Trading Rules   22
To Trade or Not to Trade   25
Conclusion   26
Note   27

Chapter 2
Practical Applications of the Elliott Wave Theory   28

Targets for Major Movements   30
Corrective Waves or Phases   31
Case Study in Crude Oil   33
How to Trade A or ABC Corrections to a Thrust   34
Trading Plan   35
Other Works on Cycles   36
Summary   36

Chapter 3
Bar Charts and Their Forecasting Ability   37

How to Use Short-Term Patterns for Profit   39
Entry Techniques   43
System Development Based on Closing Prices   43
Three-Day Equilibrium Reverse   55
Pattern Gap   59
Hook Closing   60

Narrow Range Bars   64
Trading the Narrow Ranges   68
Trading the Wide Range Bar   68
Buy Zones   69
Stop Point   70
Taking Profits   71
Anticipation   71
Time Breakout Rule   72
Gap Higher/Low Openings   73

Chapter 4
Channel and Trendline Trading   76

Trend Lines and Parallel Movements   76
Trading the 0–2 Line   78
Trendline and Four-Close System (TL4C)   80
Trend Channel System   81

Chapter 5
Swing Trading   83

Swing Charts   83
Anticipation   86
Move Ending   87
Pullback Buys   87
Action and Reactions   88
Preliminary Demand   88
Time and Space   89
Sell Tops after a Trend Change   89
Three Bar Rallies   90
Holding Gain and Rally from Support   91
Setups for Trend Change   92
Trend Continuation   94
Three Drives to a Bottom   95
Support/Resistance Zones   95
Time and Price Projections   97
Trend   99
First Day in Rally   100

Chapter 6
Patterns   101

Opening Range Breakouts   102
Trend Up Confirmed   104
Spring Reversal Pattern   105

Upthrust Reversal Pattern   106
Yum-Yum Continuation Pattern   108
L Formation and Reverse L   109
Double Tops and Bottoms   110
Small Morning Tails   111
Clear Out Patterns   114
Overlapping and Non-Overlapping Bars   114
Two-Day Intersection   116
Channel Trading Systems   116
The Pullback   121
High of Low Bar for Buying/Low of High Bar for Selling   123
Three Bars Up/Down   124
Dynamite Triangle   125
Narrow Range/Wide Range   126
Two-Day Flip (2DF)   127
Tight Formation Breakout   128
The Importants of Exits   128
Use of Tools in Trading the S&Ps   134

Chapter 7
Drummond Geometry and the PLdot:
An Introduction to the Fundamentals   139

What is Drummond Geometry?   139
Conclusion   152

Chapter 8
Introduction to Mechanical Trading Systems   153

Why Use a Trading System?   155
Throw Those Ads Away   157
Should I Buy a Trading System?   159
Myths and Facts Concerning Trading Systems   160
Conclusion   163

Chapter 9
Where to Start   164

Hardware   164
Software   164
Data   166
Indicators   171
Five Approaches Used by the Best Trading Systems   185
Anatomy of a Trading System   185
Conclusion   206

Chapter 10
Historical Testing—A Blessing or a Curse   208

Simulated Analysis	208
Curve Fitting	209
Periodic Reoptimization—Does It Work?	214
Alternative to Optimization—Adaptive Parameters	216
You Design the Trading System, Not Your Computer	219
How to Evaluate Trading System Performance	220
How to Evaluate Trading System Portfolio Performance	224
Conclusion	226

Chapter 11
Money Management   228

Statistics—A Necessary Tool	229
Risk of Ruin	230
Capital Allocation Model	231
Compounding Returns	240
Placement of Protective Stops and Profit Targets	241
Conclusion	251

Chapter 12
Turnkey Systems and Portfolios   252

Portfolio 1 $10,000 Initial Capital	252
Portfolio 2 $25,000 Initial Capital	253
Portfolio 3 $50,000 Initial Capital	254
Portfolio 4 $100,000 Initial Capital	255
Portfolio 5 $300,000 Initial Capital	256
Conclusion	257

Chapter 13
Top Ten Systems of All Time   258

Bibliography	283
Appendix: Easy Language Source Code	285
Index	293

PREFACE

All speculative markets are governed by the law of supply and demand. Economics have proven that a fair market will determine the equilibrium point between the supply and demand of goods or services. This equilibrium point is the price where buyers and sellers agree on a value of the product being traded. The price of a stock or future is constantly changing. This price movement, also known as market action, is often represented by a simple bar chart that provides five different statistics for the market that it represents: open, high, low, close price, and the range of market movement for that day.

The bar chart represents the war that is fought between buyers and sellers (bulls and bears). If the market closes up from the open, the bulls have won. If just the opposite happens, then the bears are the victors. The range of the bar chart represents the battles that were fought during the day. If the price of a stock advances by one point, that stock was worth an extra point in price. A collection of the latest bar charts of a certain market gives a longer term view of the supply and demand for that underlying market. Market technicians believe that future prices of a stock or future can be determined by following the map of supply and demand that is portrayed by the bar chart. If one can master the art of proper chart interpretation and uncover the law of supply and demand, it can lead to profitable trading.

The first part of this book is dedicated to the art of deciphering the bar chart. The authors present several approaches to reading the charts that are based on years of watching the markets. We learn best when we concentrate on one idea at a time. Take any chart and mark specific entries under each idea presented. The ideas presented will not work in isolation, but will contribute to an overall trading plan. There are only three parts to a trading plan: entry, exit, and stop loss when the entry is wrong. Each one of these three parts has a basket of techniques. By learning these techniques, you will develop your own key indicators and eventually you'll have the ability to navigate any chart and recognize a potential edge that suits your trading style. You can develop an edge in the markets, but you will never master the monster.

The second part of this book is dedicated to the multimillion dollar industry of mechanical trading systems. The advent of the computer and inexpensive data has given everyone the ability to test trading ideas. Since most of the trading public are inexperienced traders, they have searched out the gurus and experts in trading systems. Many gurus and experts promise wealth to anybody wanting to trade stocks or futures. Unfortunately, many people followed their advice, purchased their trading systems, and failed miserably at trading. The large gap between what was promised and what was actually achieved has given this industry a bad name. Futures Truth Company has been testing and evaluating trading systems since 1985. This company was organized to provide hard cold facts on the many trading systems that are available to the public. Futures Truth began as a watchdog company, but over the years it has become a medium for good and honest trading ideas. A mechanical approach to the markets can be successful and this is backed up by the fact that approximately 80% of the $30 billion in the managed futures industry is traded by exact systematic methods.

Well over 80% of traders and speculators lose money. Computers have incorrectly been used to show hypothetical performance statistics. A trading system cannot be dreamed up by a computer; it must be based on a reasonable chart interpretation of supply and demand. The computer, with the benefit of hindsight, can be used to massage data to show any desired return. This is known as curve fitting. Such trading systems have no relationship to the real world, but do make impressive promotional pieces. That is why it is extremely important for a trader to understand the forces of supply and demand that operate in the markets. The purpose of this book is to show you how to make money in the markets by providing:

1. A framework for chart interpretation based on solid supply and demand characteristics of the charts . . . and how to use this knowledge for profit.
2. The education and tools necessary for developing trading systems that will work not only in hindsight but in the future.
3. Trading systems and money management schemes that can get a trader on the right track.

The ideas and trading tools presented are bound to initiate controversy, even provoke disagreement. This seems appropriate since no one trading tool is right for everyone. Take what is useful and discard the rest. Read and study the ideas with healthy skepticism. Test the ideas and patterns against your own experience. Our interest is not that you trust and/or believe the ideas and trading plans presented herein but that you trust your own approach to trading the markets.

DISCLAIMER

It should not be assumed that the methods, techniques, or indicators presented in this book will be profitable or that they will not result in losses. Past results are not necessarily indicative of future results. Examples in this book are for educational purposes only. This is not a solicitation of any order to buy or sell. The National Futures Association requires us to state that "Hypothetical or simulated performance results have certain inherent limitations. Unlike an actual performance record, simulated results do not represent actual trading, also, since the trades have not actually been executed, the results may have under- or overcompensated for the impact, if any, of certain market factors, such as lack of liquidity, simulated trading programs in general are also subject to the fact that they are designed with the benefit of hindsight. No representation is being made that any account will or is likely to achieve profits or losses similar to those shown."

JOHN HILL
GEORGE PRUITT
LUNDY HILL

ACKNOWLEDGMENTS

If it weren't for the following people I would have never entered into the trading business. I owe all of my success to the Hill family:

John Sr. and Carol

John Jr.

Holly and Chris Hurd

Lundy

John Fisher (who taught me how to program and test trading systems). Special thanks to Minty Norris and Donna Fiskeaux.

G.P.

THE
ULTIMATE
TRADING GUIDE

INTRODUCTION:
THE SEARCH FOR TRUTH

A young engineer with a wife, three kids, a big house mortgage, and $1,000 began his search for market truths in the late 1950s. At that time he was buying a few shares of Westinghouse and other stocks when one day someone mentioned 95% leverage and the futures market. Engineers generally believe they are smarter than most people because they took the toughest courses in college. This belief is far from true when it comes to successful investing, as this engineer found out the hard way. He took his $1,000 and ran it up to $18,000 within a 3-month time span by trading in and out of the sugar market. It should have been $200,000 according to his paper studies if it had been traded in a more logical manner. He then began his search for the next great market and someone mentioned soybeans and the impending drought in the Midwest. All $18,000 went into soybeans and he began calling the weather bureau every hour to get the latest forecast. Each time the market would move up he would buy more beans to the full extent of the margin available. Within a very short time the equity was up to $80,000 and he was long 200 contracts. On Friday, the weather reports were still predicting the big drought and he was proudly telling his wife that there was very little difference between $80,000 and 0 but this thing could turn into a million bucks as he smoked a big cigar and drank a glass of champagne. (Young corporate executives at that time could not think or hold effective meetings without a big cigar.) On Saturday night the Midwest had a weather phenomena that had not occurred in the last 100 years. A huge weather front from out of nowhere came through. By Monday morning instead of drought, the country was going to produce a record crop of beans. He ended up with $5,000 and was extremely lucky he did not lose his house and earnings for the next 10 years. Three things were apparent: There was a big element of stupidity, he had to get some "smarts," and if money could be made one time, it could be made again.

This started a search for knowledge. Weekends were spent in the Library of Congress in Washington and the New York Public Library looking for any and all publications on technical analysis. He would knock on the door of anyone who was a recognized authority. Many doors were closed, but a few were open. The bull markets and silver in the early 1970s enabled him to escape the corporate world. An avocation became a profession. He wrote the Paine Webber market letter on futures for a couple of years and wrote a couple of books on technical trading.

Futures Truth was started in the mid-1980s. The author was tired of buying worthless trading methodologies, spending many thousands of dollars in this search for knowledge. One individual copied a section of the author's earlier publication and sold it for $100. It was a good technical tool but not a system unto itself. Futures Truth Company was organized for the express purpose of showing the actual performance of systems after they were released for sale to the public. The Futures Truth publication is now sold around the world. It tracks performance of about 130 different methodologies. The performance of "rainbow merchants"—venders who sell products that have far more hype than value—is no longer shown. Private opinions are still available. Sadly enough, numerous phone calls are received from people who have purchased systems and traded them without full understanding. The systems generally cost much more than the initial outlay. You can easily lose up to $10,000 on a purchased system before you decide it is not for you. Futures Truth has been threatened with lawsuits many times. Futures Truth could always count on the big lawyers from New York and Chicago calling when particular vendors ran full-page ads in trade publications extolling the beautiful profits to be made by trading their methodologies. Futures Truth showed the hard cold facts regarding these systems. Futures Truth was sued once when we showed that a vendor's systems would have lost several million dollars if you had traded them after they were released for sale. (The Judge dismissed the suit.) Futures Truth has cramped the style of many rainbow merchants, but you never really put them out of business. After some time, the honest and reputable vendors came to Futures Truth and asked the publication to track their systems. The general public wants rainbows; they generally will not buy a system that shows realistic profits and draw downs. Honest vendors simply cannot compete on a short-term basis, however, long term they are the only survivors. Look at any publication that is five years old and see how many rainbow merchants are no longer around. This has been an interesting area. The methodology has to be revealed to Futures Truth for programming into their Excalibur Testing Software to track performance. Over the years, we have seen just about every imaginable approach to trading the markets. There is simply no Holy Grail or magic formula that will make you rich. If anything, the Holy Grail is the realization that it simply does not exist. There definitely are methodologies that will give you an edge in the markets and that is what this book is all about: How to recognize that edge and then how to exploit it to make money in the markets.

The advent of massive computer power in the early 1980s unleashed a powerful force for trading stocks and futures. Trading ideas,covering many years of data, can now be tested in a matter of minutes. Unfortunately, this has lead to statistical flukes in that systems may be manipulated to curve fit the systems to yield unbelievable returns. This is simply not the real world. Late night television has infomercials that promise great riches if you only follow the statistical curve-fitted system. This book will examine the fallacies of this approach and present an outline and a basket of trading ideas that should give you a statistical advantage in trading the markets.

Technical analysis is simply reviewing historical data in an effort to understand the forces of supply and demand. This effort can give you a slight edge in the markets that may lead to consistent an profitable trading results. Technical analysis is a viable and effective force in trading the markets.

This is a story of the very best trading system of all time. The author owns a farm in North Carolina. One day while trading, he noticed that when his cows moved to the north pasture, the price of wheat moved up. This did not attract too much attention on the first day, but this phenomenon seemed to occur on every occasion when the cows went to the north pasture. The excitement was hard to contain. The ultimate trading system had been found. A PhD agronomist was hired to study this strange situation and seek out the answers to this recurring event. This went on for several months. Finally, this high-priced employee was fired. Two high school kids were employed to drive the cows to the north pasture any time the author was long wheat.

Wild isn't it, but no more so than the pundits who claim that the position of Saturn in the universe directs the price of silver or that the seasonal pattern of British Pounds is to buy British Pounds on February 15 and sell on March 3 and you will be 80% correct.

A bar chart of price action reveals underlying supply/demand factors in the market. Some of you may be familiar with the Donchian breakout theory: Buy a four-week breakout to new highs in the market and sell a four-week breakout to new lows. This basic theory has consistently made money in the markets since it was first introduced several decades ago. The computer now allows testing of these various theories with great rapidity.

Timing is the essential ingredient for success in trading. Enormous financial rewards are available if the problem of timing is solved. This book is primarily concerned with the problem of timing. The book is 100% technical. Fundamentals are not covered. Proper chart interpretation will reveal all the fundamentals that you need to know. A chart represents all the bulls and bears in a given market. When you read a fundamentalist's summary of a given situation, you are always influenced by how the author slants the article. A chart will contain not only his viewpoint (providing he has money in the market), but all the other financial interests in the market.

By studying and applying the technical approach, you can cover all the active commodity markets or many stocks. This is not possible if you are a fundamentalist. There are simply too many variables, some of which will be in conflict.

Futures Truth Company has been testing and evaluating commodity and stock trading systems for over fifteen years. A systematic mechanical system can produce profits in trading over the long term. A large number of traders have the same belief as evidenced by the $30 billion being traded in managed futures using a systematic approach. Unfortunately 90% of traders lose money year after year in trading systems. It has been our task at Future Truth Company to show the hard, cold facts concerning trading systems. Some of the true reasons behind this devastating statistic will become apparent.

TRUTH 1: THE NAME OF THE GAME IS MONEY

The first and foremost thing to remember is that the name of the game is money—or at least the acquisition thereof. This is not only the name, but the object of the game. If you have any other purpose in mind, then the game and this book are not for you.

As in all good games there are two teams. There is the "we" team; naturally enough, that's our team. The "they" team can be a large syndicate (although this is seldom true now) or, more frequently, can be a group of unrelated professional traders acting in concert.

The object of the game is the acquisition of the available money that is used to fuel the game. The gambits, feints, and intricate plays used are endless and would cause Knute Rockne to turn green with envy.

Technique number one is the lie—or, to be charitable, the loose truth. Breathes there a man, woman, or child in the continental United States who is not familiar with the television picture of sad Farmer Brown holding a black ear of corn in his calloused hands? True, there was the corn blight of 1971 which saw corn rise from $1.40 per bushel to $1.67 per bushel for a 27¢ rise.

It looked for a while as though we would need ration cards to get corn, but surprise! The production was a full third over anything seen before in history and corn went down like the Titanic to the tune of 47¢ per bushel.

This is a principle as old as the hills, Brunswick and AMF, Inc. in the late 1950s and early 1960s rose from obscurity to the $60 to $70 area and then fell back to 6 for Brunswick and to 14 for AMF. For a period, it appeared that there would be a bowling alley for every third family in the world, including new nations.

Computers, too. Levin-Townsend at 1½ in 1965. Now the tom-toms are heard and it's 1968. The stock, LTX, is at 68½. There's a good story going in computer technology, but two years later in 1970, LTX's fortunes are at a low ebb. The stock later dropped to $3.00 per share—something to do with accounting procedures and dull pencils.

Of more recent vintage, take the example of current companies that have ".com" as part of their names. One such company is The Globe.com, Inc. Their stock was initially offered at around $25 in November, 1998. It immediately went to about $48.5 per share in a matter of days. Only, one year later the price has dropped to around $7 per share.

The point is that in all four cases there was a good story—lie—going: No corn. Everybody's bowling. Computer technology is the wave of the future. Buy anything with ".com." Maybe so, but the true facts were on the bar chart. The lesson to be learned here is to ignore all news, tips, and garbage that are constantly being put out by the "they" team in an effort to deceive us. The only thing that counts is the chart. That is fact. That is the only truth.

TRUTH 2: HE WHO KNOWS NOT WHAT HE RISKS, RISKS ALL

A second basic truth in trading is risk threshold. Broadly defined this means the amount of proof required before the individual investor will move—that is, act on the basis of his convictions. The author knows several very capable market technicians who couldn't reach a decision even if a gun were pointed at them. One, in particular, will cite a number of astute observations relative to a given situation and then when pressed for a hard buy-sell decision will cop out; by saying, "I don't know. Let's watch the pattern unfold." By the time the unfolding has taken place, the opportunity is lost.

What this means in practical terms is that by the time our market operator has gathered enough proof to make a decision to buy or sell, the move is probably over. The lesson here is that when you see that something should be done—do it! Don't wait! Don't even look back!

TRUTH 3: PERSONAL PSYCHOLOGICAL MAKEUP DETERMINES HOW YOU GO ABOUT MONEY MANAGEMENT AND RISK CONTROL

Remember that risk is absolutely the only thing you can control. Some traders risk 1% to 5% of total capital on a single trade whereas others will ride a given situation into the ground. If I may quote Larry Williams: "Rich people don't take big risks." You must do some clear hard-nosed thinking in this area before you begin trading. The idea that big losses only happen to the other fellow is simply not true if your guard is down. This is an area where positive thinking can and often is your downfall. The market simply does not care how positive you feel about a given stock or future. Stifle that ego and learn to love small losses. If you don't have small losses, it is positively guaranteed that you will have huge losses.

A person may have all of the finest technical tools available at his disposal and yet be unable to make money at this business because of his personal psychological makeup. If you are to be successful in this business, you must learn who you are—how you make decisions. Personal financial decisions can be highly emotional.

Take the case of a man shopping for a car. One person will decide on the spur of the moment to buy—another person will spend months studying designs, different makes, and so on, before deciding; and then he generally has to be pushed into making a decision. The same is true of traders. You have the person who shoots from the hip—buys on the first whim. Then 15 minutes later, he changes his mind. The other extreme is the person who studies a given situation and waits until everything falls into place, including the move. He will enter the market after it has made its move, and it is too late. One author calls this risk aversion. Failure to transform into action the results of good speculative thinking is as fatal to success as a habit of hastily making decisions on purely emotional impulse.

Successful trading is dependent on developing a sound trading strategy and the ability to stick with that strategy. Always, the speculator must be on guard to maintain mastery over himself.

Another question you should ask yourself is: Why am I trading stocks or commodities? Trading is certainly different from gambling and serves a very vital function in our economy. However, the players are not necessarily different. If you have not put forth time and study in trading, you have less chance than throwing dice. There the odds are fairly predictable. What is suggested is that you read books on gambling and the instinct of gamblers, to be sure you are not addicted to trying to "make the fast buck." Compulsive gamblers want to lose to punish themselves, so some psychologists say.

You must find out where you fit in and what your psychological makeup is if you want to be successful in this business. When you know your internal strengths and weaknesses, you can build on the strengths and work to overcome the weaknesses.

To sum up the psychological aspects of trading, know who you are and why you are trading. This combined with the technical knowledge in this book should put you on the road to success.

Conrad Leslie is one of the most respected grain statisticians in the country. At a conference, I gave him a copy of a small book I published in 1977. Several months later I visited with Conrad and asked him if he liked my book. Conrad remarked that it was the best book ever written about markets and I should not be selling it. He specifically mentioned that one of the ideas in the book had made him a considerable amount of money. I asked what page in the book the idea was on. Conrad said that it was a secret, but if I searched hard enough I would find it. If anyone reading this book has Conrad's *Great Fortune,* please remember your authors and tell us what page it is on.

Good Trading and remember: A speculator who dies rich dies before his time.

1

THE SET-UPS OR THE BIG PICTURE

Trading is easy. Only buy stocks that are going up. If they don't
go up, then don't buy them.

—Will Rogers

This chapter covers the *set-ups* for profitable trading—looking at the big
picture to determine where the market is in its overall development.
After this, technical tools are used to pick exact entry techniques, stop
loss protection in the event you are wrong, and likely targets for the
move. Just as is true for real estate, the most important factor in trading
is location, location, location. In addition, add timing, timing, and
timing. The set-up gives you an overall picture on where the market is
in its stage of development—a key factor when looking at short-term reversal
and continuation patterns. Ideally, you enter the market in the
zone that has the greatest probability of being a successful trade. Expressed
another way: Go long in the buy or support zones and short or
take profits in the sell or resistance zones. Ideas such as accumulation,
distribution, buy zones, and sell zones will be explained in this chapter.

TRADING VERSUS INVESTING

The first step in investing is to study the basic market fundamentals.
Economic factors may take a number of years to be reflected in the
market so a longer term view is important. However, trading involves a
study of the technical factors that govern short-term market movements
as well as the psychological makeup of the buyers and sellers in the
market. Trading involves more risk than long-term investing, but it also
offers opportunity for greater profits.

8

THE ULTIMATE TIMING TOOL FOR ALL MARKETS

Short-term trades that have gone sour or ones that I failed to get out of become my long-term investments. You may have heard the expression: "You know it has to go back up." Let me assure you that the market does not have to do anything. If I had to tell you the exact time and price that the market will turn back up, it would be when I abandon the trade and not one minute before. Learn this market principle well because it will save you many dollars. This principle has, in fact, made me many dollars. I have had investors call me hoping for some assurance that the particular market they are in will turn back up. My response is always the same, "Let me know when you liquidate because that is the time I will buy." If a trade is not acting right, get out. Don't stay with a position. Your capital will remain intact for another trade. Learn to love small losses.

TECHNOLOGY REVOLUTION

We occasionally hear people say: "Markets have changed since the technology revolution" or "If I get enough expensive software and computers tracking all these indicators, surely I can make money in these markets." Markets have always behaved in the same manner because human nature is constant. The same forces are still at work: fear and greed and supply and demand. Markets go through cycles. Nothing has changed. Two equity charts, one from today and one from 1950 with the prices removed would have similar characteristics. Markets in 1950 were just as volatile on a percentage basis as they are today.

The technology revolution has not made a difference in trading except execution cost and ease of order placement. Although information is available more rapidly, traders' win/loss ratio remains at around 80% losers/20% winners. One important big difference is the execution cost and ease of order placement. The execution cost can make a big difference in the bottom line. Ease of execution may actually hurt your bottom line. Having fast computers, expensive software, or working with the latest hot techniques such as "chaos" or "space age technology" will not necessarily add to your bottom line.

Many indicators that massage market data come up with indexes providing essentially the same information. They tell you the extent of an overbought/oversold situation. Indicators are usually lagging, thus, you enter the market late and exit late—a losing situation. Learn to read the forces at work by studying the charts and chart patterns.

The technology revolution has put a damper on the "Rainbow Merchants" who promise instant riches if you follow their formulas. The average stock owner now has the capability of checking the formulas with inexpensive software such as Omega®. However, the promise of instant wealth lures even the best of us. The Holy Grail simply does not exist. If it did someone would have taken all the "chips" and we would no longer have markets. You can achieve a technical edge by studying the charts, but you must deal with your own psychological makeup. Some people could not make money if you gave them next week's *Wall Street Journal*. Know who you are.

A successful trader must have knowledge. However, having knowledge does not automatically make you a successful trader. There is a giant chasm between knowledge and a successful trader. Few of us are able to make that leap and those that do must be on the alert or they will fall back into the abyss. One of the authors has been up and down the investment mountain so many times he has lost count. The last time he came down he made a promise that if he ever got even half way back up the mountain he was not coming back down. Incidentally, if enough of you buy this book, it will take that author out of the valley.

Money buys us freedom, nothing more and nothing less. Once you achieve a certain level of wealth, collecting additional "things" does not add to your happiness or give added freedom. If you collect too many things, you actually lose some freedom. Trading markets can be fun, but like a golf game, it may become an obsession.

STAGES OF MARKET ACTION

All speculative markets have the following basic movements:

1. Accumulation (congestion)—the bottom of a market.
2. Run up or thrust up.
3. Distribution (congestion)—the top of a market.
4. Run down or thrust down.

A fundamental understanding of these different stages of market action is critical if you are to be successful as a trader (Figure 1.1). About 85% of the time markets are in the congestion phase and you should trade for modest profits. Different phases of market action will be examined so that you will know the stage of the market, when to trade for quick profits during the congestion phase and when to hold on for the big run up or run down. First, examine the big picture and look for set-ups. This is normally done by studying the longer time frame bar charts. Next, fine tune your analysis by studying the shorter time frame charts for the final part of the picture. This will assist you in knowing where to enter the market, where to take profits, and most importantly, when to abandon ship when one is obviously on the wrong side of a

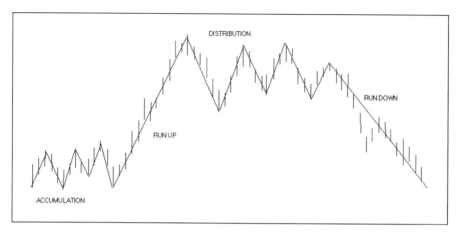

FIGURE 1.1   Four states of market action.

trade. By closely examining bar charts, you can see which direction the market is likely to take. Reading the news is generally dangerous. Read the charts instead and always think supply or demand or greed and fear. A chart reveals a number of things: When demand is greater than supply, the market goes up until the two are in balance. A chart also is an expression of greed and fear. Compare the two emotions and ask yourself which is the stronger one:

- *Greed:* "Gee, I wish I had bought more, this trade could have been worth a million bucks."
- *Fear:* "Oh brother, if this market goes down any more, I will lose everything I have."

Fear is a stronger emotion than greed and that is why markets fall faster than they go up.

Markets may enter reaccumulation and/or redistribution phases after a run up or run down. Newton's theory is at work here. A body in motion tends to remain in motion. Translated, a trend once started tends to continue with periodic periods of rest or digestion. The basic Wave Theory of 5 waves up or down (covered more extensively in Chapter 2), expands on this type of market action. That is the reason markets normally go out of a phase in the same direction as they entered. Until further evidence based on chart action suggests otherwise, you should trade in the direction of the market prior to its entry into congestion. Be alert for trend change after a second or third mark up/mark down in one direction.

These patterns may differ in specifics but repeat over and over again in all speculative markets. Some stocks remained locked in congestion for years. These are generally ones that simply have poor fundamentals. They are likely to remain there. Trade stocks that are moving.

Accumulation Set-Up

Phase 1 Selling Climax

The accumulation set up generally begins with a *selling climax* (Figure 1.2). This is the first sign of market selling exhaustion and the beginning of accumulation. A selling climax is characterized by several down bars of relatively wide ranges with the last bar having the biggest range with a big increase in volume.

A *sharp rally* follows the selling climax. This rally exceeds any previous rally in the prior down move in both time and distance. This is a requirement prior to the market entering into accumulation action. Unless you have this sharp rally, the question is still open regarding whether or not the downturn is over.

A *test of the low* after this sharp rally follows. This movement down may hold at a higher level or make a slightly lower bottom.

Phase 2 Zones of Support and Resistance

The market will now enter a stage where supply and demand are essentially equally balanced. Zones of support and resistance are established during this phase. A zone of support is in the range of the low bar of a selling climax or a subsequent low as shown in Figure 1.3. A zone of resistance is the exact opposite. If this is accumulation, volume will begin

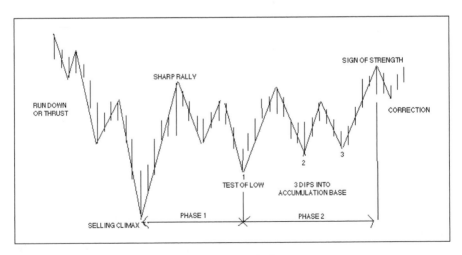

FIGURE 1.2 Accumulation stage.

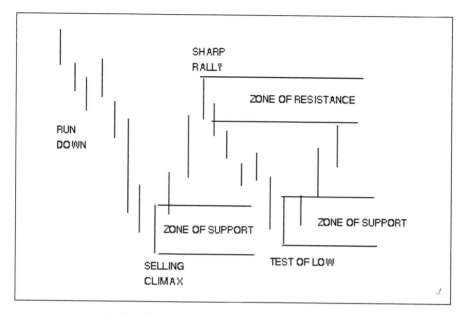

FIGURE 1.3 Zones of support and resistance.

to increase on the up days and be somewhat less on the down days. Toward the end of this phase, the market tops and bottoms may be higher than previous rallies and reactions.

Several attempts are made at new lows with significant rallies in between after the sharp rally. After two to three attempts to make new lows without success, be particularly alert for a wide range bar up. This type action indicates people are buying strongly each time the market approaches these lows. The third time signifies that the market has a high probability of a break out to the upside. A rallying tendency toward the end of the accumulation set-up is probable. A potential buying point is on the second or third dip into the accumulation zone.

A *sign of strength* occurs when the market exceeds one or two previous tops by a significant amount. A significant amount is defined as at least one average bar range above one or more previous tops. The magnitude of the top penetration of one or more prior market tops is indicative of accumulation set-up completion. A small penetration of prior tops with quick fall back implies some supply and a possible move back to the lower zone of support. Conversely, a significant penetration that has follow through implies demand. The market should hold above these prior tops for several bars for added confirmation. This indicates accumulation is over and the market may enter the run up phase.

After the sign of strength, markets generally move back to about the 50% correction point of the prior market swing. This is the beginning of the run up phase. Run up or run down is frequently referred to as *thrust*. Resist the urge to buy when the market is making new highs. Impulsive buyers who believe they will not be on board for the big move frequently do this. There are innumerable opportunities in other stocks that are in the accumulation phase in preparation for a breakout to the up side. Enter the market on your terms rather than chasing it. Chasing the markets and buying at tops often results in being stopped out when the market has its normal correction.

To summarize:

1. First rally after a selling climax rarely holds.
2. If any buys are made in the early accumulation set-up, small profit opportunities are likely until accumulation is complete.
3. The best profit opportunities are from buying toward the end of completion of the accumulation set-up.
4. The greatest profits are achieved during the run up and run down phases of the markets.

Take Profits

If the market is in obvious congestion, the profit-taking points are in the zone of resistance. Liquidation orders should be placed ahead of time as these zones are frequently entered and immediately drop away. The profit opportunity may quickly disappear if the liquidation order is not in the market. A bad trading habit is to wait and see how the market acts when it reaches the target or resistance zone. This may be done if the lower time frame is closely monitored.

Terminal Shakeout

A market may have a *terminal shakeout* at the end of the accumulation set-up (Figure 1.4). This is characterized by the market breaking below the entire range of accumulation with an increase volume. This is followed by an equally rapid recovery of the entire loss. It may then back off slightly, go dead and then take off with expanded volume and thrust. The terminal shakeout traps the crowd who sells new lows. These trades can quickly result in significant loss. This type action is also called a *V bottom*.

Distribution Set-Up

Phase 1 Buying Climax

The distribution set-up generally begins with a *buying climax* (Figure 1.5). This is the first sign of market buying exhaustion and the beginning

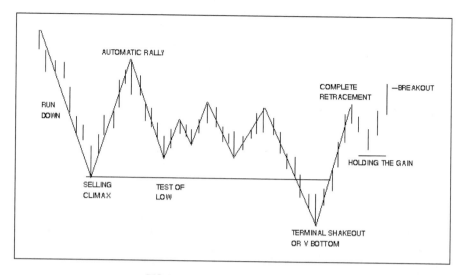

FIGURE 1.4   Terminal shakeout.

of distribution. A buying climax is characterized by several up bars of relatively wide ranges with the last bar having the biggest range with a big increase in volume.

A *sharp reaction* follows the buying climax. This reaction exceeds any previous reaction in the prior up move in both time and distance. This is a requirement prior to the market entering into distribution.

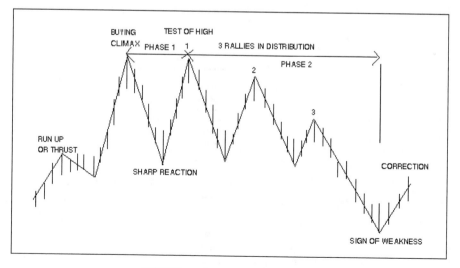

FIGURE 1.5   Distribution stage.

Unless you have this sharp reaction, the question is still open regarding whether or not the up move is over.

A *test of the high* after this sharp reaction follows. This movement up may hold at a lower level or make a slightly higher top.

Phase 2 Zones of Support and Resistance

The market will now enter a stage where supply and demand are essentially equally balanced. If this is distribution, the volume will begin to increase on the down bars and be somewhat less on the up bars. Toward the end of this phase, the tops and bottoms may be lower than previous rallies and reactions.

Several attempts are made at new highs with significant reactions after the sharp reaction. After two to three unsuccessful attempts to make new highs, be alert for a wide range bar down. This type action indicates aggressive selling each time the market approaches these highs. The third rally failure signifies that the market has a high probability of a break out to the downside. A potential selling point is on the second or third rally to the zone of resistance.

A *sign of weakness* occurs when the market falls below one or two previous bottoms by a significant amount. A significant amount is defined as at least one average bar range below two to three previous bottoms. The magnitude of penetration off one or more prior market bottoms is indicative of distribution set-up completion. A small penetration of prior bottoms followed by quick rallies implies demand and a possible move back to the higher resistance levels. Conversely, a significant penetration that follows through implies supply. Market should hold below these prior bottoms for several bars for added confirmation. This indicates the distribution stage is over and the market may enter the run down phase.

After the sign of weakness, markets generally move back to about the 50% correction point of the prior market swing. This is the beginning of the *run down phase*. You should resist the urge to buy when the market is making new lows. Impulsive sellers who believe they will not be on board for the big move frequently do this. There are innumerable opportunities in other stocks that are in the distribution phase in preparation for a breakout to the down side. Enter the market on your terms rather than chasing it. Chasing the markets and selling at bottoms often results in being stopped out when the market has its normal correction.

Summarizing:

1. The first reaction after a buying climax is generally followed by a significant rally. However, remember markets fall faster than they climb.

2. If any sells are made in the early distribution set-up, then small profits are likely until distribution is complete.

3. The best profit opportunities are selling toward the end of the accumulation set-up phase.

4. The greatest profits are achieved by trading the run up and run down phases of the markets.

Take Profits

If the market is in obvious distribution, the profit-taking points are in the zone of support. The zone of support is in the area around the prior bottoms of the congestion area. Liquidation orders should be placed ahead of time because these zones are frequently entered and immediately move away. If the liquidation order is not in the market, the profit opportunity may quickly disappear. A wait and see approach when markets enter the support zone has its hazards. Monitoring the lower time frame may be of assistance.

Reaccumulation

Trading the markets would be easy if you could assume that after a buying climax the market enters a distribution set-up and that the next move will be down. This is not reality. True, the market will enter congestion, but this area of congestion may be reaccumulation. A market may have a buying climax which signifies the run up is over. This does not mean that the market is going to go down. This is simply an area of digestion or resting while supply-and-demand forces decide whether the next move will be

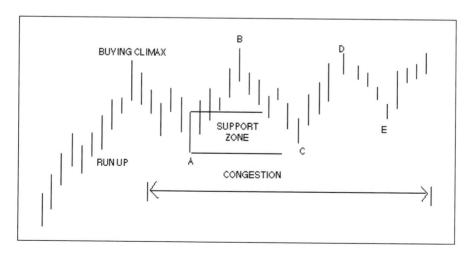

FIGURE 1.6 Reaccumulation.

up or down. Look for the market to have several rallies and reactions. After the second or third rally in this congestion, the range and location of the bars in the trading zone will frequently give an indication on direction of the next move. Markets generally move out of congestion in the same direction that they entered congestion. Figure 1.6 on page 17 shows a stock entering congestion after a buying climax. If you trade at all in this zone of congestion, buy dips and sell rallies until point E. Note that the lows are higher and the market is trading and holding for several bars near the top of the trading rage. This implies reaccumulation with another run up likely. The basic ideas are the same, only in reverse for redistribution.

Run Up and Run Down Stages

The *run up and run down* phases are the most profitable (Figure 1.7). However, these moves occur only about 15% of the time between the congestion zones. The parallel movement theory works extremely well in running markets. Fundamentally, this theory is that rallies and reactions will equal previous rallies and reactions. Buy on equal reaction points and take profits at equal movement rallies or thrusts. The run down phase is roughly the mirror image of the run up phase. Down markets generally fall quicker and deeper than up markets. Fear is a greater emotion than greed.

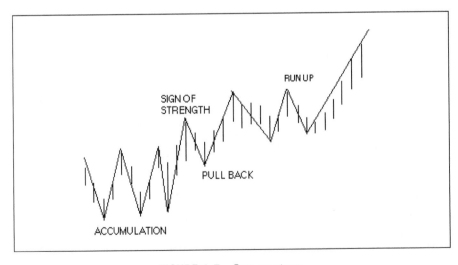

FIGURE 1.7   Run up stage.

Market Exhaustion

After an extended up move or even a move of three bars in one direction, the markets are often in their most vulnerable position and subject to a correction and may be the beginning of a new trend. A strong reversal bar at this point is the place to take a nibble on the short side. Get out of the position if the market fails to follow through in the next couple of days. A lower opening is the first sign of exhaustion and perhaps end of move.

Five ways to tell when an up market may be entering congestion:

1. Market has 2 wide-range bars down.
2. The market is unable to make a new high for 10 bars.
3. The market has non-overlapping days counter to the prevailing trend. A non-overlapping bar is when the high of a bar is less than the low of the top bar. This may occur three to four bars after the top bar.
4. The market has a sharp spring or upthrust after an extended run. A spring is when the market goes to a new low, finds no supply, then aggressively rallies. An upthrust is when the market goes to a new high, finds no demands, and falls rapidly. Chapter 6 discusses these concepts in more detail.
5. The market has a 75% retracement or greater of last thrust.

End of Move

The end of a price movement is signaled when the high price of a move cannot be exceeded by three attempts to breakthrough to new highs. This is usually preceded by shortening of the upward thrusts. This is presumptive evidence that the upward move is over either temporarily or permanently. This is a point to either take profits or move stops in tight.

HOW TO MAKE MONEY WITH THIS THEORY

The big question is how does one use the preceding information to make money in the markets. Before you are through with this book, this question will have some answers. The goal is for you to see and recognize the set-ups and patterns at the time they occur and not in hindsight. Anyone can see them after the fact. What follows is a method that might be used. Rules are given. Charts show patterns and places to use the rules for buy/sell entries.

Identify the congestion action as one of reaccumulation or redistribution by the direction of the last run up or run down. Markets generally

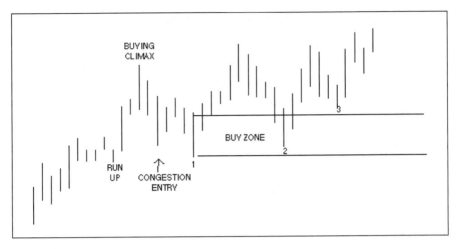

FIGURE 1.8   Reaccumulation.

go out of congestion in the same direction from which they entered. Assume this to be the case until the congestion pattern suggests otherwise.

Figure 1.8 shows a stock in reaccumulation. Buy zones (Figure 1.9)
may be defined as follows (sell zones are the opposite):

- At or below a 50% correction of the run up, or
- In the support zone.

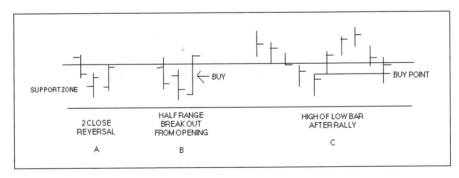

FIGURE 1.9   Buy entry patterns.

Long entry is made once the market enters the support zone by using the following rules:

- Closing above two or more prior closes with a wide range bar and expansion of volume. A wide range bar is one that is greater than the 10-day average range of the bars.
- Buy on a half range breakout from the opening. Compute 50% of the prior days range and add that to the opening.
- Buy on the second or third pullback to the support zone. Beware of doing this on the fourth pullback as markets usually break through on the fourth testing of an area.
- A close on day of entry above the prior day's high and opening is further confirmation of strength.
- A market unable to make a new high for 10 bars raises a red flag.
- Buy after a two to three bar movements into the support zone. You must be alert and have the ability to act quickly or the opportunity will be missed on the good trades. The bad trades will give you plenty of time to act. The time window for good trades is frequently very narrow.

Stop

Two stop points are suggested: An average range below the prior reaction point low, or an entry bar range below the low of entry bar. This stop is moved up as soon as some breathing room develops. Liquidate the position if market does not respond within about three bars. Do not wait for the stop to be hit.

Target

The target or profit objective shown in Figure 1.10 is:

- *Box target.* The width of the box of the accumulation pattern (B = A), or
- *Swing target.* 50% of the run-up movement or thrust added to the high of the move for first objective or 100% for second objective.

Once the market reaches the target zone, either liquidate at market or on evidence that supply is overcoming demand.

These targets will be used throughout this book. If in a position and the market enters the objective area, you should be alert to either take profits or at least tighten the stops.

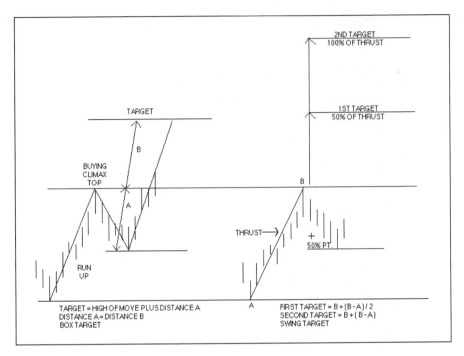

FIGURE 1.10   Targets for moves.

CASE STUDY OF TRADING RULES

Figure 1.11 is a chart of General Motors demonstrating the use of these rules for trading during a 12-month period (July 1998–July 1999). General Motors went from 61 down to 39, up to 78, and back down to 62. Buying and holding the stock would have produced a 5 point profit. Trading by the techniques, as outlined above, yielded a profit of around 30 to 45 points. Marked on Figure 1.11 are the principles used. Five trades were made during this time (Figure 1.12).

Trade One

The thrust that penetrated the support point at 58 turned the trend down. Congestion is forecast with an eventual breakout to the downside. Two rallies were made in this zone. A short position was taken at 60 on the second rally upon the appearance of the outside day (a day where the high and low is outside the range of the prior day). Initial stop was one entry day range day above the high of entry day. Profits were taken at the target of around 48 for a profit of about 12 points.

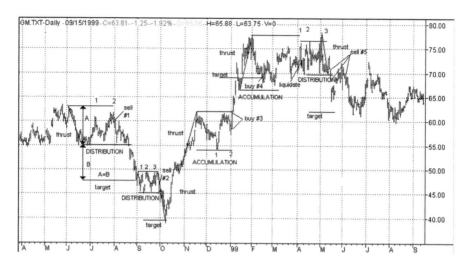

FIGURE 1.11 GM.TXT-Daily (September 15, 1999). Created with TradeStation 2000i by Omega Research © 1999.

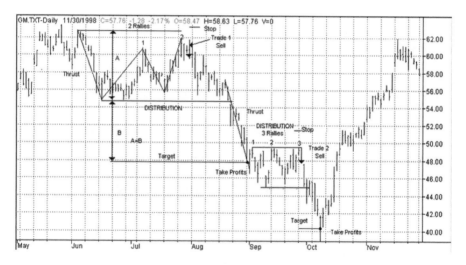

FIGURE 1.12 GM.TXT-Daily (November 30, 1998). Created with TradeStation 2000i by Omega Research © 1999.

Trade Two

The market had three rallies in this second zone of congestion. Short was taken on the wide range down bar after the third rally at 48. Profits were taken at the target for a profit of about 7.5 points. A wide range down bar is one where the range is greater than the average range and market closes below the opening and prior close.

Trade Three

Congestion did not take place again until the market reached 62 (Figure 1.13). A buy was made at either the 50% point of the correction or on the wide bar up from the 50% point. Profit taken at target of 9 to 13 points.

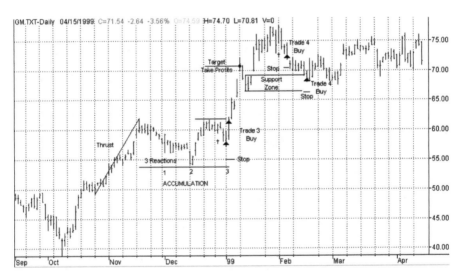

FIGURE 1.13 GM.TXT-Daily (April 15, 1999). Created with TradeStation 2000i by Omega Research © 1999.

Trade Four

This trade (Figure 1.14) was a loser if purchased at the 50% point of the run up. However, if bought at the high of the low bar of the prior thrust, it yielded a small profit. The position was liquidated when it was noted that the wide range down bar implied distribution and not accumulation. The profit at most was 4 points, loss may have been 3 points with a one range stop from point of entry.

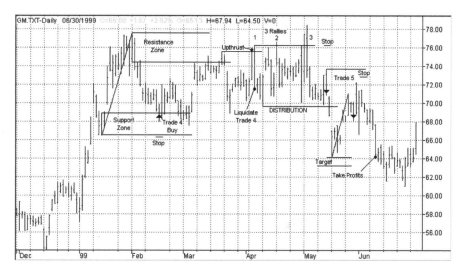

FIGURE 1.14 GM.TXT-Daily (June 30, 1999). Created with TradeStation 2000i by Omega Research © 1999.

Trade Five

The up thrust on the third rally with subsequent movement to the low of the range clearly defined this area as distribution. A short was made on one of the two pull backs. Note that short was made on a pullback or rally. The trade was liquidated at the 64 area for a profit of 5 to 7 points.

TO TRADE OR NOT TO TRADE

Your money is not at risk when it is not in the market. This style of trading limits exposure to around 10% to 15% of the time. You will be out of the market 85% to 90% of the time. A position may be held through an accumulation/distribution period. There is nothing wrong with this approach. However, by so doing, the potential exists for giving back a substantial amount of the profits. The pattern may be distribution rather than reaccumulation. You must examine many charts to prove to your satisfaction that this is a valid approach and is suitable to your style and comfort level of trading.

This approach involves some judgment. You should attempt to mechanize as many rules as possible to keep the judgment down to a minimum.

Trade the Markets That Are Moving

For active trading, you should look for stocks and/or futures that are moving or trending and not dull sideways moving equities. The definition of a moving equity is somewhat subjective. There are many sources that rank stocks that are out performing others and are moving. *Investors Business Daily* is a great source for finding stocks that are moving.

Moving equities might be vehicles that:

- Have expanded volatility.
- Have made new four-week highs.
- Stocks that are in the run up phase
- Slope of a 20-day moving average of closes is decidedly up/down.
- The leaders in their particular sector of the market.

CONCLUSION

Remember, the name of the game is to be profitable, not to catch 90% of every move. Learn to be satisfied with small chunks of the market. Enter the market on pattern set-ups and take profits at targets or at the first sign of supply overcoming demand.

These same principles work in any time frame, including day trading. There is something here for every time-frame trader. If your perspective is longer term, go to the weekly charts. Many false moves will be made, but that is what stops are for. The only way you will make money with trading is to look at numerous charts and mark your buy/sell, take profits, and stop loss points on them. This makes the idea yours rather than ours. You might then be successful in your trading. One of the most difficult things you will ever do is liquidate a position toward the end of the run up phase or at a buying climax. Develop the attitude of being a nice person: When everyone is wanting to buy, sell them some.

The General Motors study is only an example of how you build a trading system based on the supply/demand forces of the market. Mark up many charts with the things you see relating to supply/demand or buying and selling climaxes. Read *Popular Delusions and the Madness of Crowds* by Charles Mackay. Written 160 years ago, the principles are just as true today as in 1841. Don't trust your memory. Keep a log book on your trading activities. Write down what you see every day and frequently review your notes. Keep two charts: One on what you did, another one on what should have been done. Learn by comparing. Show the principles occurring at market turning points. Hindsight analysis is usually at least 90% correct. The goal is to see the patterns as they are taking place and take appropriate action.

NOTE

Some of the ideas regarding supply and demand are based on the pioneering studies of Wyckoff, Tubbs, and Larsen. Further studies by Wyckoff are available from the Stock Market Institute in Phoenix, Arizona and *Stocks and Commodities Magazine*. The Tubbs and Larsen courses came from a private collection.

2

PRACTICAL APPLICATIONS OF THE ELLIOTT WAVE THEORY

The Elliott wave theory has confused many traders. This chapter does not attempt to address the ambiguities in the theory. Instead, the theory is used in a viable trading plan that may lead to a successful trading approach. This is one of the best cycle theories there is because it allows for nonharmonic action.

There are many different approaches to speculating in the markets. Broadly speaking, they are broken down into technical and fundamental methods. Some technicians like to blend the two as an optimum way to approach a market. The fundamental approach involves counting bushels, acres, consuming units, earnings, book value, and so on. The technical approach analyzes past market movements and projects future actions. Some of the great masters in this field have been Schabacker, Gartley, Dow, Gann, Livermore, Wyckoff, and others, including R.N. Elliott. In 1939, Elliott prepared a series of articles describing the *Elliott Wave Principle*. This series of articles has long baffled the investment community. Most casual students of the market read them and quickly discard them. They are one of the most useful technical approaches to the market and the serious market student would do well to include them in his or her studies.

Can the Elliott wave theory be used to advantage in predicting price trends for profitable trading? The answer to that question is a guarded yes, provided you do not try to make an exact science of this theory. The Elliott wave theory allows for harmonic and nonharmonic movement. Many of the popular cycle theories use wave principles based on harmonics. You get into trouble when a nonharmonic movement comes along.

The following condensation of the Elliott wave theory reduces the concepts to a useful format:

1. Bull moves are composed of five waves, two of the waves are corrections. Bear moves are in the opposite direction. Odd waves are in the main direction. Even waves are against the main direction. Wave 2 corrects wave 1. Wave 2 corrects wave 4. After the fifth wave, the entire movement is subject to a correction. Plot your equity growth in trading. You will be amazed at how it conforms to the Elliott wave theory. How many times have you been in wave 5 of your equity growth, only to get careless in your trading? Your psychology at that moment is that trading is a money machine. You get careless and make trades you should not make. A movement does not have to correct after the fifth wave. Many will be as great as nine or higher. Elliott gets around this by calling such movements *extensions*.

   A wave is a movement from a chart low point to a high point or vice versa. They are subjective and you should not expect the exactness that Elliott demands. It simply is not there.

2. Termination of wave 4 is greater than the high of wave 1 (Figure 2.1). Elliott has very specific rules such as wave 3 has to be shorter in price length than waves 3 and 5. We have found that this is not necessarily true.

   These movements are broken into waves of one lower degree. What is a lower degree? That is a difficult question to answer. It is one of the reasons for the great difficulty is applying the theory. A suggestion is to look at the different time frames for the next lower degree. If Figure 2.1 is a daily bar chart, then look to the 30 minute point for the next lower degree. For instance, the next lower degree has five waves to complete wave 1 of the higher degree. It is identical to Figure 2.1. It is shown as Figure 2.2. The bars have been left out for simplicity.

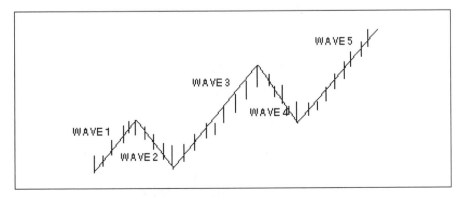

FIGURE 2.1   Elliott wave theory.

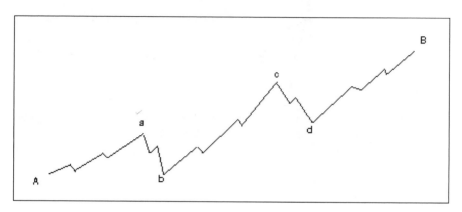

FIGURE 2.2   Elliott wave—lower degree.

TARGETS FOR MAJOR MOVEMENTS

The idea shown in Figure 2.3 is probably as good as any method for anticipating targets for waves three and five:

1. The target for wave 3 is 50% of the range of wave 1 added to the high of wave 1.
2. The target for wave 5 is 100% of the range of wave 1 added to the high of wave 1.

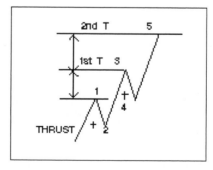

FIGURE 2.3   Wave targets. First target = (Thrust × 50%) + High at 1. Second target = (Thrust × 100%) + High at 1. If Wave 2 is a simple correction such as an A leg only, then Wave 4 will be complex and vice versa.

The practical use is to provide guidelines for overbought and over-sold conditions.

CORRECTIVE WAVES OR PHASES

Corrections generally take the form of three waves (ABC) but occasionally only consist of a single wave (A). The following three categories in Figure 2.4 show the types of corrections: A zigzag correction, Figure 2.4A, is the weakest type of correction and can lead to trend reversal. Note that the high of wave B is less than the high of wave 1 and the low of wave C is lower than the A wave low.

An irregular type has the high of B going above point 1 (Figure 2.4C). It is the strongest, particularly when the low of wave C terminates above the low of wave A.

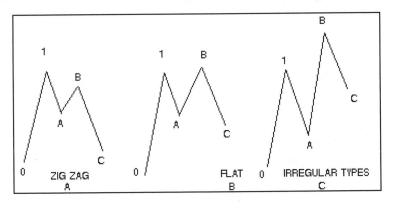

FIGURE 2.4   Types of counter waves or corrective phases.

Triangle Corrections

Triangle corrections are composed of a 5-point pattern, labeled as ABCDE, after an impulse move or thrust. The type and location of this pattern can often be revealing as to whether or not a trend reversal is taking place.

Figure 2.5A is a flat correction with all the action above the 50% point of the 0 to 1 thrust or run up wave. Strong demand for this stock appears each time the market approaches the 50% correction point at A,B,C,D, and E. Termination of wave E generally points the direction out of the correction or congestive phase. If wave E terminates above point C, be alert for an upside breakout. Figure 2.5B is a bearish looking

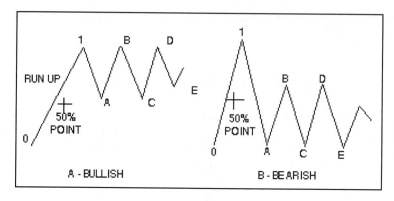

FIGURE 2.5 Triangle corrections.

corrective pattern because most action is below the 50% point. A down-side breakout is more likely.

A-Leg Corrections

The first correction wave or the A wave correction to a run up wave or thrust is composed of both time and space. The length and time of the A wave correction is of extreme importance in judging the nature of the entire corrective movement and the probabilities of a trend reversal.

Figure 2.6 demonstrates the use of the A-leg (or first counter wave against the run down wave) in judging the type of correction and the likely direction of the market when the correction is completed. Four

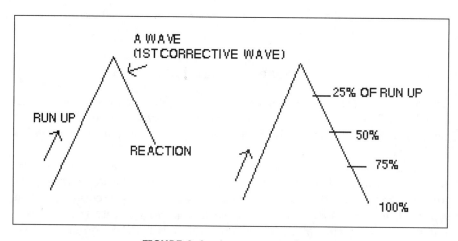

FIGURE 2.6 A wave correction.

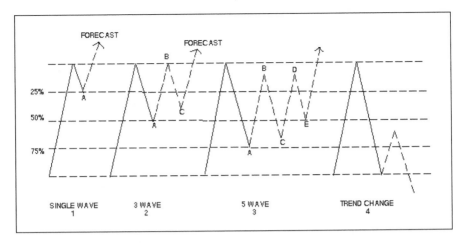

FIGURE 2.7   Forecast of corrections.

possible outcomes of market action are shown in Figure 2.7. If the magnitude of the A-leg rally is:

- 25%–35% reaction: Forecasts a single wave correction before continuation.
- 35%–50% reaction: Forecasts a 3 wave correction before continuation.
- 50%–75% reaction: Forecasts a 5 wave correction before continuation.
- Greater than 75% reaction: Often is a possible trend change.

This type action can lead to a trend reversal. This is supply and demand forces at work. A 75% reaction away from a point established a stronger point of resistance than does an anemic 25% reaction.

CASE STUDY IN CRUDE OIL

The crude oil chart, Figure 2.8, demonstrates the beautiful utility of trading the A-leg correction to a thrust in a strongly trending market. This is best traded by going to a lower time frame to aid in judging the termination of the A-leg and timing your market entry. A simple reversal bar after several bars against the trend would have been very profitable. A reversal bar is one that reverses the direction of the prior bar. A 1.0 range stop from the low (or high for sell) of the bar of entry is recommended. Nine out of 11 examples would have been successful on a short-term basis.

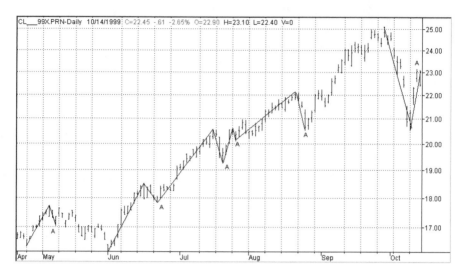

FIGURE 2.8 CL 99XPRN—Daily (October 14, 1999). Created with TradeStation 2000i by Omega Research © 1999.

Statistical studies on wave action show the following:

- A-leg or single wave movement only—32%.
- ABC or 3 wave movement—50%.
- ABCDE or 5 wave movement—14%.
- Greater than ABCDE—4%.

Only 18% of the waves exceed an ABC wave counter movement. The conclusion is obvious. Buy or sell after an ABC wave correction to a thrust. Only 18% of the time do markets go beyond the ABC correction.

HOW TO TRADE A OR ABC CORRECTIONS TO A THRUST

This is a useful tool in your bag of technical tools. Shortcomings are:

- Sometimes it is difficult to know which ABC to use.
- Corrections may go to the ABCDE variety.
- The thrust may be the termination of a move.

Enter the market on corrections rather than on breakouts as most breakouts fail. Buying a pivot point penetration or breakout requires a much larger stop to prevent loss than does buying on the corrections.

TRADING PLAN

Nothing is easy in this business but the following is one possible approach. The basic idea is to purchase a stock or commodity on the A-leg or C-leg correction to a demand thrust (or vice versa for shorts). Entry is made on a correction rather than chasing a running market. Three possible methods of exact entry are:

1. Enter a buy order at the 50% correction to the demand thrust, but never on the first bar in the correction.
2. Enter the market on the C-leg correction when the market shows evidence of supply exhaustion such as a narrow range period with market closing off the low. Buy an opening range breakout of 50% of the prior bar's range.
3. Enter the market when the lower time frame charts give a buy/sell signal and market is in buy/sell zone.

A stop loss order is entered at one average range below the low of the bar when purchase is made. The position is liquidated when market reaches the target. If the market fails to reach target, then liquidate the position on evidence of supply overcoming demand. If the A-leg goes to the 75% or lower after a buy at the 50% point, forget about profits. Scratch the trade or liquidate as close to break even as possible.

Figure 2.9 demonstrates these simple principles. Note that five waves to a top are marked on the chart. After a five wave movement to

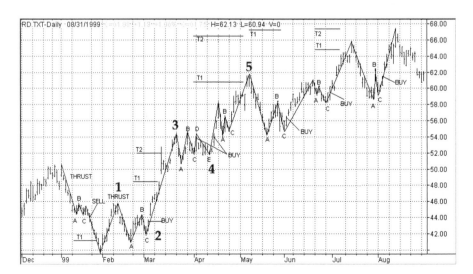

FIGURE 2.9 Royal Dutch Petroleum. Created with TradeStation 2000i by Omega Research © 1999.

a top, a correction is likely to occur, however, this action forecasts higher prices will be forthcoming. The basic idea is to buy after a sign of strength (thrust), but only on a reaction to a logical support point. Buy on temporary weakness and liquidate on strength.

OTHER WORKS ON CYCLES

In addition to Bob Prechter, Tom DeMark was one of the early technicians to recognize the value of Elliott's work. You might wish to take a look at his interpretation of this work (see bibliography). Tom has many excellent ideas in his books. They are not presented as trading systems. However, with a little imagination, many good trading systems can be developed. Others who have done excellent work on cycles include J.M. Hurst, Welles Wilder, and Walt Bressert (see bibliography). Walt was an old friend until I took him bear hunting when he visited me in North Carolina. We were in the deep underbrush when a bear startled us and we both dropped our guns and started running. Walt remarked that we had a problem in that we had to outrun the bear. I advised Walt that he had his facts incorrect. All I had to do was outrun him. The chase continued for some distance when I turned around to see Walt had stopped and had his head bowed in prayer. I was deeply impressed. I also noticed that the bear had stopped and assumed a prayerful position. I overheard the bear saying, "Oh Lord, thank you for this meal I am about to receive." Somehow, we both survived.

SUMMARY

An attempt has been made to show how to trade with the Elliott wave theory. Don't get hung-up on the many facts of Elliott. Put 10 Elliott students in a room with one chart and you are likely to get 10 different answers on where the wave stands. Bob Prechter Jr. and one of the authors spent an evening arguing this point and neither one of us convinced the other. Look at Bob's work. You may reach a different conclusion. A thrust is a very simple structure that is likely to have a correction. This chapter has attempted to provide you with some entry techniques on the corrections. After corrections, a market is likely to have another thrust. We have shown the likely targets for the next thrusts and where you should either take profits or at least tighten stops.

3

BAR CHARTS AND THEIR FORECASTING ABILITY

This chapter presents a road map for constructing and interpreting bar charts. How do you know where you are going if you do not know where you have been? Charts are only a history lesson. The technician attempts to take this history and build a viable trading plan. This chapter takes the basic bar chart formations and uses a computer to see if there is a trading edge from the many common patterns. Only the buy side is considered in the stock tables.

In studying market action, nothing is more fundamental than bar charts reflecting a history of past market action. There is, however, no life in the charts; they do not give you information about the psychology of investing. The charts come to life when past market action is used to project the future course of price movement. Bar charts are like a road map, showing you how to travel from one point to another. Bar charts depict the actions, emotions, and ideas of mass speculation.

All of nature is controlled by innate laws. There is also an inexorable law of price. We might use the medical profession to explain this. Starting with the human body and studying the needs of each function of the body, medicine built up data that became an action-reaction concept. we can apply the same thinking to price and market action. This is where a bar chart of past market action comes into play. Fluctuations in price movement lead to logical conclusions that these actions and reactions were caused by the psychology of the masses. The student of market action will find that a certain sequence of events on a bar chart will normally lead to a given response. Such actions occur with enough frequency that they suggest a law. It is not absolute because a person's mind cannot be reduced to an exact science. However, recognition of the probability of a market response places the student ahead of the vast majority of traders.

Speculation is anticipation. Market action discounts coming events before they happen. The function of price is to integrate supply-demand relationships.

Since the beginning of time, man has been largely controlled by fear and greed. When a student of market action allows these emotions to influence his or her market response, many opportunities in the market are lost. These two emotions must be resisted. Confidence and courage are required to overcome fear and greed. Courage is inborn. Confidence is gained by study, study, and more study.

One of the great little books on this subject was written by George Cole in 1936. The authors are indebted to this man and his work.

Figure 3.1A represents one day's price action. The horizontal bar to the left represents the opening and the bar to the right is the close. The dashed line is the 50% point on the day's price range. This one day's action tells you:

- The opening was above the halfway point and above the close.
- The close was in the lower part of the price range.

From these two factors you might conclude that the market should sell lower the next day, as the available evidence indicates a heavy market.

Figure 3.1B shows the same day; the previous day's action is also shown. We now know that the entire day's price action is above the previous day's action and, also, it closed above the previous day's range. These factors would be considered bullish and might warrant a purchase instead of a sell on a lower opening the next day.

In another example, suppose the action of the two days is as shown in Figure 3.1C. This indicates momentum building up for a down move, and it may be a candidate for a short sell, depending on other conditions.

This type of discussion could continue under various assumed conditions and with many days added. The main idea here is to encourage thinking about supply/demand and dominant force or trend.

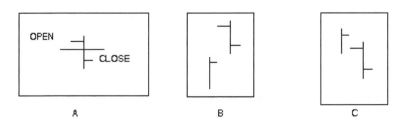

FIGURE 3.1   Daily bar chart analysis.

HOW TO USE SHORT-TERM PATTERNS FOR PROFIT

The primary key to successful use of single-day patterns is that they are only used when other market factors support the one bar indication of a movement. This simple idea will not work in isolation. That is why the big picture was presented first. To use these short-term patterns successfully, you must be cognizant of the overall market picture. Two basic ideas are suggested:

1. Trade only in the direction of the trend when the market is in the run up or run down stage.
2. When in congestion, buy when the market is in the support zone and sell when the market is in the resistance zone.

Remember that these short-term patterns are generally valid for no more than 3 to 5 bars. When trading with short-term patterns, it is wise to have a target and exit order in the market, unless, you are using this as an entry technique for a bigger movement. Otherwise, another reversal pattern may set up and quickly erase any profit that may have been taken.

Closing Price Graph

A closing price graph is very neces-sary in proper market analysis. Some market students feel this is the most revealing of all graphs. The closing price is the most impor-tant one of the day. This represents the final sentiment after the total day's activities. At a later time, a close becomes a support or resis-tance point. The more closing prices there are in a zone on the chart, the

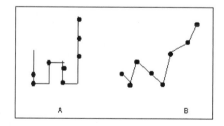

FIGURE 3.2   Closing price charts.

more important this level becomes as an area of support or resistance. There are two types as shown in Figure 3.2. In Figure 3.2A, a vertical line is continuous until a price closes in the opposite direction. Figure 3.2B plots each day's closing price on alternate vertical lines.

Pivot Points and Swings

A top pivot point is the highest price in a movement prior to penetration of the low of the top bar. A bottom pivot point is the lowest price in a movement prior to penetration of the high of the low bar. A top pivot

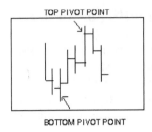
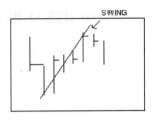

FIGURE 3.3   Pivot points and swings.

point becomes a resistance point. A bottom pivot point becomes a support point. The movement from one pivot point to the next is called a swing (Figure 3.3).

Trend Direction

Trend is up as long as new price highs and higher price lows are being made. It changes from up to down when the last low prior to the new high is broken (Figure 3.4).

FIGURE 3.4   Trend signals.

Price Closes

A number of closes in a relatively narrow range is a market that is in a state of equilibrium. Movement away from this band of closing prices represents disequilibrium with demand overcoming supply or vice versa. Patterns can be developed based on this idea. They can give a technical edge when trading with the trend. Caution must be exercised in using this pattern as an entry against the prevailing trend. Minimum risk is accomplished by taking action on pull backs after closes point the direction.

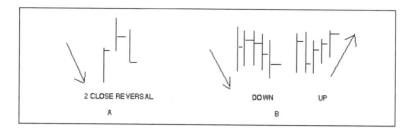

FIGURE 3.5 Close direction.

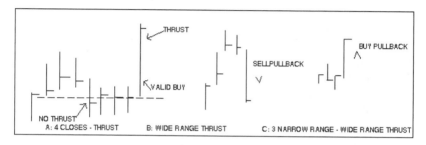

FIGURE 3.6 Tight closings followed by thrust.

Two-bar close reversal with widening spread is likely to signal a significant reversal if it is in the trend direction. Odds increase when the close is below the low of the previous bar (Figure 3.5).

When several closing prices occur together in a tight range, the latest closing price often points the direction of the move out of the state of equilibrium (Figure 3.6).

The first thrust out of a tight formation of several closes by a wide range bar generally points to the short-term direction of the market.

Figure 3.7 shows tails in close proximity on three price bars that overlap. The close each day is below the opening and mid-range. This is called a *tail*. Supply occurred each day after the market opened. This is a sign of distribution with a strong possibility of lower prices.

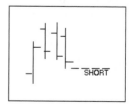

FIGURE 3.7 Tails—close < open.

Figure 3.8A shows a four-bar reversal that is not as strong an indicator of a reversal as the preceding examples. It may be just a one-bar correction.

Figure 3.8B is a weak appearing four-bar pattern. The first three bars show weakness. The fourth bar is a correction.

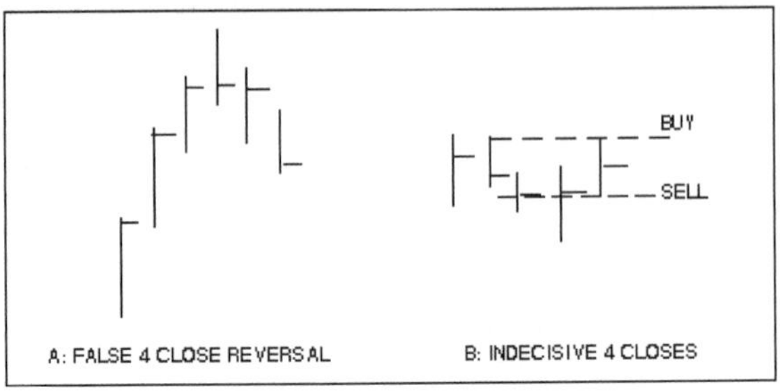

A: FALSE 4 CLOSE REVERSAL   B: INDECISIVE 4 CLOSES

FIGURE 3.8 Indecisive closes.

Closes with Non-Overlapping Bars

A still weaker pattern is the three-bar movement which includes a non-overlapping bar (NOL)—one where the high of the current bar is less than the low of the most recent pivot point high bar (Figure 3.9).

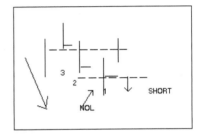

FIGURE 3.9 Non-overlapping bars.

Trend Direction

A price bar that reverses four prior closes may be a trend reversal. If the four closes are in close proximity and not all up, the shift is to down. If four prior closes are all up, the one-bar reverse may only be correcting an overbought condition, thus, the shift is to neutral (Figure 3.10).

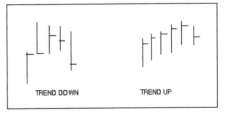

TREND DOWN   TREND UP

FIGURE 3.10 Trend direction.

Once the market reaches a target, profits may be protected by:

1. Liquidating at objective.
2. Carrying a stop under each bar's low by at least three ticks.
3. Carrying a stop one tick below a reaction equal to the preceding reaction.
4. Hold on to the position and wait for a four-bar close reversal before liquidating.

5. Liquidate on any three to four bar higher close.

6. Liquidate on pattern reversals in a lower time frame.

ENTRY TECHNIQUES

After a sign of strength enter the market by one of the signals shown in Figure 3.11:

- Buy on stop above three-bar high if this point is below the high of prior movement (Figure 3.11A).
- Buy on close of a pullback bar (Figure 3.11B).
- Buy on a 50% reaction after the sign of strength (Figure 3.11C).
- Buy on a 50% movement off the opening of the prior bars range once the market has a correction to the sign of strength (Figure 3.11D).

Another possibility is to buy on entry signals in a lower time frame once market corrects the thrust. For instance, if trading the daily bar, look for an entry pattern in the 30-minute bar.

Initial stop is below the four-bar low or one average bar range below low of entry bar. A potential loss of this magnitude is livable. Our inclination is never to let our trades get into deep water.

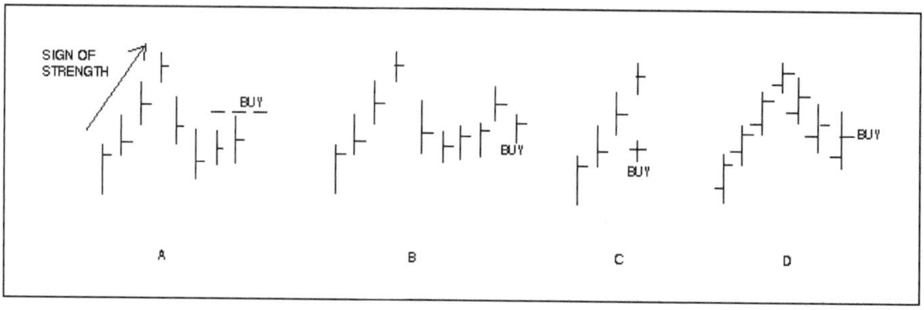

FIGURE 3.11 Entry points.

SYSTEM DEVELOPMENT BASED ON CLOSING PRICES

Successful trading systems can be developed by using the close patterns as an entry technique. The four prior closing prices are used to demonstrate the power of this formation (Figure 3.12). There is nothing sacred about four bars. The basic idea is that the range of the recent band of

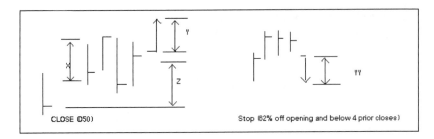

CLOSE (D50)   Stop (62% off opening and below 4 prior closes)

FIGURE 3.12   Four-close system.

closes is less than the average true range of 10 days. This is a form of narrow congestion. This particular pattern occurs about 15 to 25 times per year per market. A simple system to utilize the frequency of this formation use the following rules for the buy side (sell side is exactly opposite):

1. *Range.* The range of four closes is less than the 30-day average bar range.
2. *Trend.* The closing price of the prior day is greater than the closing price 50 days ago.
3. *Breakout.* The market must move 62% of the prior days range from the opening. This point must also be above the highest close of the prior four days.
4. *Liquidation.* Position is liquidated by a stop below any four prior closes but must trade 62% below the opening.

In Figure 3.12,

X = Range of last four days closing prices (less than 30-day average daily range);

Y = Open of day plus 62% of prior day's range;

Z = Close of prior day is greater than close 50 days ago;

YY = Open of day minus 62% of prior day's range;

Stop = maximum of open – 62% of prior day's range on any day after entry and four prior day's closes.

Table 3.1 on page 45 and Table 3.2 on page 46 demonstrate the effectiveness of these simple rules. Every market except two showed a profitable return in futures and all but one in stocks. This is not a viable trading system as the numbers do not make allowance for commission and slippage. It *could* be the basis for a successful trading system. A trading system is made up of three components: entry, stop loss, and

TABLE 3.1   Four Closes in Tight Range—Stocks

OPENING RANGE BREAKOUT—100 SHARES PER SIGNAL
TEST PERIOD 1/1/96–10/30/99
$0 ALLOWED FOR COMMISSION AND SLIPPAGE

Individual Stocks	Total PL ($)	Avg PL ($)/Yr	Max DrawDn ($)	Trds /Yr	Win%	TIM%	W:L
AT&T	764	199	1,011	8	41.9	18	1.5
Amazon	2,909	1,518	2,650	13	44	37	1.7
COMPAQ	1,013	264	927	9	48.6	21	1.8
Dell	3,378	881	728	9	61.1	37	5.3
General Elec	2,098	547	2,311	14	45.5	32	1.4
IBM	4,551	1,187	1,727	11	51.2	32	2.2
Coca Cola	72	19	1,408	10	52.5	23	1
Merk	(469)	(122)	1,639	10	28.2	24	0.9
Microsoft	2,281	595	859	12	53.2	32	2
Royal Dutch	61	16	1,291	8	46.7	23	1
Excite	1,792	935	1,344	10	50	28	3
Yahoo	5,322	2,777	4,890	12	39.1	35	2.1

Definitions: Total $PL = Total profit or loss; Max DrawDn = The highest down movement in equity from any new equity high; % TIM = Percent of time in the market; W:L = Total profit ($) divided by total loss ($).

Summary	Net PL ($)	Max DrawDn ($)	Return on $50,000*(%)
Average/Year	6,201		12.4
Full run total	23,772	6,404	

* $50,000 should be more than adequate to trade the 12 stocks in view of the infrequent trading and short time in the market.

exit (either through a profit objective or by a trailing stop). These three items must combine to be an effective method of trading. This is just one approach. Further studies on exit techniques and stop loss might yield a satisfactory approach to this entry and exit technique.

Swing Charts

Swing charts are extremely useful in giving clarity to price action by leaving out the bars (Figure 3.13). This simplifies the chart. This type of graph will be used in analysis of moves including angles, time, distance, and envelope studies. It is made by extending a line from a previous low of a move to the next high. It reverses when the low of a previous bar is broken. A variation to this is to reverse the line when a set amount of movement occurs in the opposite direction.

TABLE 3.2 Four Closes in Tight Range—Futures

OPENING RANGE BREAKOUT—ONE CONTRACT PER SIGNAL
EXIT: MAX OF OPENING RANGE BREAKOUT OF 62% OF PRIOR DAYS RANGE
AND LOWEST LOW OF 4 PRIOR CLOSES
TEST PERIOD 1/1/84 – 6/30/99
$0 ALLOWED FOR COMMISSION AND SLIPPAGE

Individual Future	Total PL ($)	Avg PL ($)/Yr	Max DrawDn ($)	Trds /Yr	Win (%)	TIM (%)	W:L	Gain/Mr +DD (%)	
British Pd.	31,744	2,048	19,719	16	35.1	35	1.3	9.7	BP
Deutsche Mark	51,763	3,340	12,688	14	46.8	33	1.8	23.8	DM
Japanese Yen	85,600	5,523	14,313	12	43.9	33	2	32.7	JY
Swiss Franc	56,425	3,640	16,538	16	38.5	34	1.6	19.9	SF
US$ Index	(3,460)	(255)	14,510	16	35	32	1	−1.6	DX
US Bonds	55,270	3,566	15,080	18	45.9	41	1.5	20.1	US
Treasury Note	41,610	2,685	8,300	15	43.8	41	1.6	27.4	TY
Muni Bonds	50,190	3,628	8,570	15	51.4	40	1.8	35	MB
Euro $	13,625	879	6,600	7	47.2	41	1.6	12.4	ED
Gold	9,800	632	5,660	19	35.7	36	1.2	9	GC
Silver	(5,260)	(339)	25,480	22	32.6	37	0.9	−1.2	SV
Soybeans	29,120	1,879	5,010	17	39.6	34	1.5	29.5	SD
Wheat	17,988	1,161	7,475	17	41.5	38	1.4	14.1	WD
Corn	17,363	1,120	3,738	10	42.2	33	1.9	26.2	CN
Soybean Meal	31,120	2,008	4,821	18	44.1	39	1.9	33.3	SM
Cotton	53,090	3,425	10,440	17	40.4	36	1.9	29.9	CT
Live Cattle	13,144	848	5,252	18	39.5	35	1.3	14.6	LC
Live Hogs	20,904	1,349	6,552	18	38.6	38	1.4	17.7	LH
Pork Bellies	21,228	1,370	11,212	17	40.2	34	1.2	10	PB
Crude Oil	47,170	3,043	6,130	14	48.4	34	2.4	37.3	CL
Heating Oil	15,179	985	8,421	16	36.1	30	1.2	9.4	HO
Natural Gas	47,190	5,148	9,430	15	45.7	39	2.4	38.3	NG
Coffee	151,725	9,789	44,438	18	42.2	38	1.9	19.8	KC
S&P 500	49,000	3,161	29,725	21	39.1	42	1.2	7.7	SP

Summary	Net PL ($)	DrawDn ($)		Avg.Mrgn Req'd ($)
Average/Year	58,163	24,811	Average	21,474
Full run total	901,526	39,628	Maximum	21,474
Avg trade	175			

	Trades	Percent	Ratio Win/Loss	P/L ($)	Avg Trade P/L ($)	Avg Time In Trade	Total (%)
Long side	2,561	41.7	2.3	571,832	223	6.3	63.4
Short side	2,578	39.9	2.1	329,628	128	5.9	36.6

	Return (%)	Capital Req'd for % Return ($)
Average drawdown is the average of last 15:		
1. Return on margin plus average drawdown	84.5	46,285
2. Return on margin plus maximum drawdown	69.5	61,102
3. Return on five times average margin required	54.2	107,370
4. Return on max drawdown limited to 20% of capital	29.4	198,140

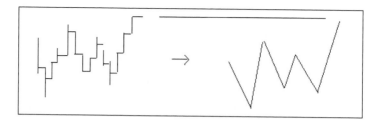

FIGURE 3.13   Swing chart.

Daily Range

Figure 3.14 shows three days of market action with different highs, lows openings, and closing prices. Figure 3.14A indicates the market should sell lower the next day as it closed in lower part of range and below the opening. Figure 3.14B is a neutral day as it closed in mid-range. Figure 3.14C indicates the market should sell higher the next day as it closed above mid-range and the opening.

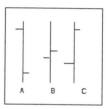

FIGURE 3.14   Daily range forecast.

It is widely believed that if a market closed above the opening and mid-range, it is bullish for the underlying stock or future. Statistically,

TABLE 3.3   Daily Range—Stocks

BUY DOWN CLOSES—100 SHARES PER SIGNAL
BUY OPENING FOLLOWING DOWN CLOSE, LIQUIDATE ON CLOSE
TEST PERIOD 1/1/96–10/30/99
$0 ALLOWED FOR COMMISSION AND SLIPPAGE

Individual Stocks	Total PL ($)	Avg PL/ Yr ($)	Max DrawDn ($)	In PL ($)	Last 12mn DrawDn ($)	Trds /Yr	Win (%)	TIM (%)	W:L
AT&T	(3,705)	(967)	4,149	−3,086	3,951	222	43.8	47	0.9
Amazon	829	433	4,328	2,893	4,121	236	49.6	48	1
COMPAQ	(1,410)	(368)	3,719	−2,758	3,719	225	49.1	47	0.9
Dell	2,891	754	952	787	952	227	52.8	47	1.2
General Elec	1,302	340	3,381	75	3,381	227	47.3	47	1
IBM	(3,704)	(966)	4,523	−1,973	4,523	225	47.2	47	0.9
Coca Cola	5,665	1,478	1,504	949	1,104	224	52.1	47	1.2
Merk	2,544	664	2,064	669	1,088	229	50.9	48	1.1
Microsoft	4,344	1,133	2,572	1,320	2,572	232	53	48	1.1
Royal Dutch	3,385	883	1,815	1,286	738	223	50.9	47	1.2
Excite	(8,872)	(4,629)	9,900	−8,201	9,003	231	46.2	48	0.8
Yahoo	(4,239)	(2,212)	16,386	−4,781	16,386	232	49.9	48	0.9

Summary shows a breakeven in profit/loss.

TABLE 3.4   Daily Range Study—Futures

BUY DOWN CLOSES, SELL UP CLOSES—ONE CONTRACT PER SIGNAL—DAY TRADE
TEST PERIOD 1/1/84–6/30/99
$0 ALLOWED FOR COMMISSION AND SLIPPAGE

Individual Returns	Total PL ($)	Avg PL/ Yr ($)	Max DrawDn ($)	In PL ($)	Last 12mn DrawDn ($)	Trds /Yr	Win (%)	TIM (%)	W:L	Gain/Mr +DD (%)
British Pd.	(18,200)	(1,174)	30,531	−25	4,288	203	49.3	45	1	−3.8
Deutsche Mark	29,013	1,872	24,163	1,963	4,663	208	52.1	46	1.1	7.5
Japanese Yen	41,763	2,694	14,900	−4,113	7,538	207	50.5	45	1.1	16.6
Swiss Franc	48,950	3,158	27,588	2,213	6,738	209	52.2	46	1.1	11.1
US$ Index	57,730	4,250	11,160	5,250	3,580	211	52.3	46	1.1	35.9
US Bonds	94,370	6,088	16,830	7,430	8,590	213	51	46	1.1	33.5
Treasury Note	43,180	2,786	13,990	250	6,590	203	49.8	45	1.1	18.9
Muni Bonds	(11,680)	(844)	47,730	11,940	2,800	207	47	45	1	−1.7
Euro $	18,525	1,195	3,450	−775	1,225	158	46.8	39	1.1	32.4
Gold	53,380	3,444	9,900	550	960	199	54.2	45	1.2	32.6
Silver	55,450	3,577	29,945	1,675	4,045	201	55	45	1.1	11.5
Soybeans	90,845	5,861	7,625	−1,180	3,430	212	52.8	46	1.2	70.6
Wheat	5,438	351	10,063	1,038	1,600	207	48.2	46	1	3.4
Corn	1,638	106	6,813	−1,175	2,238	204	47.8	45	1	1.5
Soybean Meal	10,990	709	15,540	110	2,080	208	49.8	46	1	4.4
Cotton	16,600	1,071	20,810	−955	8,705	201	52.2	45	1	5
Live Cattle	26,952	1,739	6,244	5,336	2,616	213	50.1	46	1.1	26.8
Live Hogs	(2,352)	(152)	15,236	−1,888	5,116	208	50.4	46	1	−1
Pork Bellies	56,604	3,652	11,108	3,672	8,940	206	52.2	45	1.1	29.6
Crude Oil	18,880	1,218	29,870	−6,170	9,090	212	50.2	46	1.1	3.9
Heating Oil	(1,151)	(75)	37,170	−3,163	8,875	207	49.9	46	1	−0.2
Natural Gas	25,740	2,808	17,090	8,360	5,830	204	48.8	45	1.1	14.7
Coffee	73,144	4,719	51,881	−38,906	42,938	208	51.4	46	1.1	8.7

Composite Returns	Net PL ($)	Drawdown ($)		No. of Trades	TIM (%)	Avg.Mrgn Req'd ($)
Average/Year	47,471	37,713	Average	4,577	100	15,801
Full run total	735,808	72,719	Maximum	70,936	100	15,801

		Return (%)	Capital Req'd for % Return ($)
Average drawdown is the average of last 15:			
1. Return on margin plus average drawdown		88.3	53,514
2. Return on margin plus maximum drawdown		53.60	88,520
3. Return on five times average margin required		60	79,005
4. Return on max drawdown limited to 20% of capital		13.1	363,595

this is false on a one-day basis as demonstrated in the tables. It does not mean that the market may not trade higher in the early part of the day. The trading rules for Table 3.3 on page 47 and Table 3.4 on page 48 are:

1. Buy the opening if the market on the prior day closes *below* the opening and mid-range of the day.
2. Sell the opening (on futures only), if the market on the prior day closes *above* the opening and mid-range.
3. Liquidate on the close (day trade).

No stops are used. The tables demonstrate that there is a very definite advantage in buying futures on down days (and vice versa). It is essentially a break even in stocks.

These tables suggest that you should consider buying the markets on down days rather than up days. The exception to this is when the market is breaking out of a trading pattern. The statistics should not be too surprising as markets are in a trading range about 85% of the time.

Inside Day

An inside day (ID) is one in which the entire day's price action is within the range of the previous day (Figure 3.15). The closing price is not as significant for forecasting purposes as any other day unless there are two to three previous closes in the same general area. The close might then point the direction of the next minor move. Usually, a movement that breaks the high or low of the inside day points the direction of the next minor swing.

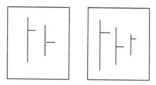

FIGURE 3.15   Inside days.

Sometimes there will be two inside days. A movement outside the range of the second day is usually more pronounced and points the direction of the next minor move, particularly if it closes outside that range.

An inside day is indecisive from a supply/demand standpoint. The theory is that when the market overcomes this indecision by penetrating either the high or the low it is an evidence of demand/supply and should lead to a profitable trade. Inside days occur about 12% of the time. Statistically, you cannot make money by day trading on this pattern alone as Tables 3.4 and 3.5 clearly show. These studies were designed to demonstrate that a slight technical edge is gained by using this as an entry technique. This is a beautiful pattern to use in your trading with other filters because it enables you to enter the market with a close stop. The way to trade the inside day is to have a buy order three ticks

TABLE 3.5 Inside Bars—Stocks

BUY BREAKOUT FROM INSIDE BARS—100 SHARES PER SIGNAL
TEST PERIOD 1/1/96–10/30/99
$0 ALLOWED FOR COMMISSION AND SLIPPAGE

Individual Stocks	Total PL ($)	Avg PL/ Yr ($)	Max DrawDn ($)	In PL ($)	Last 12mn DrawDn ($)	Trds /Yr	Win (%)	TIM (%)	W:L
AT&T	(206)	(54)	386	−325	386	9.1	57.1	4	0.8
Amazon	(256)	(134)	556	−209	556	4.7	55.6	2	0.6
COMPAQ	25	7	313	−163	247	6.3	50	2	1.1
Dell	151	39	31	−27	31	6.5	56	3	3.3
General Elec	978	255	305	1,273	103	9.9	55.3	4	2.1
IBM	79	21	559	−123	485	6.5	48	3	1.1
Coca Cola	(157)	(41)	546	389	181	10.7	46.3	4	0.9
Merk	377	98	113	226	100	7.6	58.6	3	1.8
Microsoft	984	257	146	594	146	7.0	66.7	3	4.2
Royal Dutch	656	171	112	210	9	7.8	63.3	3	4.6
Excite	201	105	187	297	0	6.8	69.2	3	1.6
Yahoo	(1,403)	(732)	2,728	−2,172	2,728	9.4	55.6	4	0.7

Summary	Net PL ($)	Max DrawDn ($)	Return on $50,000(%)
Average/Year	373	1,420	0.7
Full run total	1,429	3,059	

above the high of the bar with a sell order three ticks below the low of the bar. Again, the primary time to trade this formation is:

1. Trade with the trend.
2. When market is in congestion, buy in the buy zone and sell in the sell zone.
3. Trading in the direction of the close of the bar immediately preceding the inside bar. This is frequently a clue as to whether the penetration is valid.

Tables 3.5 and 3.6 show that it is statistically significant and does give one a slight edge if the preceding bar showed evidence of demand by closing above the opening (item 3 above). This edge is not sufficient to overcome slippage and commission by day trading. Further studies could be made by holding the position for a profit objective and using a close stop. This is how profitable trading systems are developed.

TABLE 3.6 Inside Range Bar Performance—Futures

BUY/SELL BREAKOUT FROM INSIDE BAR—ONE CONTRACT PER SIGNAL—DAY TRADE
TEST PERIOD 1/1/84–6/30-/99. DAY TRADE
$0 ALLOWED FOR COMMISSION AND SLIPPAGE

Individual Future	Total PL ($)	Avg PL/ Yr ($)	Max DrawDn ($)	In PL ($)	Last 12mn DrawDn ($)	Trds /Yr	Win (%)	TIM (%)	W:L	Gain/Mr +DD (%)
S&P 500	5,245	338	10,578	3,638	10,273	17	49.6	6	1.1	2.1
British Pd.	15,494	1,000	3,838	−1,369	1,406	17	49.4	6	1.4	21.8
Deutsche Mark	3,075	198	4,438	−650	1,100	16	47.8	6	1.1	3.9
Japanese Yen	8,838	570	4,288	−3,400	3,925	17	47.9	6	1.3	10.2
Swiss Franc	463	30	7,838	−2,138	2,388	15	50.4	6	1	0.3
US$ Index	(680)	(50)	5,510	−1,840	3,140	18	49.6	7	1	−0.8
US Bonds	12,990	838	6,520	4,180	1,210	18	51.1	7	1.3	10.6
Treasury Note	7,520	485	4,270	1,770	370	18	48	7	1.2	9.7
Muni Bonds	10,750	777	7,810	2,900	950	18	55.5	7	1.3	8.9
Gold	(1,400)	(90)	6,760	−510	640	21	44.7	8	1	−1.2
Soybeans	(9,765)	(630)	11,695	−1,025	1,455	17	50.4	6	0.7	−5.1
Wheat	5,825	376	2,075	1,063	388	17	56.2	6	1.4	15.3
Corn	2,700	174	1,763	−600	738	15	55.1	6	1.3	8.6
Soybean Meal	1,949	126	2,222	−342	849	18	52.7	7	1.1	4.5
Cotton	6,555	423	2,855	−95	2,000	17	53.4	7	1.2	12.6
Live Cattle	1,984	128	2,648	508	468	15	52.6	6	1.1	4.4
Live Hogs	6,516	420	1,356	−160	1,356	15	54.4	6	1.4	22.2
Pork Bellies	(508)	(33)	5,032	324	1,132	17	48.3	7	1	−0.5
Crude Oil	13,180	850	2,010	420	930	14	59.4	5	1.9	28.1
Heating Oil	(1,961)	(127)	6,724	−1,281	1,495	16	52	6	0.9	−1.6
Natural Gas	7,190	784	2,720	1,130	1,120	15	53.5	6	1.5	16.6
Coffee	9,600	619	20,119	−4,594	5,531	20	53.3	8	1.1	2.7

Summary Performance	Net PL ($)	Drawdown ($)		No. of Trades	TIM (%)	Avg.Mrgn Req'd ($)
Average/Year	6,810	8,358	Average	362	68	18,100
Full run total	105,558	24,112	Maximum	5,604	68	18,100
Average trade	19					

		Return (%)	Capital Req'd for % Return ($)
Average drawdown is the average of last 15:			
1. Return on margin plus average drawdown		25.7	26,458
2. Return on margin plus maximum drawdown		16.1	42,212
3. Return on five times average margin required		7.5	90,500
4. Return on max drawdown limited to 20% of capital		5.6	120,560

Outside Days or Bars

An outside bar is one where both the high and low of the day exceeds the high/low of the prior day. It occurs about 10 to 15 times per year per future. This usually represents a one-day change to aggressive demand from supply or vice versa. The theory is that one should go with the latest expression of demand or supply. This simple formation was tested by various methods on the computer in an effort to see if trading this formation gives one a technical edge. Testing was done by buying on the close of the outside day and liquidating 1 to 3 days later. It simply is not an effective entry filter.

Reversal Day

Reversal day (RD) patterns occur between 15 to 30 times/year with a trend filter (Figure 3.16). A reversal bar is a one-day change in sentiment from bull to bear or vice versa. Statistically, there is no way you can make money day trading this pattern alone. However, it can be very useful in trading provided these patterns are combined with other technical indicators and it is not a day trade.

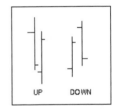

FIGURE 3.16   Reversal day.

A reversal day is one where the price trades below (above) the previous day's range and then closes above (below) the previous day's low/high and opening (Figure 3.17). This type of price action can mark the temporary or permanent end of the minor trend then in effect.

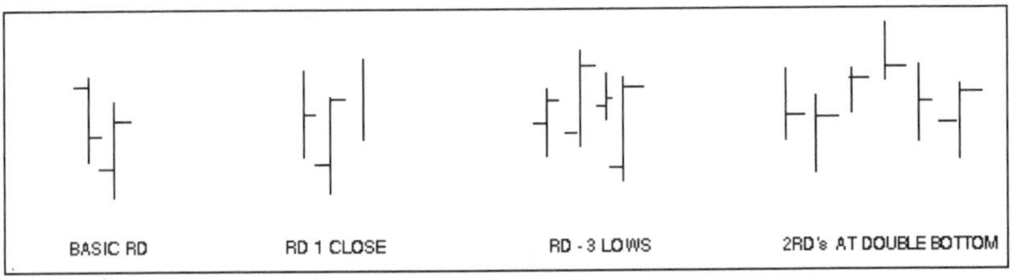

BASIC RD   RD 1 CLOSE   RD - 3 LOWS   2RD's AT DOUBLE BOTTOM

FIGURE 3.17   Reversal days.

Types and Location of Reversal Days

In Figure 3.18, the RD-3 lows is great for a trending market and this is the pattern in the correction to a thrust. The second reversal day at a double bottom is much more powerful than a single reversal day.

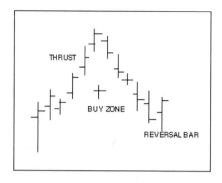

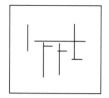

FIGURE 3.19   Reversal day at two daily highs.

FIGURE 3.18   Reversal day in buy zone.

A reversal day up when the market is in the buy zone is more likely to be successful than one in the sell zone.

Figure 3.19 illustrates a minor upthrust with a reversal day. The market went above two daily highs and fell back and closes below them. The sign of buying pressure is gone. The range on a reversal day determines its validity. Its position in the pattern is significant. The reversal

TABLE 3.7   Reversal Day Bars—Stocks

BUY ON CLOSE OF DAY OF PATTERN COMPLETION—100 SHARES PER SIGNAL
TEST PERIOD 1/1/96–10/30/99
$0 ALLOWED FOR COMMISSION AND SLIPPAGE

Individual Stocks	Total PL ($)	Avg PL/ Yr ($)	Max DrawDn ($)	In PL ($)	Last 12mn DrawDn ($)	Trds /Yr	Win (%)	TIM (%)	W:L
AT&T	(170)	(44)	1,046	−684	1,046	9.7	32.4	9	0.9
Amazon	4,096	2,137	629	2,914	554	15.1	51.7	18	4
COMPAQ	1,385	361	398	716	192	11.0	40.5	12	2.6
Dell	1,839	480	438	829	438	18.5	50.7	24	2.2
General Elec	(2,844)	(742)	3,136	−1,719	2,003	21.1	29.6	16	0.4
IBM	(868)	(226)	2,161	−1,275	1,745	16.4	47.6	16	0.8
Coca Cola	(1,454)	(379)	2,092	367	470	16.2	25.8	15	0.6
Merk	487	127	1,765	−955	1,765	16.7	39.1	16	1.2
Microsoft	159	41	1,193	794	1,067	21.9	35.7	20	1
Royal Dutch	(1,279)	(334)	1,575	−814	911	15.4	33.9	16	0.6
Excite	2,500	1,304	523	1,763	523	13.6	38.5	12	2.7
Yahoo	8,599	4,486	5,593	4,836	5,593	21.9	42.9	26	2.3

Summary	Net PL ($)	Max DrawDn ($)	Return on $50,000(%)
Average/Year	3,248	4,425	6.5
Full run total	12,450	7,397	

TABLE 3.8 Reversal Day (Futures)

BUY/SELL ON CLOSE OF DAY OF PATTERN COMPLETION
LIQUIDATE ON OPENING RANGE BREAKOUT OF 0.5 RANGE OF PRIOR DAY
TEST PERIOD 1/1/83–6/30/99—ONE CONTRACT PER SIGNAL—DAY TRADE
$0 ALLOWED FOR COMMISSION AND SLIPPAGE

Individual Performance	Total PL ($)	Avg PL/ Yr ($)	Max DrawDn ($)	In PL ($)	Last 12mn DrawDn ($)	Trds /Yr	Win (%)	TIM (%)	W:L	Gain/Mr +DD (%)
British Pd.	26,956	1,634	19,281	4,506	1,488	23	46.2	22	1.3	7.9
Deutsche Mark	25,113	1,522	13,038	9,075	1,050	28	41.3	25	1.3	10.6
Japanese Yen	27,788	1,684	14,513	−3,163	8,800	26	46.1	24	1.2	9.9
Swiss Franc	39,700	2,406	12,525	6,550	1,788	29	43.5	24	1.3	16.9
US$ Index	(3,970)	(292)	12,090	−680	2,860	28	38.2	24	1	−2.2
US Bonds	37,450	2,270	16,990	6,880	3,050	31	43.1	29	1.3	11.5
Treasury Note	42,690	2,587	5,990	9,670	1,970	29	46.3	28	1.6	34.6
Muni Bonds	80,300	5,805	7,910	1,090	2,380	27	48.7	30	2.2	59.8
Gold	11,380	690	7,950	320	1,190	29	39.8	26	1.2	7.4
Soybeans	15,380	932	9,320	1,720	1,760	30	36.9	26	1.2	8.7
Wheat	18,400	1,115	4,400	275	863	27	40.5	25	1.5	21.7
Corn	21,175	1,283	2.313	−550	738	26	44	26	1.9	45
Soybean Meal	32,220	1,953	4,325	180	1,130	28	44	27	1.8	35.3
Cotton	24,875	1,508	9,020	−2,730	3,260	29	38.8	26	1.3	15
Live Cattle	18,216	1,104	6,360	−2,636	3,424	29	40.7	27	1.4	16
Live Hogs	24,112	1,461	3,844	1,756	2,404	29	40.5	28	1.5	29.7
Pork Bellies	13,384	811	12,672	−7,472	10,052	29	36.6	27	1.1	5.4
Crude Oil	29,410	1,857	10,020	410	1,890	31	44.1	29	1.5	15.4
Heating Oil	18,824	1,147	9,232	−4,196	4,351	29	39.6	27	1.2	10.2
Natural Gas	48,280	5,267	4,470	2,950	4,470	28	49.8	30	2.3	62.2
Coffee	87,638	5,311	19,913	−12,000	13,688	31	44.2	29	1.5	21.4

Summary Performance	Net PL ($)	DrawDn ($)		Avg.Mrgn Req'd ($)
Average/Year	38,747	16,563	Average	13,166
Full run total	639,320	35,196	Maximum	13,166
Avg trade	71			

	Return (%)	Capital Req'd for % Return ($)
Average drawdown is the average of last 15:		
1. Return on margin plus average drawdown	130.3	29,729
2. Return on margin plus maximum drawdown	80.1	48,362
3. Return on five times average margin required	58.9	65,830
4. Return on max drawdown limited to 20% of capital	58.9	175,980

day at a double bottom has more significance than one at a single bottom if the range is the same or greater than prior day.

Factors affecting validity of reversal day include:

- Range of the bar.
- Number of closes reversed.
- Number of pivot points below/above it.

Computer studies were made using the reversal day pattern as an entry setup. Additional filters were added:

1. Buy/sell on close of day of basic reversal day pattern setup.
2. Exit. After entry, exit is made on any day that the market had a 50% opening range breakout of the previous day's range.
3. Trend filter. A buy entry is made only if the close of the prior day was greater than the close 50 days ago (and vice versa).

Table 3.7 on page 53 and Table 3.8 on page 54 show the results of this study on futures and stocks. No commission or slippage was allowed. These tables clearly demonstrate that you gain an edge in the markets by use of the reversal day pattern. However, the profit is insufficient to take care of slippage and commission. Further study in this area could yield a profitable trading system.

THREE-DAY EQUILIBRIUM REVERSE

The last three days' action of a stock or commodity can often be used to point the direction of the next minor effort. A turn in the minor trend can take many forms. There are certain characteristics in three-day patterns that can occasionally be used advantageously for evaluating potential turning points in the minor trend.

In any given three days' action, there are nine potential support/resistance points, three highs, three lows, and three closes. One rule might be to buy on the close of the third day if the closing price is above the average of these nine points. Although a set of rules can be put down, you must recognize they are not absolute. This is intended to be an additional tool and is not a trading system.

The requirements for a reversal to the upside are:

1. Three days' action with the first two days' closing prices in close proximity to each other.
2. First two days have a smaller range than the third day.

3. Close on third day is above the 62% point of the daily range and is above the two previous closes.

4. Low on third day is above low of second day.

5. Added significance of a possible minor turn is present if market is in the buy zone for a buy. Note the third day has a wider spread and a high close with the low above the second day's low.

The strongest three-day equilibrium (3DE) upside reversal is where the high and close on the current day are above the high of two previous days, and the close is greater than the open. The reverse of the above is true for a reversal to the downside Figure 3.20 shows a few three-day equilibrium reversals on Advanced Digital Information Corp.

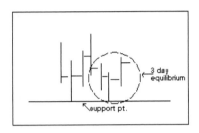

FIGURE 3.20   Three-day equilibrium reverse.

The pattern in Figure 3.21 is a change from supply to demand over a three-bar time frame or vice versa. This pattern occurs between 35 to

FIGURE 3.21   Change from supply to demand. Created with TradeStation 2000i by Omega Research © 1999.

40 times per year per futures or stock. The key to successful use of this pattern by one method is to wait one day for entry and buy on the close of the following day. Markets generally have a pull back after a strong day in either direction. The numbers below are based on:

- Buy on the close of the day following the three-day equilibrium.
- Exit. A 0.5 range breakout off the open on any day after entry.
- Trend: The closing price of two days ago is greater than the closing price of 50 days ago.
- Closing price of second day back is less than closing price on fourth day back.

These simple rules produce profits in all but three markets out of 21 for futures, and 9 out of 12 for stocks, as shown in Tables 3.9 and 3.10. It is not a stand-alone system but with some work on the exit rule and when to take the signal could yield a very profitable system. Figure 3.22 gives the combined equity on 21 futures in trading this pattern.

TABLE 3.9   Three-Day Equilibrium—Stocks

BUY ON CLOSE OF DAY OF PATTERN COMPLETION—100 SHARES PER SIGNAL
TEST PERIOD 1/1/96–10/30/99
$0 ALLOWED FOR COMMISSION AND SLIPPAGE

Individual Stocks	Total PL ($)	Avg PL/ Yr ($)	Max DrawDn ($)	In PL ($)	Last 12mn DrawDn ($)	Trds /Yr	Win (%)	TIM (%)	W:L
AT&T	1,099	287	275	574	275	8.1	45.2	8	2.9
Amazon	(745)	(389)	1,353	−485	1,028	12.5	41.7	11	0.5
COMPAQ	880	230	437	659	149	10.7	36.6	11	1.9
Dell	960	250	884	−166	884	14.6	44.6	15	1.7
General Elec	(103)	(27)	1,495	964	1,495	14.4	32.7	11	1
IBM	281	73	995	−203	995	13.3	33.3	11	1.1
Coca Cola	245	64	1,064	−465	465	12.3	38.3	13	1.1
Merk	(1,052)	(274)	1,503	−363	776	11.5	27.3	9	0.5
Microsoft	1,354	353	726	1,369	726	15.4	44.1	14	1.7
Royal Dutch	(1,134)	(296)	1,621	−338	708	12.5	31.3	11	0.6
Excite	1,217	635	620	530	620	11.5	40.9	10	1.9
Yahoo	753	393	3,171	−1,718	3,171	13.6	57.7	15	1.3

Summary	Net PL ($)	Return on $50,000(%)
Average/Year	980	2.0
Full run total	3,755	

TABLE 3.10 Three-Day Equilibrium—Futures

BUY/SELL ON CLOSE OF DAY FOLLOWING PATTERN COMPLETION
LIQUIDATE ON OPENING RANGE BREAKOUT OF 0.5 RANGE OF PRIOR DAY
TEST PERIOD 1/1/83–6/30/99—ONE CONTRACT PER SIGNAL—DAY TRADE
$0 ALLOWED FOR COMMISSION AND SLIPPAGE

Individual Performance	Total PL ($)	Avg PL/ Yr ($)	Max DrawDn ($)	In PL ($)	Last 12mn DrawDn ($)	Trds /Yr	Win (%)	TIM (%)	W:L	Gain/Mr +DD (%)
British Pd.	7,800	473	13,325	–2,556	2,619	20	44.5	16	1.1	3.2
Deutsche Mark	8,100	491	15,163	–513	1,800	18	41.3	14	1.1	3
Japanese Yen	3,388	205	14,863	–1,463	5,563	17	44.5	14	1	1.2
Swiss Franc	15,600	945	9,575	3,288	463	19	42.5	15	1.2	8.4
US$ Index	(2,170)	(160)	11,700	1,770	2,160	18	38.1	16	1	–1.2
US Bonds	37,940	2,299	6,390	1,400	3,490	22	44.1	19	1.5	25.3
Treasury Note	8,300	503	9,590	310	1,480	22	39.4	18	1.1	4.5
Muni Bonds	42,480	3,071	3,960	–540	2,390	23	45.6	22	1.9	53.3
Gold	14,230	862	3,120	130	520	12	44.3	11	1.6	19.3
Soybeans	15,450	936	9,750	1,025	1,185	16	45.1	14	1.4	8.4
Wheat	10,913	661	4,375	–313	563	18	41.6	16	1.4	12.9
Corn	5,275	320	3,050	–475	538	15	37	13	1.3	8.9
Soybean Meal	22,855	1,385	6,255	690	570	16	46	15	1.8	18.5
Cotton	(4,375)	(265)	13,175	–695	1,995	20	36.7	16	0.9	–1.9
Live Cattle	1,276	77	4,172	284	764	25	36.9	21	1	1.6
Live Hogs	(868)	(53)	7,640	452	948	21	34.9	16	1	–0.6
Pork Bellies	26,252	1,591	5,508	–1,396	5,020	17	37.8	14	1.5	20
Crude Oil	11,460	724	4,990	100	2,220	22	40.1	19	1.3	10.3
Heating Oil	6,157	375	10,088	–1,961	2,444	19	41	16	1.1	3.1
Natural Gas	11,070	1,208	4,790	510	1,730	20	40.4	17	1.3	13.7
Coffee	91,988	5,575	14,869	–3,956	6,375	19	46.7	17	1.8	28.2

Composite Performance	PL ($)	DrawDn ($)		Trades	TIM (%)	Avg.Mrgn Req'd ($)
Last 6 months	–13,223	12,870	on 990629	126	95	5,243
Last 12 months	–4,189	16,701	on 990629	296	96	6,382
Average/Year	20,189	13,646	Average	382	98	7,997
Full run total	333,120	21,744	Maximum	6,301	98	7,997
Avg trade	55					

	Return (%)	Capital Req'd for % Return ($)
Average drawdown is the average of last 15:		
1. Return on margin plus average drawdown	93.3	21,643
2. Return on margin plus maximum drawdown	67.9	29,741
3. Return on five times average margin required	50.5	39,985
4. Return on max drawdown limited to 20% of capital	18.6	108,720

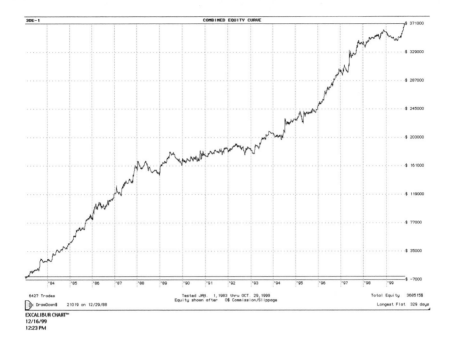

FIGURE 3.22 3DE combined equity for futures.

PATTERN GAP

There are a number of different types of gaps. The pattern gap is one that occurs more frequently than other gaps, and has the most utility in trading (Figure 3.23).

The up pattern gap is where the low of the bar is greater than the close of the prior bar. The down pattern gap is where the high of the current bar is less than the close of the prior bar. For the up pattern gap, the market is sufficiently strong such that it is unable to move

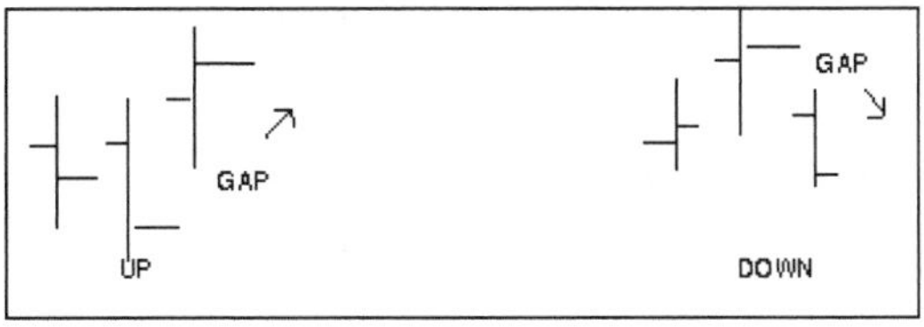

FIGURE 3.23 Pattern gaps.

FIGURE 3.24 Pattern gaps on Royal Dutch. Created with TradeStation 2000i by Omega Research © 1999.

back to the close of the prior day. The strongest pattern gaps have the following characteristics:

- Range of bar is greater than the range of the two prior bars.
- Close of bar is greater than the opening of the bar.
- Close of bar is greater than the closes of the two prior bars.

Early entry may be possible if the market is significantly above the opening at midday and the other requirements are in place. Sell signals are the opposite. This is not a system into itself and some judgment should be exercised on which signals to take. The exit and stop loss points have not been identified on Figure 3.23 but it is apparent that most signals lead to immediate profit opportunities. The entry signal is great for getting on board a running market or catching a move coming out of congestion. The best moves are the ones that have followed through within two days after entry and the two prior bars are narrow range bars. Figure 3.24 show some of the more obvious pattern gaps on Royal Dutch.

HOOK CLOSING

A hook closing is a strong expression of demand or supply. It consists of one or more bars in one direction followed by a relatively narrow range

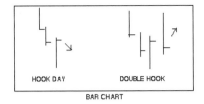

FIGURE 3.25   Hooks and double hooks.

bar that closes against the trend. The theory is that the market will continue on the following day in the direction of prior bars. A double hook, shown in Figure 3.25, reverses the trend.

A hook coming after only a one-day move is not as reliable as a hook coming after a two-day movement. The hook shown in Figure 3.26A is more likely to go up than is the one shown in Figure 3.26B.

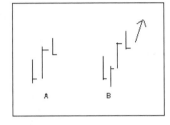

FIGURE 3.26   Hook comparison.

TABLE 3.11   Hook Closing—Stocks

BUY ON OPENING OF DAY FOLLOWING PATTERN COMPLETION—100 SHARES
PER SIGNAL DAY TRADE
TEST PERIOD 1/1/96–10/30/99
$0 ALLOWED FOR COMMISSION AND SLIPPAGE

Individual Stocks	Total PL ($)	Avg PL/ Yr ($)	DrawDn ($)	In PL ($)	DrawDn ($)	Trds /Yr	Win (%)	TIM (%)	W:L
AT&T	(755)	(197)	799	−462	799	12.8	40.8	5	0.6
Amazon	1,643	857	1,079	1,590	1,079	20.9	47.5	8	1.9
COMPAQ	62	16	594	−381	594	17.0	44.6	7	1
Dell	439	115	426	256	272	18.0	55.1	7	1.4
General Elec	(256)	(67)	881	138	624	19.3	48.6	7	0.9
IBM	385	100	572	403	265	17.5	53.7	7	1.2
Coca Cola	(94)	(25)	1,070	298	270	17.2	47	7	1
Merk	304	79	717	2	384	18.0	52.2	7	1.2
Microsoft	1,118	292	539	286	539	17.0	61.5	6	1.8
Royal Dutch	417	109	482	426	163	12.8	65.3	5	1.4
Excite	(1,970)	(1,028)	2,027	−1,848	1,965	15.7	43.3	6	0.5
Yahoo	1,436	749	4,429	815	4,429	20.9	62.5	8	1.2

Summary	Net PL ($)	Max DrawDn ($)	Return on $50,000 (%)
Average/Year	712	2,467	1.4
Full run total	2,729	5,584	

TABLE 3.12 Hook Closing—Futures

BUY/SELL ON OPENING OF DAY FOLLOWING PATTERN COMPLETION
LIQUIDATE ON CLOSE
TEST PERIOD 1/1/84–6/30/99—ONE CONTRACT PER SIGNAL—DAY TRADE
$0 ALLOWED FOR COMMISSION AND SLIPPAGE

Individual Market	Total PL ($)	Avg PL/ Yr ($)	Max DrawDn ($)	In PL ($)	Last 12mn DrawDn ($)	Trds /Yr	Win (%)	TIM (%)	W:L	Gain/Mr +DD (%)
British Pd.	6,981	450	8,975	−3,350	3,613	32	51.1	11	1.1	4.6
Deutsche Mark	12,588	812	4,400	750	1,138	30	56.2	11	1.2	16
Japanese Yen	(13,413)	(865)	20,575	−2,513	2,950	31	48.2	11	0.8	−4
Swiss Franc	14,825	956	8,763	550	1,925	33	55	12	1.2	9.9
US$ Index	18,650	1,373	5,910	280	1,230	32	53.3	12	1.3	20.9
US Bonds	36,760	2,372	4,000	−2,530	3,060	30	54.8	11	1.5	44.3
Treasury Note	24,600	1,587	3,980	230	1,350	29	52.7	10	1.5	33.6
Muni Bonds	32,000	2,313	2,710	1,980	910	28	51.4	10	1.6	64.1
Euro $	1,175	76	2,400	225	75	18	46.7	7	1.1	2.9
Gold	7,730	499	3,170	−20	370	33	49.4	12	1.2	13
Silver	24,015	1,549	5,965	−1,040	1,900	32	54.9	11	1.4	21.6
Soybeans	13,245	855	3,780	−820	1,120	29	51.1	10	1.3	19.2
Wheat	(2,475)	(160)	6,100	−588	1,500	31	44.4	11	0.9	−2.5
Corn	7,213	465	1,025	213	675	28	54.7	10	1.4	35.9
Soybean Meal	2,125	137	4,950	1,500	310	30	47.9	11	1.1	2.5
Cotton	(7,310)	(472)	9,790	−4,860	5,230	35	47.9	12	0.9	−4.6
Live Cattle	5,172	334	4,380	484	1,464	29	50.6	11	1.1	7.2
Live Hogs	3,856	249	3,220	−768	2,284	33	51.6	12	1.1	6.6
Pork Bellies	3,952	255	7,824	−1,936	5,044	31	49.6	11	1	2.8
Crude Oil	18,250	1,177	2,960	250	870	32	53.2	11	1.4	29.6
Heating Oil	4,326	281	6,859	−2,012	2,579	35	47.1	12	1.1	3.6
Natural Gas	4,980	543	5,310	160	2,700	29	52.4	11	1.1	7.4
Coffee	22,275	1,437	18,319	−16,556	17,550	32	50.9	11	1.1	6.9
S&P 500	13,525	873	20,675	7,075	17,900	35	49.4	12	1.1	3.3

Composite Performance	PL ($)	DrawDn ($)		Net PL ($)	Max DrawDn ($)	No. of Trades	Avg.Mrgn Req'd ($)
Last 6 months				−9,374	19,481	349	3,209
Last 12 months				−23,296	26,738	715	3,269
Average/Year	16,454	13,022	Average	16,454	13,022	715	3,163
Full run total	255,045	28,084	Maximum	255,045	28,084	11,090	3,163
Avg trade	23						

	Return (%)	Capital Req'd for % Return ($)
Average drawdown is the average of last 15:		
1. Return on margin plus average drawdown	101	16,185
2. Return on margin plus maximum drawdown	52.7	31,247
3. Return on five times average margin required	104.1	15,815
4. Return on max drawdown limited to 20% of capital	11.7	140,420

Hook closing prices as an effective trading vehicle was popularized by James T. Kneafsey in 1984. Computers can be used to determine the validity of the hook pattern. There are a number of variations to the hook pattern. The following computer study was designed to determine if the hook pattern gives a statistical edge on a one-day basis. The rules for the study were:

- The market has two consecutive up closes.
- A down close follows that is below the close of the prior day but above the close of the second day back.

A purchase is made on the opening the following day and liquidated on the close. The reverse is true on sell orders (futures only). Table 3.11 on page 61 and Table 3.12 on page 62 demonstrate that this can be an effective entry technique as it produced profits in all but three markets in futures, and 8 out of 12 in stocks. This pattern sets up around 18 to 30 times per year and it is in the market about 6% to 11% of the time. You cannot make money on this pattern alone; however, it can be an effective entry technique when combined with other technical tools.

The bar chart in Figure 3.27 points out the occurrences of the hook closing. Possible conclusions are:

- 4 of the 5 occurrences would have yielded a profit the following day.

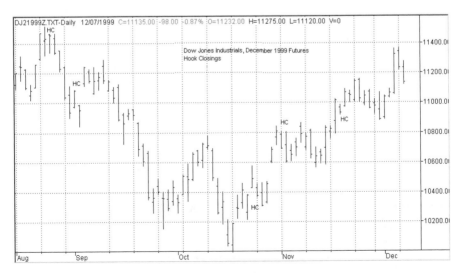

FIGURE 3.27 Dow Jones Industrial average illustrates hook closings.

- It seems to work best to buy in the buy zone of a congestion pattern or when the market is in the run-up phase. The opposite is true for sell entries.

NARROW RANGE BARS

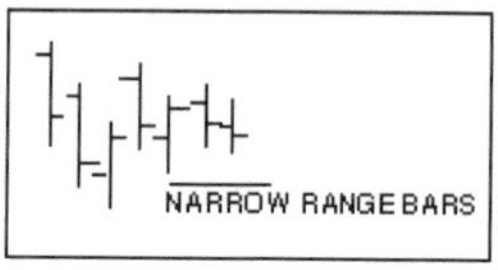

A narrow range bar is one where the range of the bar is less than the preceding number of bars. No one set amount is required. Figure 3.28 illustrates that the last three bars have a smaller range. This represents a market coming to rest with supply and demand about equally balanced. Penetration of the high of the last bar accompanied by an opening range breakout is a strong indication of

FIGURE 3.28 Narrow range bars.

TABLE 3.13 Narrow Range—Stocks

BUY ON OPENING BREAKOUT OF DAY FOLLOWING PATTERN
COMPLETION—100 SHARES PER SIGNAL
LIQUIDATE ON 0.5 RANGE BO ON ANY DAY AFTER ENTRY
TEST PERIOD 1/1/96–10/30/99
$0 ALLOWED FOR COMMISSION AND SLIPPAGE

Individual Stocks	Total PL ($)	Avg PL ($)/Yr	Max DrawDn ($)	Trds /Yr	Win (%)	TIM (%)	W:L
AT&T	(417)	(109)	417	3.1	25	2	0.1
Amazon	3,032	1,582	399	6.8	53.8	8	13.5
COMPAQ	(67)	(17)	429	2.6	50	3	0.8
Dell	1,243	324	259	5.2	65	9	7.4
General Elec	884	231	734	4.4	52.9	4	2.1
IBM	(1,881)	(491)	2,173	5.7	45.5	5	0.3
Coca Cola	567	148	469	4.2	56.3	4	2.1
Merk	(365)	(95)	581	3.9	46.7	3	0.6
Microsoft	1,452	379	599	5.5	52.4	5	3
Royal Dutch	336	88	652	5.5	52.4	4	1.4
Excite	2,656	1,386	278	6.8	69.2	8	10
Yahoo	1,723	899	831	5.2	60	7	9

Summary	Net PL ($)	Max DrawDn ($)	Return on $50,000*(%)
Average/Year	2,390	1,401	4.8
Full run total	9,163	1,648	

*$50,000 should be adequate for the limited time in market per stock.

TABLE 3.14 Narrow Range Trading—Futures

BUY/SELL ON OPENING BO OF DAY FOLLOWING PATTERN COMPLETION
LIQUIDATE ON 0.5 RANGE BO ON ANY DAY AFTER ENTRY
TEST PERIOD 1/1/83–6/30/99—ONE CONTRACT PER SIGNAL—DAY TRADE
$0 ALLOWED FOR COMMISSION AND SLIPPAGE

Individual Market	Total PL ($)	Avg PL/ Yr ($)	Max DrawDn ($)	In PL ($)	Last 12mn DrawDn ($)	Trds /Yr	Win (%)	TIM (%)	W:L	Gain/Mr +DD (%)
S&P 500	47,343	2,869	13,493	26,100	12,338	13	45.9	12	1.6	11.5
British Pd.	(10,325)	(626)	29,319	138	3,088	9	39.6	8	0.8	-2
Deutsche Mark	3,163	192	17,513	-425	850	8	42	7	1.1	1
Japanese Yen	1,588	96	8,525	-7,513	8,525	9	41.9	8	1	0.9
Swiss Franc	9,900	600	14,750	5,475	1,225	8	41.4	8	1.2	3.6
US$ Index	5,620	414	6,870	-1,070	2,150	9	42	9	1.2	5
US Bonds	36,140	2,190	7,270	5,980	1,990	10	53.8	10	2	22
Treasury Note	13,670	828	4,000	610	1,600	11	51.1	10	1.5	15.1
Muni Bonds	28,820	2,083	5,240	3,400	1,200	12	45.9	12	1.9	29.6
Gold	4,440	269	5,670	200	110	6	42.6	5	1.3	3.8
Soybeans	14,175	859	4,445	-10	570	8	49.3	7	1.6	14.8
Wheat	5,950	361	1,900	-638	638	8	47.8	8	1.4	13.6
Corn	2,213	134	3,525	100	500	9	50	8	1.2	3.3
Soybean Meal	16,120	977	2,305	-520	765	8	52.3	8	2.1	27.8
Cotton	22,840	1,384	5,565	2,270	650	10	50.9	10	1.8	21.1
Live Cattle	(4,624)	(280)	6,272	768	588	13	42.3	11	0.8	-4.1
Live Hogs	3,536	214	5,220	1,184	792	11	45.7	9	1.2	3.4
Pork Bellies	29,688	1,799	4,096	276	4,064	8	51.6	7	2.2	27.6
Crude Oil	11,740	741	2,610	2,860	770	9	50	8	1.7	16
Heating Oil	10,370	632	5,011	-449	1,344	9	50.3	7	1.5	9
Natural Gas	9,920	1,082	3,210	-700	1,550	8	50	7	1.7	15
Coffee	66,525	4,032	17,363	1,463	1,069	9	53	8	2.3	18.1

Composite Performance	PL ($)	DrawDn ($)		Trades	TIM (%)	Avg.Mrgn Req'd ($)
Last 6 months	9,671	15,756		70	81	4,973
Last 12 months	39,889	16,695		155	80	5,129
Average/Year	19,928	10,074	Average	199	86	5,854
Full run total	328,810	32,236	Maximum	3,281	86	5,854
Avg trade	105					

	Return (%)	Capital Req'd for % Return ($)
Average drawdown is the average of last 15:		
1. Return on margin plus average drawdown	125.1	15,928
2. Return on margin plus maximum drawdown	52.3	38,090
3. Return on five times average margin required	68.1	29,270
4. Return on max drawdown limited to 20% of capital	12.4	161,180

buying pressure entering the market with an up move likely. A trading edge is gained. Table 3.13 on page 64 and Table 3.14 show the computer generated numbers for this edge. Eight of 12 stocks produced profits. They were even more impressive on futures. The rules for the tests were as follows (long side only, sell side exact opposite):

- The range of the previous day is less than the range of any of the five prior days.
- Entry. Buy at the maximum of an opening range breakout of 0.5 range of prior day and the high of the prior day.
- Trend: The close of the prior day is greater than the close of 50 days ago.
- Exit the trade on any day at the market that has a 0.5 opening range breakout.

Narrow Range after Strong Demand or Supply

This is a great tool for entering a running market. After a strong run, markets will frequently digest the movement by holding the gain for several days in a relatively narrow range. The urgent demand is likely to resume the movement after the third bar (Figure 3.29). The set up rules for trading are (buy side only—sell side is the opposite):

- The market has a sign of strength or a strong movement.
- The slope of the 10-day moving average is up.
- Market has corrected for one to three bars.
- Range of one of the last several bars are less than the 10-day average bar range.
- The last bar may slightly penetrate the low of the prior bar. This is not entirely necessary but it does show lack of supply.

Buy on penetration of the narrow range bars high. Enter a stop below the low of the narrow range bar. Take profits at targets or by a trailing stop. Figures 3.30 and 3.31 show this method in action.

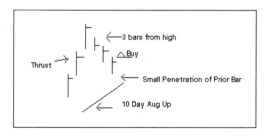

FIGURE 3.29 Narrow range in correction.

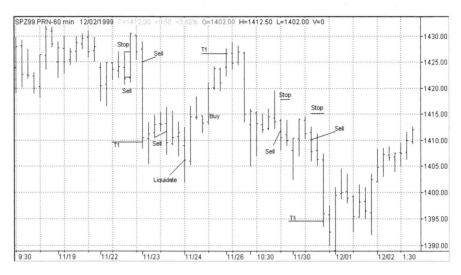

FIGURE 3.30 S&P's 60-minute chart (December 1999). Created with TradeStation 2000i by Omega Research © 1999.

FIGURE 3.31 S&P's 60-minute chart (December 1999). Created with TradeStation 2000i by Omega Research © 1999.

TRADING THE NARROW RANGES

Narrow ranges can be a useful tool in a trading plan. They must be integrated into the overall pattern for successful trading. The basic concept is to enter the market as it breaks away from a state of equilibrium, which is characterized by one or more narrow range bars. If the market rallies away from this point and later comes back to it, demand is expected to enter the market. This is a classic double bottom. This becomes a significant trading plan if you then combine this with the accumulation/distribution set-up. Only take the trades in the direction of the thrust. Stops are entered on the other side of the narrow range bar. For instance, Figure 3.32 shows entry points at either the A- or C-leg correction to the latest thrust.

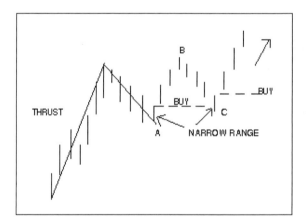

FIGURE 3.32   Trading the narrow ranges.

TRADING THE WIDE RANGE BAR

A wide range bar may be either bullish or bearish depending on where it takes place in the set up. If it comes at the end of a buying climax, it is bearish. However, it is positive if it is breaking out of a formation. Figure 3.33 shows it coming out of a pattern. Most of the wide range bars have a pull back on the following bar. The buy zone is in the lower 50% of the range of the bar. Conversely the take profit zone is 50% to 100% added to the high of the wide range bar. This obviously is for short-term trading. The market tends to rotate by having a narrow range bar after a wide range bar. This is not 100% objective and the definition of a wide range bar is subjective.This is where the art of chart reading comes into focus. This talent is developed only by looking at many charts over a long period of time.

BUY ZONES

The buy zone is in the lower 50% of a thrust, as shown in Figure 3.34. As higher thrusts are made, the buy zone is at a higher level. These are the areas to look for patterns for taking a long position. Prior to entering the market, know where the stop should be and establish a target level. Mark the buy, sell, and take profit zones on your charts. Do *not* chase a running market. There are always candidates for market entry out of the vast number of stocks. Pick your zone of entry. A step-by-step procedure might be:

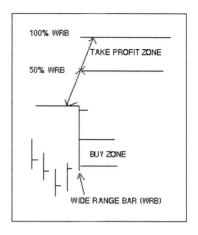

FIGURE 3.33   Trading the wide range bar.

1. Buy only in the buy zones.
2. Enter stop loss immediately after market entry.
3. Liquidate the trade if it enters the take profit zone. Do you come out on a stop or simply liquidate in the zone? This question is a trade off. If you come out at the target, the market may go much higher. If you come out on a stop, often significant profits are given up.
   The solution might be:

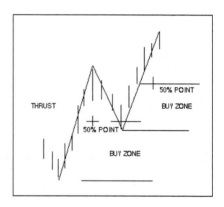

FIGURE 3.34   Buy zones.

- Tighten the stop.
- Liquidate half your position and be either half right or half wrong.
- Liquidate on the first sign of supply overcoming demand (for longs).
- Use a lower time frame for stop placement. For instance, if trading the daily bar and market enters the target zone, use the 30-minute chart for moving a stop in tight.

STOP POINT

He who knows not what he risks, risks all.

No one stop loss method is satisfactory for everyone. One must seek his own comfort level in the area of risk versus reward. A number of suggested ways of placing a stop order are:

1. Three ticks below the low of the most recent one to two pivots.
2. One average range below either the low or close on the day of purchase.
3. 50% opening range breakout after the date of entry. This particular stop works exceedingly well when combined with the other possible stops. For instance, a market may open below a stop level and this turns out to be the low for the day. We like to see some movement away from the opening such as about eight ticks or a half range of prior bar.
4. Three ticks below the lowest low or close of the two prior bars.
5. Liquidate the trade after three bars if it is not profitable.
6. Scratched the trade at break even, if possible, if it moves too far against you after entry and your stop has not been hit. Forget about profit at this point. All you are trying to do is protect your stop and prevent significant loss.

It is exceedingly important to have a plan in place for your investments. When you enter the market, ask yourself if this is a long-term investment which you will hold for five to ten years. Do not panic on short-term market fluctuations. Are you a trader? Unfortunately, many people base their liquidation point or stop loss on the following:

1. The stop is located at the point where they lose big time.
2. The stop is based on the overall stock market movements. When the overall market tanks, they will liquidate my investments.
3. When everyone else is liquidating their positions in panic in your particular investment, you will liquidate your investments.
4. Some analyst or broker said liquidate. This brings up a story.

I had the honor of being on *The Mark Haynes Show* on CNBC a few years ago. Mark introduced me as an expert in the futures market. He asked me what gold was going to do. I replied that I knew exactly the future movement of gold. However, before I answered that question his listeners should be aware that I was only correct 23% of the time, but lately it had been improving. Thus, I am dangerous as I am sometimes right. If the truth were known, I was having a hard time getting bus fare back to North Carolina. Needless to say, after that interview, CNBC initiated a closer scrutiny of invited guests.

The point of the story is to be careful of people who know all the answers. If you are going to be a trader, recognize that to be successful involves a considerable amount of work and is a lifetime pursuit of a monster you will never master, however you might learn to live with it and extract more than you give.

TAKING PROFITS

If long and the market moves to the target area, profits may be protected by:

- Liquidating position at market.
- Liquidating if a close is below opening.
- Liquidating position by a half range breakout to the downside from the opening.
- Carrying a stop below each day's low.
- Liquidating on a close below two prior closes and below opening.
- Liquidating on the third strong up period of the next lower time frame. For instance, if the weekly bar chart reaches its target, get out on three up days on the daily chart.

ANTICIPATION

These factors are useful in anticipation of pattern completion and reversal. One might take nibbles on a position prior to a close. Remember, the name of the game is to be profitable and not catch 90% of every move. Learn to be satisfied with small chunks of the market. What you are doing is either taking profits at market or taking them at the first sign of supply overcoming demand.

The seven possible action points for Anticipation (Figure 3.35) of a pattern completion:

1. On the close of the bar if a narrow range indicating lack of supply or demand.
2. Opening in the direction of a pattern completion.
3. Opening range breakout in the direction of a pattern completion.
4. 30-minute breakout in the direction of a pattern completion.

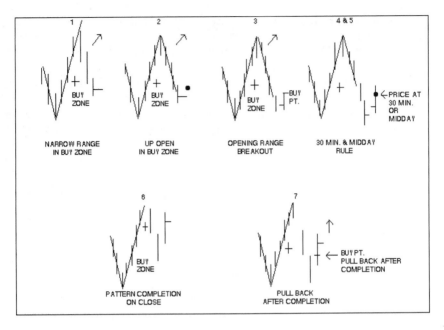

FIGURE 3.35 Entry techniques.

5. Mid-day price above opening and in the direction of a pattern completion.
6. On close when the pattern completion is in place.
7. On a pullback bar after pattern completion.

It also is apparent on many patterns that the market will dip into the buy zone but pattern completion will be above the buy zone. Taking action at such points is a question of judgment.

TIME BREAKOUT RULE

A popular theory is to trade the breakout of the first 30-minute bar with a stop loss on the other side of the 30-minute bar. This theory was tested on intraday S&P market data over a 14-year period. Trading this rule will result in colossal losses as demonstrated on the equity curve in Figure 3.36. One should note that it has made money in the last couple of years. This clearly points out the hazard of reaching trading conclusions on a limited amount of data.

This tool, buying/selling the breakout of the first 30-minute bar, can be an effective means of entering a trade. A pattern set up must be in place. As with most of the tools, it cannot be used in isolation.

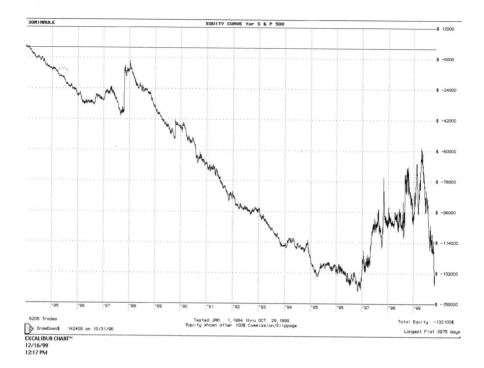

FIGURE 3.36 Thirty-minute rule trading S&Ps.

GAP HIGHER/LOW OPENINGS

Markets open on a gap either above or below the previous day's high or low about 20 to 25% of the time or about 80 to 100 times per year per market (Figure 3.37). The normal reaction to a gap up opening is that this is a sign of strength and the market should be purchased. The

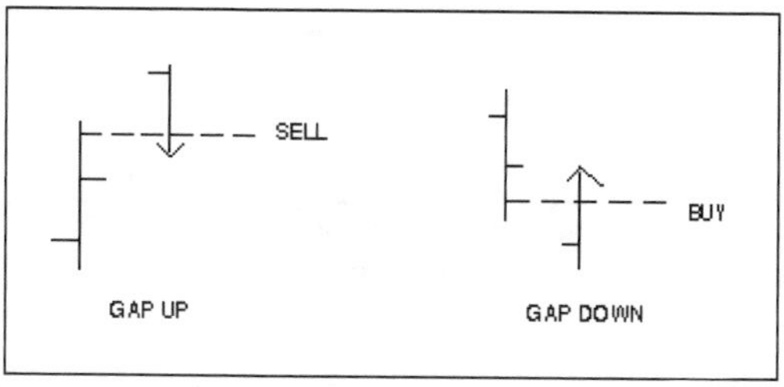

FIGURE 3.37 Gap openings.

TABLE 3.15   Gap Openings—Futures

BUY ON PULLBACK TO HIGH OF PRIOR DAY ON DOWNSIDE GAP
OPENING (OPPOSITE FOR SELL)—DAY TRADE. NO STOPS
TEST PERIOD: 1/1/77–6/30/99. ONE CONTRACT PER SIGNAL. DAY TRADE
$0 ALLOWED FOR COMMISSION AND SLIPPAGE

Individual Future	Total PL ($)	Avg PL ($)/Yr	Max DrawDn ($)	Trds /Yr	Win (%)	TIM (%)	W:L	Gain/Mr +DD (%)
US Bonds	108,170	5,012	10,600	62	54.7	20	1.5	41.9
Treasury Note	31,490	1,843	7,630	61	50.9	20	1.3	22
Euro $	22,025	1,271	1,850	51	49.8	17	1.5	60.9
T.Bills	29,300	1,256	3,925	49	49.4	16	1.4	29.9
Muni Bonds	30,320	2,192	4,820	51	49.4	17	1.3	38.3
British Pd.	14,213	590	10,113	59	47.6	19	1.1	5.4
Deutsche Mark	35,463	1,473	6,963	63	52.5	20	1.3	19.3
Japanese Yen	7,188	322	22,150	62	47.4	20	1	1.4
Swiss Franc	21,638	898	13,038	62	52.2	20	1.1	6.5
Canadian $	5,120	229	8,610	70	47.3	22	1.1	2.6
US$ Index	(8,780)	(646)	14,940	49	48.9	16	0.9	−4.1
Copper	45,925	1,728	6,313	60	53.2	19	1.4	23.4
S&P 500	30,113	1,798	43,450	44	56.2	15	1.1	3.7
NYFE Index	67,900	3,975	28,750	44	56.1	15	1.3	12.3
Live Cattle	42,320	1,447	3,596	50	52	17	1.5	37.4
Pork Bellies	63,076	2,108	11,852	53	53.8	18	1.3	16.1
Live Hogs	30,660	1,036	4,312	47	54.2	16	1.3	21.4
Soybeans	62,850	2,049	15,075	53	53.5	18	1.3	13
Soybean Oil	41,754	1,365	2,610	50	53.5	17	1.5	47.4
Soybean Meal	49,960	1,634	5,730	50	53.1	17	1.4	25.8
Wheat	24,126	789	5,863	50	48.8	17	1.2	12.6
Crude Oil	44,370	2,802	4,410	63	55.1	20	1.6	51.7
Unleaded Gas	31,357	2,163	4,557	57	53	19	1.4	38.8
Heating Oil	28,627	1,468	10,550	63	51.6	21	1.2	12.7
Coffee	242,981	9,406	12,413	59	58.7	19	1.7	63.3
Sugar	81,458	3,045	5,141	59	56.3	19	1.6	55.5
Cotton	77,940	2,914	5,945	60	55.6	20	1.4	45.2
Cocoa	24,480	1,300	5,310	56	53.2	19	1.3	22.1
Orange Juice	30,150	1,131	6,038	54	53.6	18	1.3	17.3

Summary	Net PL ($)	Max DrawDn ($)		Avg.Mrgn Req'd ($)
Average/Year	42,919	14,302	Average	20,000
Full run total	1,316,192	53,792	Maximum	20,000

	Return (%)	Capital Req'd for % Return ($)
1. Return on margin plus average drawdown	126	34,000
2. Return on margin plus maximum drawdown	58	73,792
3. Return with maximum drawdown limited to 20% of capital	16	268,960

1. $20,000 assumed as this is a day trade

exact opposite is true when placed under computer scrutiny. This idea was tested by 2 methods:

1. Sell a gap up opening.
2. Sell a gap up opening but only if it pulls back to the prior day's high.

The opposite was applied to the buy side. Both ideas were run on a computer with no stops and as a day trade. The second approach was about twice as good as the first one and is shown in Table 3.15 on page 74. It trades about 60 times/year/future. It is making the market move in your direction prior to taking a position. It does show that you gain an edge on the markets by this signal. It is insufficient to overcome the commission and slippage in most markets. It could be a valuable addition to your bag of trading tools when combined with other filters and use of appropriate stops. Incidentally, the numbers show that this could be a profitable bond day trading system.

This pattern is very similar to one developed by Larry Williams called *Oops*. The basic idea is the same, but how he treats entry and exit is not known. Possible uses of this knowledge might be:

1. The signal is probably more reliable if market is extended in either direction and this could signal the end of a move. If so, this could be a beautiful way to take profits on positions and perhaps reverse positions.
2. Other studies might be to:
   • Look at entry signals on reversals of the previous close, a number of previous closes, and a number of previous highs and lows.
   • Study carrying a half range stop once entry is made.
   • Study gap openings above or below a cluster of closes.
   • Look at a half range reversal of the gap prior to taking a position.

These are simple computer studies that will quickly tell you whether the opening in relation to recent market action gives one a technical edge. Larry Williams and Toby Crabel have down some excellent work in this area. One could fill an entire book on studies of market action in relation to the opening and movement away from the opening.

4

CHANNEL AND
TRENDLINE TRADING

This chapter will be helpful in trade location because it identifies both major and minor channels. This is of value in knowing when to act on reversal and continuation patterns. Use of simple trendlines combined with basic wave theory as an entry technique is also shown. Some of the methodology in this section defies computer programming into a system. However, it becomes very clear when viewing a chart with the lines and channels on them. This can almost be a systematic approach.

One of the most useful tools in the trader's kit is trendlines. Many people use indicators put out by some elaborate computer program. These indicators generally tell you the same thing: the extent of an overbought/oversold market. Simple trendlines with a few additional rules can be extremely effective in timing your trades. Learn how to read the charts rather than the indicators. We have yet to see an indicator that tells you that a spring or upthrust took place and if you have a position, you better act promptly. A *spring* is when a market trades below a pivot low or support point, finds no supply, and rallies aggressively. An *upthrust* is when the market trades above a pivot point high, encounters no demand, and immediately falls. This is further discussed in Chapter 6.

TREND LINES AND PARALLEL MOVEMENTS

A major pivot point high is followed by at least two lower pivot points prior to a new high (and vice versa for lows). A major trend line connects two major pivot point lows or highs. The parallel movement is a parallel line drawn from major pivot points as shown in Figure 4.1. The target for the movement is where the price reaches the parallel line or the

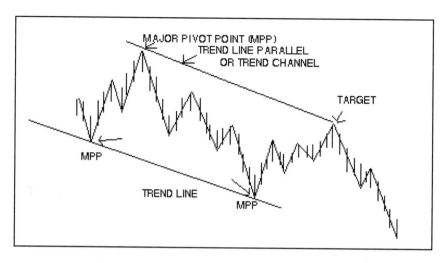

FIGURE 4.1 Trend line and parallel movements.

trend channel. Minor trend channels are the channels that connect minor pivot points.

Figure 4.2 demonstrates the use of 0–4 lines for trading. Note that the bars are not shown which simplify reading the chart. The swings go from pivot point to pivot point. The 0–4 lines connect the major pivot points with the fourth wave. Shown are 0–4 lines for both a down move and an up move with the waves marked. Trade entry is made when the

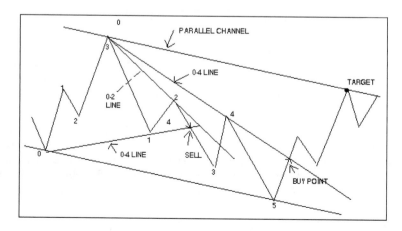

FIGURE 4.2 0–4 lines.

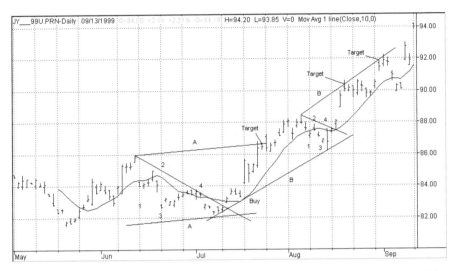

FIGURE 4.3 Japanese Yen (September 1999). Created with TradeStation 2000i by Omega Research © 1999.

market penetrates the 0–4 line provided the 0–4 line is above the 0–2 line for a buy and vice versa. A wide range bar with the close above the opening at this point is another indication of demand (long trade). The target point is at the parallel trend channel. Figure 4.3 demonstrates the use of this technique for trading the Japanese Yen.

TRADING THE 0–2 LINE

Trading set up: Market has a demand thrust and is now in the correction phase (Figure 4.4). If wave C holds above the level of minor pivot point A, then a purchase may be made upon penetration of the 0–2 line. However, if pivot point C is below A, then it is best to wait to enter the market after wave 4 sets up.

Some subjectivity is involved in trading the parallel movements, 0–4 lines and 0–2 lines. The logic for programming this into a mechanical system would be exceedingly difficult. However, the rules are relatively simple and entry and exit points are straight forward. A computer is not needed. Figure 4.3 on Japanese Yen demonstrates the use of this technique.

Figure 4.5 is an example for trading penetration of the 0–2 line. This is at the termination of an irregular correction.

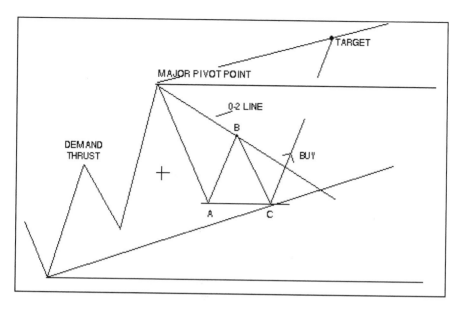

FIGURE 4.4 Trading the 0–2 lines.

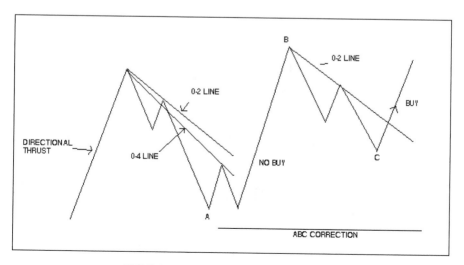

FIGURE 4.5 0–2 line trading the C-leg.

TRENDLINE AND FOUR-CLOSE SYSTEM (TL4C)

This is a simple system that does not require a computer to run (Figure 4.6). It requires judgment on the trend and whether the profit potential is worth the risk.

Setup for buy (sell is opposite):

1. Trade only in direction of thrust or trend.
2. Draw a trendline connecting the last two high pivot points.
3. There are two or more rising or equal low pivot points within the last 20 days.

Buy on movement above this line if:

- Close is above opening.
- Close is above the four prior closes.
- Range is greater than average.

Stop is below most recent pivot point low. Liquidate on evidence of false move such as a wide range reversal.

Move stop to breakeven when breathing room exists so as to have a free trade. Breathing room is a question of judgment but one simple method might be to move stop just below the low of entry day if the high of entry day is exceeded by a half range.

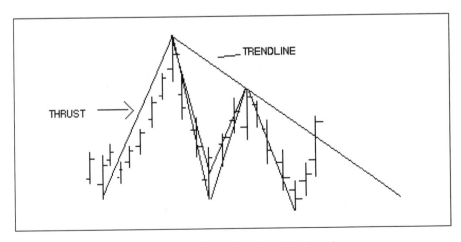

FIGURE 4.6   Four-close trendline break.

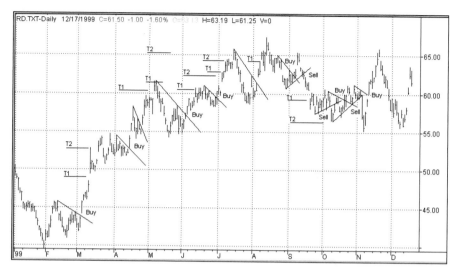

FIGURE 4.7 Royal Dutch Petroleum. Created with TradeStation 2000i by Omega Research © 1999.

Take profits at:

1. Swing objective, or
2. On a four-close trendline break that is against the trend, or
3. On a half range breakout from opening if market enters the sell zone.

These are suggestions. The basic idea is to liquidate the trade when it becomes apparent that supply is overcoming demand or it is a buying climax (reverse for shorts). Figure 4.7 on Royal Dutch illustrates these ideas.

TREND CHANNEL SYSTEM

When the market hits a lower trend channel line, buy/sell on first positive indication of a trend change, in up move:

- Buy higher opening.
- Buy on 11:30 rule (market above opening at mid-day).
- Buy on reversal day.
- Buy on minor reversal patterns.

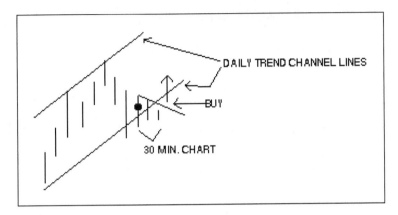

FIGURE 4.8   Use of lower time frame.

- Buy the pull back.
- Lower time frame. Keep 30-minute chart and buy at trend channel parallels (basic daily charts) on first sign of strength on 30-minute chart (Figure 4.8).

5

SWING TRADING

This chapter presents the basic approach to swing trading combined with supply/demand characteristics of the bar chart and the wave theory. These factors are utilized in a coherent manner to use past price movements to project future prices and thereby gain a technical edge for profitable trading. Elements of this chapter have been presented in other places in this book. The repetition is intentional. You cannot build a house with a hammer. Also, you cannot build a house without one. The same is true in trading. You cannot trade with only one tool. You must have many and know from looking at the big picture which one is appropriate to use at the moment.

SWING CHARTS

A swing chart is a line drawn from one pivot point to the next on a bar chart (see Figure 3.3). A movement is up as long as the bars are making new highs. It reverses to down when the low of a previous bar is penetrated. This adds clarity to the picture as openings and closing are not shown. A view of both is useful is determining which trading tools are appropriate.

Action Points for Trading the Long Side

Thrust Action

Trade in the direction of a thrust (Figure 5.1). Contrary to some wave theories, markets in one direction may have more than five waves, three of which are in one direction and two in the opposite direction. As many as eleven waves have been apparent on many charts. A movement or trend will continue in that direction until a counter wave occurs that is of greater magnitude than any of the prior waves. This is simply supply and

THE ULTIMATE TRADING GUIDE

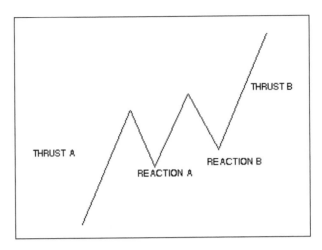

FIGURE 5.1

demand. It does not necessarily mean the market will now reverse trend. It may mean, but as a minimum, the market has shifted into congestion.

Parallel movement of up swings tend to be equal in magnitude and time. Figure 5.1 demonstrates that thrust B equals thrust A and reaction B equals reaction A. This enables the trader to forecast the termination of the next swing in both time and price.

Figure 5.2 demonstrates these ideas with Japanese Yen. Two profitable trades are shown.

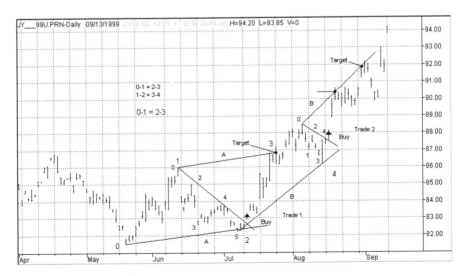

FIGURE 5.2 Japanese Yen (September 1999). Created with TradeStation 2000i by Omega Research © 1999.

- *Trade 1:* A buy is made as market penetrates the 0–1 trendline and closes above the prior 4 closes. The swing from 81.50 (point 0) to 86.00 is a thrust up. We now know the trend is up and the Yen is a buy on a reaction. The market has an orderly five-wave correction back toward the base or beginning of the move. The setup is now complete. A buy is made and profit of 5.50 points taken,

- *Trade 2:* Market continues up to above the 88.00 level confirming that the breakout of the 86.00 level is a valid one. Market enters a 1,2,3 or ABC correction pattern. A purchase is made at 88.00 on completion of the 4-close, trendline break pattern. Profits taken at 90.30 at the parallel objective.

Figure 5.3 demonstrates a number of swing chart principles. This is a chart of intraday movements of S and P's with the prices removed.

- *Spring:* A substantial movement may take place after a spring. Market frequently moves back across the trading range as it did in this case.

- *Penetration of two pivot points in close proximity:* Be alert for a larger swing. Close proximity might be defined as two points within a half average bar range of one another. This penetration led to a reversal of trend. Complete replacement of the prior down thrust shows that the market has shifted from supply to

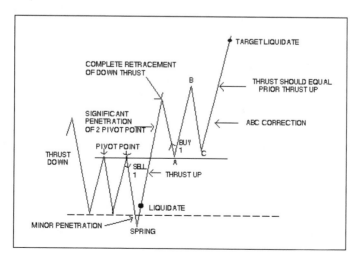

FIGURE 5.3 Swing chart analysis of intraday movements of S&Ps.

demand. Buy on a correction after a complete retracement of the prior move.

- *ABC/ABCDE correction to a thrust:* Anticipate continuation of movement after this type action following a thrust.

Two trades were possible on this movement:

- *Trade 1:* A short was taken when market tested the pivot point. Note that the prior thrust confirmed the trend as down and market should be traded from the short side only. This trade was immediately liquidated when lack of supply was apparent by the spring.
- *Trade 2:* Purchase was made on the A-leg pull back to support of the 2 prior pivot point highs. Trend is up as a complete retracement was made of the prior down thrust Target was another thrust equal to the prior directional thrust.

ANTICIPATION

Anticipation is the key to successful speculation. One must anticipate termination of a movement at critical areas of support or resistance. A swing chart and a bar chart may be used in combination for determining these zones. Two methods are available for market entry at these zones of support:

1. Buy in the logical support zone. A stop must be entered immediately at a reasonable distance below the level of support.
2. Buy on a stop above the market once the market enters the zones of support. The amount above the market should be in anticipation of a wide range bar up which would signal that the correction is over. This order should be entered upon seeing the market drop into the zones of support or slightly penetrate it. This type order is most useful when the market is in an up trend and the buy zone is entered at the termination of an ABC correction.

If the market is in obvious congestion, the take profits points are established in the resistance zone or at one of the following:

1. At swing objectives.
2. At parallel trend channel points.
3. At major pivot points particularly if a reversal pattern is signaled.
4. On penetration of trendline if time factors favor a reversal.

MOVE ENDING

A run up move ending is signaled when a reaction exceeds any previous reaction in both time and space. Figure 5.4 shows that reaction 3 is greater than both reaction 1 and reaction 2 in time and space. The reverse is true for a run down.

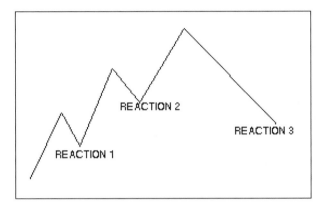

FIGURE 5.4 Move ending.

PULLBACK BUYS

When the high of bar 1 is penetrated, look for a buy on a one-bar reaction or pullback (Figure 5.5). This is particularly true if bar one is a wide-range bar and the range is greater than the range of the low bar.

When a high is penetrated, the low of bar one becomes a point of support. A purchase might be made in the lower 25% of the range with a stop below support.

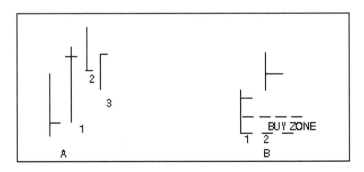

FIGURE 5.5 Pullback buys.

Before entering this trade, you should make certain that other tools or setups are in place to support the action.

ACTION AND REACTIONS

There is a reaction in both time and space for every action in the market (Figure 5.6). Reactions are not necessarily equal. They may be equal in space but not in time and vice versa. Therein lies a trading methodology and the ability to tell when there is an imbalance in the markets. For instance, say the action in a market is a 10-point rise in five days. An equal reaction in 10 points down in five days. However, if the market has only reacted 5 points in five days, then time has run out on the reaction. The next action is likely to be either a 5 or 10 point rise to the upside to equal the previous action and reaction.

This holds true for small moves as well as large moves. This is why a big correction down is likely after a five-wave movement to the upside. The entire five waves up may be corrected with three to five waves down.

This concept is why you should resist the urge to buy a 50% point correction on the first day down after an up move.

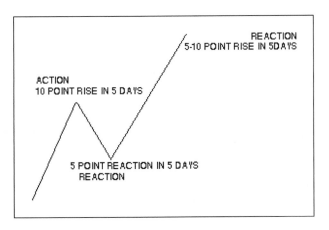

FIGURE 5.6 Action/reaction.

PRELIMINARY DEMAND

Preliminary demand is demand overcoming supply prior to a final bottom. It is characterized by a significant range rally prior to the final low. Note that rally 2 is greater than rally 1 in Figure 5.7. This action makes the shorts nervous because another type movement just might

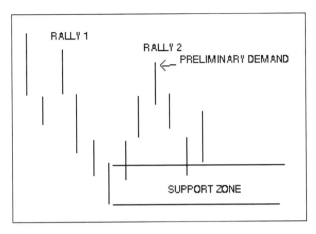

FIGURE 5.7 Preliminary demand.

occur and eliminate any profits. Demand is likely to overcome supply as the market again approaching the low or perhaps exceeds the low of the move. It's a setup for a possible spring.

TIME AND SPACE

Trend is generally at an end when a reaction exceeds any previous one in time and space (Figure 5.8). Never buy at 50% point on first bar after the time and space signal.

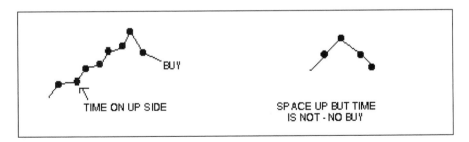

FIGURE 5.8 Space and time comparison.

SELL TOPS AFTER A TREND CHANGE

Sell short-term strength in a down trend (Figure 5.9). Buy short-term weakness in an up trend. This type trading enables one to enter markets with low risk in the event the trade is wrong. Try to develop the

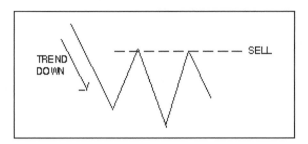

FIGURE 5.9   Sell tops after trend change.

ability to buy short-term weakness and sell on strength. This type of trading greatly enhances the profit potential.

Short Sell Points (Figure 5.10)

Point 1 to point 2. Three-day up move is positive, however, bars 2 and 3 close below opening and this is a warning sign of distribution.

Point 2 to point 3. Corrective action to the 1–2 move is normal. The wide-range bar at point 2 sets up a resistance point at the high.

Point 4. The narrow-range bar at point 4 is not demand and supply may enter the market.

Point 5. Three places are shown for taking a nibble on the short side. Note the trend line break and five-day close reversal. Stop is above the three bar high.

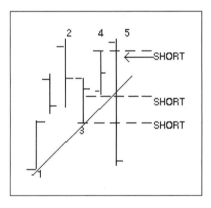

FIGURE 5.10   Three opportunities to short.

THREE BAR RALLIES

Three bar rallies do occur in major moves (Figure 5.11). If it takes place when the market is in the run-down phase, it is a warning sign but not a trend change. A three-bar counter up move places market in an exhausted overbought condition particularly if spreads are becoming shorter. A short above the high of the second day may be appropriate

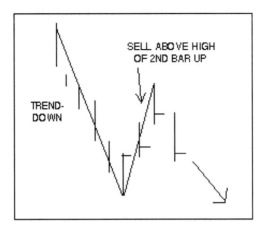

FIGURE 5.11   One- to three-bar rallies.

particularly if major trend is down. Generally the first or second day after this third bar will provide the answer. A widening range to the downside should appear or another swing up may be in the picture. You are selling into near-term strength in a down market.

A three-bar rally with increasing range after three dips into a zone of congestion is a sign of strength (Figure 5.12). A one to one and a half day reaction, into the buy zone is the time and place to take a position. The buy zone is the area between the 50% correction point and the three bar low.

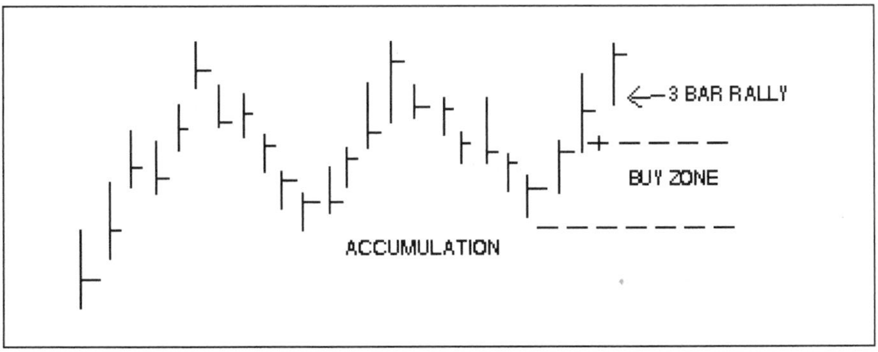

FIGURE 5.12   Three-bar rally at end of congestion phase.

HOLDING GAIN AND RALLY FROM SUPPORT

If the market breaks out above a pivot point, as shown in Figure 5.13A, and holds the gain for two to three bars, odds favor that this is a valid

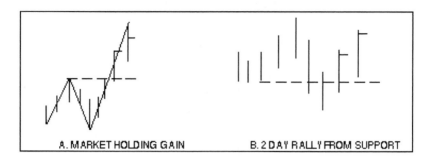

FIGURE 5.13   Holding gain/rally from support.

breakout. A two-bar rally after penetrating a series of lows, as shown in Figure 5.13B, implies no supply and bullish forces may be gaining control. A widening of the range would be positive.

Three periods after thrust reveal whether it is false or real.

Figure 5.14A is a market breakout from a tight formation. This appears to be a valid breakout. The following three bars generally confirm or deny the pattern. Figure 5.14B confirms it as the market was able to hold the gain and make new highs. Action as in Figure 5.14C would suggest failure of the breakout.

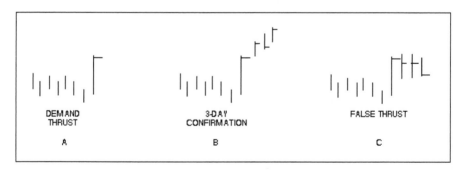

FIGURE 5.14   Three-day confirmation of a thrust.

SETUPS FOR TREND CHANGE

Swing from A–B as in Figure 5.15A is not a trend change until Point B is penetrated. In Figure 5.15B, 0–1 movement is a demand thrust. When the leg is equal to 1.5 to 2.0 times the A leg, the main trend may have turned down. This would be confirmed if point C is penetrated on the next swing down.

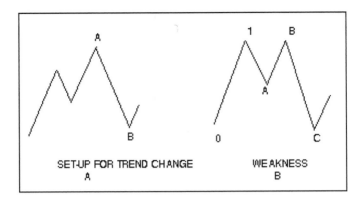

FIGURE 5.15 Setups for trend change.

Wide-Range Reversal Bar after Run Up

When the market is moving aggressively up in new high ground and the following actions take place, it is time to move stop in tight or take profits:

1. A wide-range reversal bar.
2. A narrow-range inside bar bounce.

This type action implies supply is entering the market (Figure 5.16).

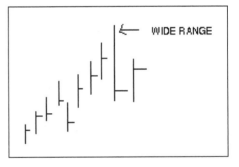

FIGURE 5.16 Wide-range reversal bar.

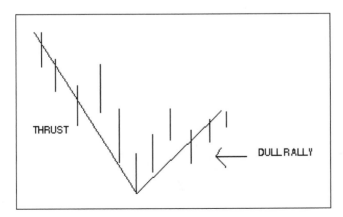

FIGURE 5.17 Dull rally after thrust.

Sell dull rallies after thrust. A dull rally is a rally with relatively small range bars that have a difficult time in reaching the 50% point of the down thrust (Figure 5.17 on page 93).

TREND CONTINUATION

Under these conditions (Figure 5.18A), expect a trend continuation:

- 0–1 is thrust down in example A:
  1. ABC up to the 75% point implies a minimum of an ABCDE correction.
  2. If ABC holds above 1, market is neutral.
  3. If ABC holds above B, market trend may be changing to up.
  4. If ABC breaks point 1, trend remains down.
- 0–1 is a directional move up in Figure 5.18B:
  1. ABCDE is a triangular correction. Note that it is holding above the 50% point of the thrust.
  2. Penetration of D would indicate resumption of up move.
- Market is in a correction to a thrust up (Figure 5.18C). When five waves down is completed and wave 5 is shorter than wave 3, an aggressive ABC rally is a possibility. Added fuel is possible if this is in the support zone.

How a market moves away from a point determines whether or not that point will hold on next testing. Always go back three to four market swings to determine market direction. Thrust after a period of inaction usually points direction of move.

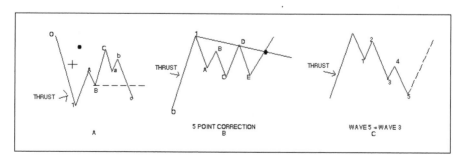

FIGURE 5.18   Trend continuation.

THREE DRIVES TO A BOTTOM

Three drives to a bottom with a shorting of thrusts places the market in an oversold condition and subject to a good sized rally (Figure 5.19). Note the difference in the three rallies. The third rally was stronger. This is the time and place to consider going long if other parts of the setup are in place.

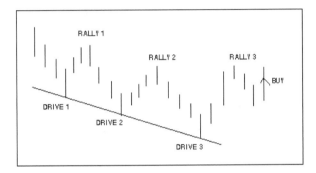

FIGURE 5.19   Drives to a bottom.

SUPPORT/RESISTANCE ZONES

The power of a support or resistance zone can be gauged by several factors:

1. The magnitude of a rally after the market has entered a zone (and vice versa) in both time and space.
2. The number of times a support or resistance zone has been tested.

These factors are a basic expression of supply or demand. If the market enters a support zone and is unable to have a significant rally within one to three bars, then the zone is unlikely to hold (Figure 5.20). A sharp rally shows that demand exists in that area and is likely to hold on the next movement back into that zone. Each time a support zone is tested, it absorbs some of the underlying demand in that area. That is why the old adage, "Markets will penetrate on the fourth testing of a support zone" is frequently true.

The logical question is how does one make money with this basic knowledge. The answer is as follows.

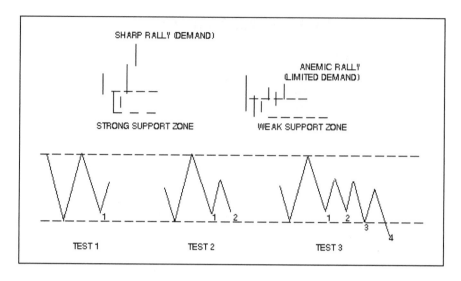

FIGURE 5.20   Tests of support.

1. *Anticipation.* You must buy the market in support zones and sell in resistance zones when you do not know the outcome. You may buy when a lower time frame shows evidence of supply exhaustion and demand entering the picture and vice versa. Use the short-term reversal patterns. You may make several attempts at entry and be stopped out before you are successful. Learn to love small losses because you know a winner is coming. Study enough charts until you realize that a number of logical support zones simply do not hold and some do.

2. *Position Exits.* Appropriate liquidation procedures must be in place if you are wrong. Have a take profit target in mind and take profits or at least some of them at such points. Remember that the time frame to take profits is sometimes a very short duration. If you do not act promptly, the opportunity may be lost.

You should develop the ability to recognize the difference between a sharp rally and a weak one. Buy on reaction after sharp rallies and not after weak one and vice versa. Figure 5.21 shows a chart of S&P's (December 1999, daily). It demonstrates the use of this knowledge. Exact buy/sell points are not given. The main thrust is to plant an approach to trading.

Trade moving markets and avoid dull sideways markets (W.D. Gann). This has been mentioned many times but the swing chart in Figure 5.22 gives you a picture of what to look for.

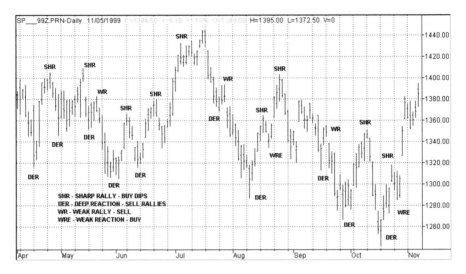

FIGURE 5.21 S&Ps daily bar chart (December 1999). Created with TradeStation 2000i by Omega Research © 1999.

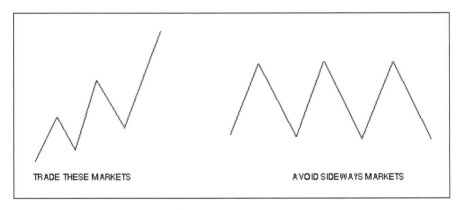

FIGURE 5.22 Markets to trade.

TIME AND PRICE PROJECTIONS

Time and price projections for the future can be made based on recent history for swings (Figure 5.23). This assumes that future market action will be a reflection of the immediate past. The last two reactions or wave 1 and wave 3 will be reflected in wave 5. This gives projection of both time and space. The last three rallies and reactions are used to

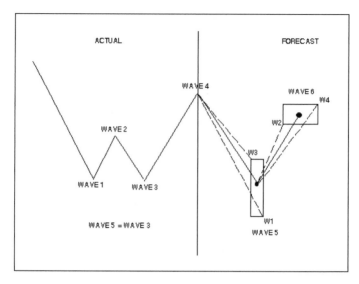

FIGURE 5.23   Time and price forecast.

project future turning points. Note that waves 1 and 2 are different, thus the projection points will differ. The boxed area in Figure 5.23 shows the zone where waves 5 and 6 should terminate in both time and space. Time projections are much less reliable than price projections. Some technicians believe that bottom to bottom and tops to tops time projections are

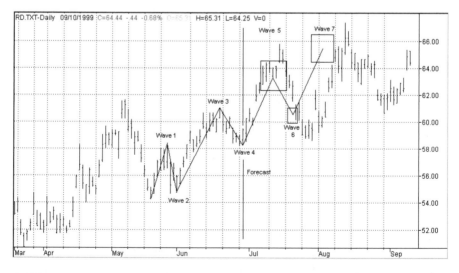

FIGURE 5.24   Royal Dutch Petroleum time and price forecast. Created with TradeStation 2000i by Omega Research © 1999.

more reliable than the above. We cannot reach this same conclusion, but can't disprove it either. Wave 6 can be projected based on wave 2 and wave 4. This is done by using the center of the wave 5 box area as a starting point.

Figure 5.24 on page 98 demonstrates this idea on Royal Dutch Petroleum. If in a position and market enters the target zone for both time and price, use the trading tools outlined in this book to take profits or move stop in tight by use of the lower time frame charts. A reversal of position might also be considered, depending on the big picture.

TREND

The trend is an elusive element subject to many definitions, all of which have elements of truth. The old adage, "The trend is your friend" is certainly true. Trading with the trend is the key element in everything discussed in this book. Some subjectivity is always present and we are certain that the readers of this book will quickly point out that we choose the trend to fit the case. This is known as hindsight analysis. We have very few losing trades when we trade in this manner. The real world is entirely different and many false analyses will be made. Trend definition has a lot to do with your style of trading. If you are trading

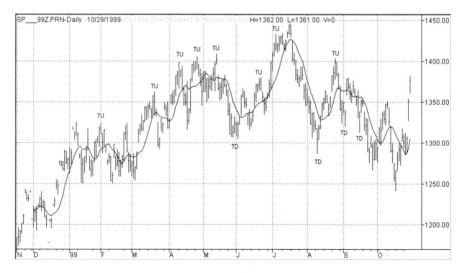

FIGURE 5.25 S&P Futures trend defination (December 1999). Created with TradeStation 2000i by Omega Research © 1999.

for the long-term trends, the definitions below are inadequate. One definition of trend is as follows:

1. *The slope of the 10-bar average:* If up, the trend is up.
2. *Major pivot points:* If the last major top pivot point is greater than the prior top pivot point then the trend is up. This gets a little fuzzy. ABC corrections to a thrust frequently will have the C-leg going below the A-leg and it is not a trend change.
3. Go with the trend direction signaled by the pivot point direction if the two are in conflict. Figure 5.25 on page 99 shows the use of this definition.

Use of multiple time frames is invaluable in your search for profitable trading methodologies. For instance, use a daily bar chart for trend and the 30-minute or 1-hour chart for trading. Just take the trades on the 30-minute chart that are in the direction of the daily trend.

FIRST DAY IN RALLY

The first day in a rally following a down wave frequently reveals technical makeup (Figure 5.26). Compare the spread and close of this one day at point 3 to the preceding one day rallies coming off the lows at points 1 and 2. A stronger day implies a shift to the upside with near term demand overcoming supply. Be alert for a trend change. If this is in a bed of accumulation, it may be worth a nibble on the long side.

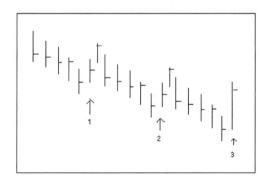

FIGURE 5.26   First day in rally.

6

PATTERNS

The mistake is not being wrong, the mistake is staying wrong.

When a woodsman enters the forest, he must pick one tree and cut it. The same is true in trading. Once the big picture is known, a trader must decide on a specific entry technique, stop point, and take profit level. This chapter covers 19 patterns relating to entry and exit techniques. In reading about these various techniques, keep in mind the basic idea of demand overcoming supply and vice versa. A chart is the reflection of the forces pulling both ways on the market until one wins out.

Patterns demonstrate the exact moment in time when demand overcomes supply (and vice versa) and "the rubber hits the road." These signals are far from 100% correct, and some do fail. Immediate failure means a false start. That is where the professional will aggressively take the other side of the trade. They know the signal is false as evidenced by market action. That is why it is so important that the stop loss and perhaps reversal order be entered immediately. Part of your arsenal of trading tools should include trading immediate pattern failures. The take profit point is just as important if not more so than the entry. Your trading plan must consist of all three elements: entry, stop, and exit.

The following trading patterns will be discussed:

- Opening range breakout.
- Trend up confirmed.
- Spring reversal pattern.
- Upthrust reversal pattern.
- Yum-yum continuation pattern.
- L formation and reverse L.
- Double tops and bottoms.
- Small morning tails.

- Clear out patterns.
- Overlapping and non-overlapping bars.
- Two-day intersection.
- Channel trading systems.
- The pullback.
- High of low bar for buying/low of high bar for selling.
- Three bars up/down.
- Dynamite triangle.
- Narrow-range/wide-range bars.
- Two-day flip.
- Tight formation breakout.
- The importance of exits.

OPENING RANGE BREAKOUTS

The opening range breakout is a movement off the opening. Studies have shown that the opening of the day is frequently either the high or low point of the day. A buy or sell order is entered a certain amount from the opening, as shown in Figure 6.1.

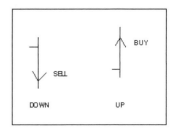

FIGURE 6.1 Opening range breakout.

There are many types of breakout trading systems. This is one of the most effective filters for getting on board at the beginning of a trend whether it is a three-bar or a 10-bar trend. Movement away from the opening frequently sets the trading tone for the day and the market will close in the direction of the opening range breakout. Combine this with pattern setups and you have the basis for an excellent trading systems. We personally know of at least $200 to $300 million being traded using opening range breakout as one of the filters for entering or exiting a trade. E. Hadady, Larry Williams, and Toby Crabel have done excellent studies on use of this tool.

How much of an opening range breakout is effective? Possible answers to this question are:

1. Use a prescribed amount such as eight ticks. This is a critical amount and anything smaller is less likely to be successful. This simply will not work on low volatility stocks or futures. This is an easy statistical study.

2. Make the breakout be a function of the volatility. The volatility might be average daily range for a past number of days or prior day's range. For instance, studies have shown that if a market moves 50% of the prior day's range away from the opening, it is likely to remain in that direction for the balance of the day.

Intraday Ranges

Divide the day into three equal time segments and develop a strategy around these three bars on an opening range breakout for each time period. One could also use hourly or smaller bars. Bob Buran has done excellent work in this area particularly with S&P's and as confirmation on whether the breakout is exhaustion or continuation.

The opening range breakout must be combined with other technical tools to be an effective entry technique. Figure 6.2 shows six examples of using a second tool to time your market entry. These additional tools are: four weeks high or low (Donchain or Turtle Breakout), trendline, tight range of closes, two prior closes, trend filter such as a 10-bar

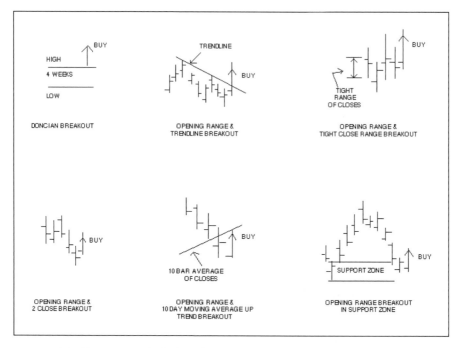

FIGURE 6.2 Technical tools to use with opening range breakout.

moving average of closes (slope must be up for a buy), and support zone buying. All of these tools are an expression of demand overcoming supply. There is no pat answer as to which one is best. A number of them can be programmed into exact trading systems. However, the other two parts of the trading plan, stop and exit must be built into the system. Both are just as important as the entry.

TREND UP CONFIRMED

Trend up confirmed is a four-step process that is present in most movements (Figure 6.3). It is a very useful tool but should not be used by itself. The rules for this formation are as follows (for up move):

1. The current bar makes a low below the prior bar.
2. The high of this bar is penetrated to the upside (trend up or sign of strength). Best if this is a wide-bar penetration with several up bars.
3. Within one to three bars, the low of an up bar is penetrated (the pullback or test of the low).
4. The high of the last bar in the reaction is penetrated and closes above it. The low must be greater that the low in step 1. This is pattern completion and your buy point.

The stop is the range of the entry bar subtracted from the low of the entry bar. Take profits at the swing target. If the swing target is not reached, then liquidate on two closes below a prior pivot point with the close on last bar below the opening. There is some flexibility in this rule. Do not let good profits turn into losses simply because the price did not quite reach the target.

This technique works exceedingly well in a strongly trending market and is a first cousin to the dynamite triangle. Trade with the trend. It sometimes takes as many as 10 bars to complete the formation. It is a simple four-step process for getting on board a move. The up bars should be relatively long with

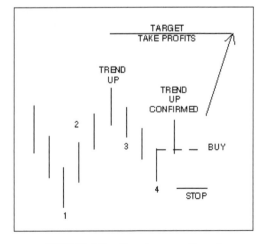

FIGURE 6.3 Trend up confirmed.

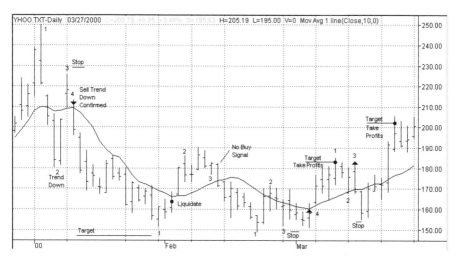

FIGURE 6.4 Yahoo trend up confirmed. Created with TradeStation 2000i by Omega Research © 1999.

high closes compared to the down bars. This implies demand or a sign of strength.

You are buying on strength in trading this pattern. Take some profits on strength rather than on a stop. The exception is when the market has a clearly defined breakout from tight congestion. Figure 6.4 shows use of this pattern on a chart of Yahoo.

SPRING REVERSAL PATTERN

The springs and upthrusts concept originated with the Wyckoff Course (see bibliography). It is another way of expressing demand exceeding supply. A set of rules have been devised around this idea in an effort to make trading as mechanical as possible. Basically, the market goes to new lows below a significant pivot point and clears out all stops (Figure 6.5). When lack of supply is apparent to the professional trader, he immediately buys it and the market

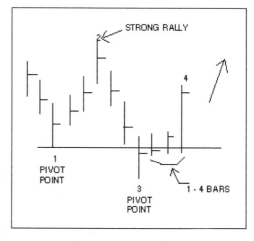

FIGURE 6.5 Spring.

aggressively rallies. The market moves up on a wide range that exceeds the two prior closes.

This pattern occurs at move endings and is generally against the current trend. It works best when the pattern has been in a zone of congestion and the market makes an attempt to resume the downward move. Overpowering demand occurs at the new low with an up move as a result. The congestion pattern proceeding the spring may be one of accumulation rather than distribution.

Spring Rules

1. A pivot point low is made. It does not have to be the last pivot point. It may be several back where strong support was in evidence.

2. A fairly strong rally takes place.

3. Market moves to a new low below the prior pivot point.

4. Within one to four days, a wide-range rally takes place with the close greater than the two previous bars closing prices. The range of this bar exceeds the range of the two prior bars. Close is above opening and mid-range of the bar.

Confirmation is when the high of the wide-range bar is exceeded. A spring that reverses two pivot points is much more significant than a single pivot reverse. The stop point is 0.5 to 1.0 range below the low of the entry bar. The first target is the prior pivot point high.

UPTHRUST REVERSAL PATTERN

The upthrust reversal pattern is essentially the mirror image of the spring reversal pattern.

1. A pivot point high is made. It does not have to be the last pivot point. It may be several back where supply was in evidence.

2. A fairly strong reaction takes place. This is not always present.

3. Market moves to a new high above the prior pivot point high.

4. Within one to four days, a wide-range reaction takes place with the close less than the two previous bars closing prices. The range of this bar exceeds the range of the two prior bars. Close is below opening and mid-range of the bar.

Confirmation is when the low of the wide-range bar is broken. An upthrust that reverses two pivot points is much more significant than a

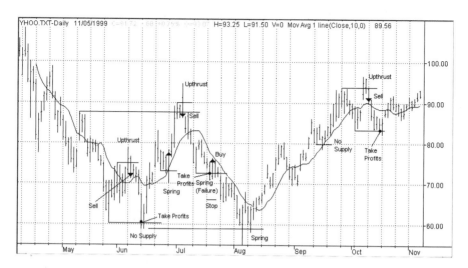

FIGURE 6.6 Yahoo spring upthrust formations. Created with TradeStation 2000i by Omega Research © 1999.

single pivot reverse. The stop point is 0.5 to 1.0 range above the high of the entry bar. The target is the prior pivot point low.

This pattern occurs at move endings and is against the current trend (Figure 6.6). It works best when the pattern has been in a zone of congestion and the market attempts to resume the upward move. Overpowering supply occurs at the new high and selling results. The congestion pattern may be one of distribution rather than accumulation.

An insignificant penetration of a pivot point implies lack of demand and a possible move back toward the lows. This is classic upthrust action. An insignificant penetration can generally be defined as one that is less than one-half range above the previous rally top. The professional will aggressively sell when he notes the lack of demand. Traders who buy on a slight penetration of rally tops are frequently handed a quick loss. The ability of the market to make a new high is positive. A potential profit point is toward the low of the bed of accumulation as the market will frequently drop back to this level after an upthrust.

Figure 6.6 shows a number of springs and upthrusts on Yahoo. One spring ended in failure and that is why a stop is always in place. Confirmation of the action should take place within three bars or it is questionable. This basic idea works in all time frames.

Spring and Upthrust Reversal Action

A spring or upthrust may have stronger implications if more than one pivot point is reversed as shown in Figure 6.7.

FIGURE 6.7   Strength of spring thrusts.

YUM-YUM CONTINUATION PATTERN

This is a pay day formation (Figure 6.8). A high pivot point is set up. Market reacts from this pivot point high for a number of bars followed by a strong thrust through the pivot point high. Rules are:

1. Pivot point high is broken with a wide-range bar that exceeds the 10-day average range bar.
2. Close is near the high of the bar and above the open.
3. Confirmation is provided when the high of the breakout bar is penetrated within one to three bars. This formation is a breakout and a sign of aggressive demand.

The downside Yum-Yum is the opposite. This formation is frequently called a *breakout*. There are more breakout failures than just about any formation. That is why it is dangerous to place stops just outside pivot points. A Yum-Yum (YY) is proof that the breakout is for real. Upon breaking a pivot point high, abundant demand is present as evidenced by the wide-range bar with a high close. The ability to hold and extend this gain for three days is further confirmation of strength. This pattern is seen frequently in trending markets. Figure 6.9 demonstrates the Yum-Yum on crude oil.

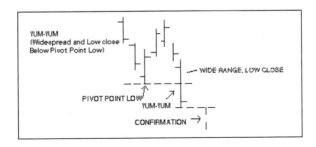

FIGURE 6.8   YUM-YUM.

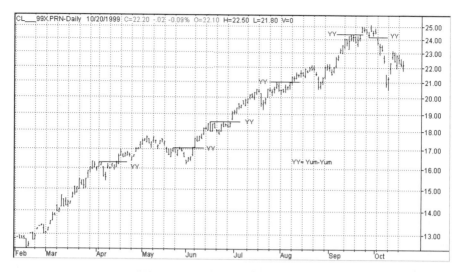

FIGURE 6.9 Crude oil futures (November 1999). Created with TradeStation 2000i by Omega Research © 1999.

L FORMATION AND REVERSE L

The L formation continuation consists of a strong thrust (Figure 6.10). If market holds the gain (or loss) for three to five bars with the ranges getting smaller, the market has adjusted to the new price zone and another thrust is in the same direction has a high probability. The open/close

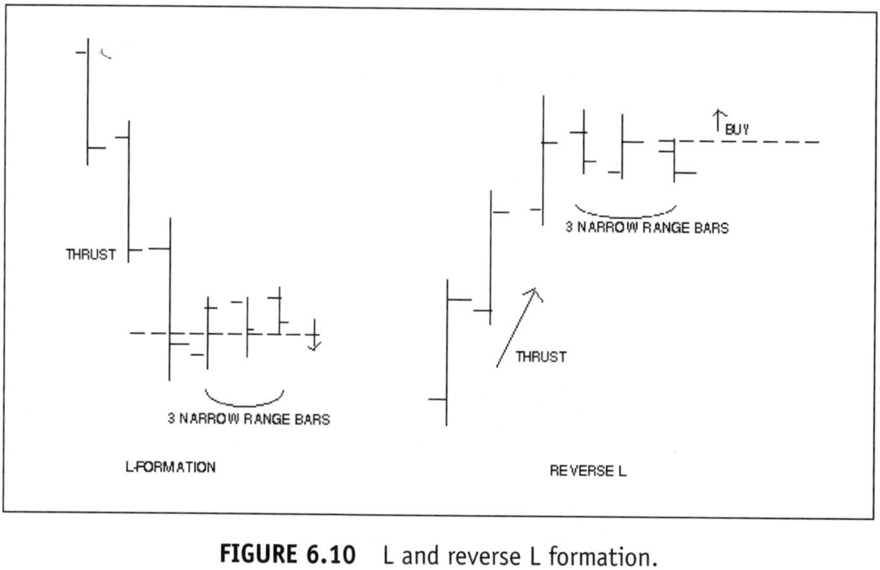

FIGURE 6.10 L and reverse L formation.

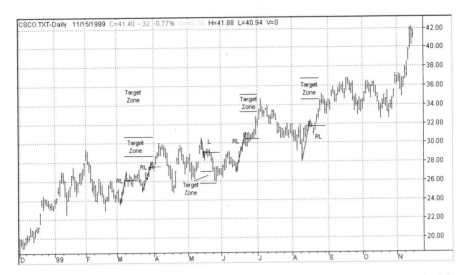

FIGURE 6.11 Cisco Systems L and reverse L continuation patterns. Created with TradeStation 2000i by Omega Research © 1999.

relationship after the three- to five-bar correction generally points the direction of the next thrust. Enter the market after the third day if close and open point to continuation of the move.

Stop is one range below the low of bar of entry. Target objective is 50% to 100% of the prior thrust added to the high of the initial thrust. Figure 6.11 demonstrates the use of this tool on Cisco.

DOUBLE TOPS AND BOTTOMS

Minute double tops and bottoms over a three- to five-day period is a very useful tool as a reversal pattern (Figure 6.12). Note that wide-range reversal bars are an important ingredient (Figure 6.13).

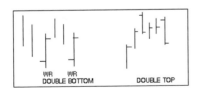

FIGURE 6.12 Double tops/
bottoms.

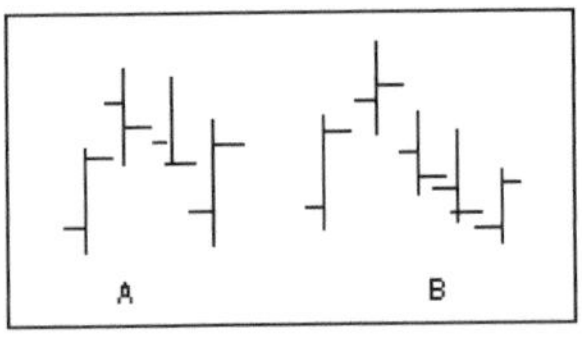

FIGURE 6.13 Double bottom/
comparison.

FIGURE 6.14 Cisco Systems double tops and bottoms. Created with TradeStation 2000i by Omega Research © 1999.

Figure 6.13A shows a valid double bottom as both days at the bottom have a wide range and high close. The double bottom in Figure 6.13B is questionable as the second bottom reversal is small range. Figure 6.14 on Cisco Systems shows this pattern.

SMALL MORNING TAILS

A trending market frequently has a counter move in the morning and then reverses and has a powerful move in the direction of the prevailing trend in the afternoon (Figure 6.15). A small tail is when the opening to low is less than the high to opening. A possible long entry setup is as follows:

1. Market moves down from the opening to about mid-day.
2. Movement down is less than a half range from the opening.
3. Enter a stop buy above the high or opening of the day.
4. If filled, enter stop of three to eight ticks below the low of the day.

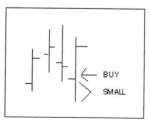

FIGURE 6.15 Small morning movements.

The move does not necessarily have to happen on the day of the tail. For instance, it may dip down in the morning, and come back above the opening and close there. The following day is when the big trend day takes place. Early confirmation of lack of supply is necessary.

Further study on early morning strength followed by late day selling (and vice versa) is available from *The Taylor Trading Technique* by George Taylor (Traders Press, 1950) and *A Journey through Trading Discoveries* by Peter Steidlmayer (1996).

A number of people have written and discussed the merits and shortcomings of these studies which should be perused by market students who uses judgmental type trading.

Taylor assumed that market momentum for the next bar would equal the momentum of the prior two bars. The forecast for tomorrow's high, low and close are a function of the two prior bars action as shown in Figures 6.16 and 6.17. He had two ways to predict the next bars action:

1. High to high movement of two prior bars for predicting the next bars high. This assumes the same momentum of the highs. The low to low momentum predicts the next bar's low. The same holds true for the close (our innovation on closes).

2. Low to high and high to low. This is also known as the *criss cross*. The low of bar one to the high of bar two projects the high of the next bar. This distance is added to the low of bar two to predict the high. The opposite is true for the low forecast. In all cases A1 is equal to A.

Markets that are up in the morning may sell off in the afternoon and (vice versa). Just as the opening on some days is the low or high of the day that gives rise to the opening range breakout, there are many

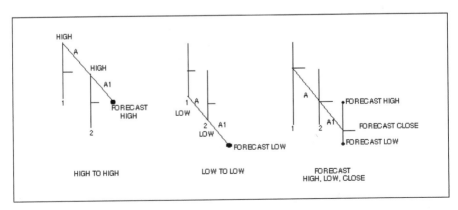

FIGURE 6.16 Next bar forecast based on high to high, up to low, and close to close.

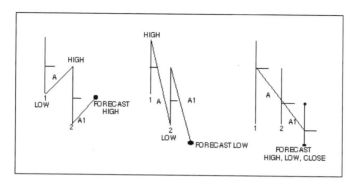

FIGURE 6.17 Next bar forecast based on low to high, high to low, and close to close.

days that go both up and down. Steidlmayer calls this a *rotating day.* These targets are potential action points for the rotating day. Position is taken with the expectation that markets will find support or resistance at these objective points. This methodology is difficult to incorporate into an exact mechanical system. However, potential action points can be clearly defined and rules may be defined such that subjective interpretation is kept to a minimum.

A suggested way to use this information is to establish zones of support and resistance where the market is likely to reach and then change directions. For instance, a zone of resistance might be the average of the high to high thrust, the low to high thrust, and the high of the prior day. You would look to sell in this zone with a half range stop. It has been our experience that the market will enter one of these zones each day. Trade with the trend and look at the next lower time frame before taking a position. This is a beautiful way to trade the two- to three-day moves. You are buying on short-term weakness and selling on strength (and vice versa) every two to three days.

Expansion of these basic ideas is to use a three-day average for projections of zones of support and resistance. Drummond geometry has expanded on this work by trading around the three-bar average and by use of multiple time frames.

The last three bars may also be used to predict the zone of support as shown in Figure 6.18. The

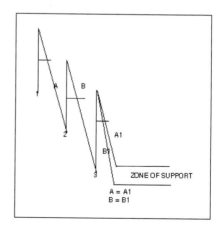

FIGURE 6.18 Zone of support based on three prior bars.

high to low forecasts of the prior two days are used to forecast the expected low range for the next bar. This is the zone to consider a long position or liquidate a short.

CLEAR OUT PATTERNS

This powerful tool is a form of spring or upthrust (Figure 6.19). The primary difference is that it happens all in one day. Conditions are:

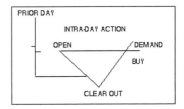

1. The market opens above a prior resistance point such as a prior day's low.

FIGURE 6.19   Clear out action.

2. It moves down and takes out the low by a small amount (less than a half range). Stops are taken out.

3. It reverses direction and takes out the high or opening of the day. This is the point to enter. New shorts are trapped.

Beware if the market moves down a half range below the prior day's low and just gets back to around or slightly above the low. The opening and first move off the opening the next morning holds the key.

Anticipation is the key to using these patterns. At mid-morning enter stop buy at what may seem a very high price. When and if it gets there later in the day, you are on board.

OVERLAPPING AND NON-OVERLAPPING BARS

Overlapping bars is where all of the bars are inside the range of the previous bars (Figure 6.20A). Non-overlapping bars is where a bar or bars are not inside the range of the previous bars. Figure 6.20 shows that the low of bar one is greater than the high of bar three. Some judgment is involved in trading in this manner. This is a simple market principle that will let you get on board a market when it is slightly oversold in an uptrending market and vice versa. The fundamental idea for a buy is to wait until a correction shows the high of a correction bar is less than the low of

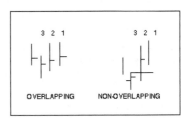

FIGURE 6.20   Overlapping and non-overlapping bars.

the top bar in the thrust. You then buy on some expression of market downside exhaustion or a sign of strength such as:

1. A narrow-range period implying supply exhaustion.
2. An up bar that closes above two prior closes.
3. Movement away from the opening and above two prior closes.

Stops and take-profit orders should be placed upon entry into the market. Strong uptrending markets have few non-overlapping downside bars.

Non-Overlapping Top and Bottom

A non-overlapping top is when a day sells completely below the low of the top bar (Figure 6.21). This may be the first day or several days later. A bottom is the mirror image. These are only guidelines. You must have a trading plan in place for market entry, stop, and liquidate or take profits.

Uptrending markets have few downside non-overlapping bars as shown in Figure 6.22A. A non-overlapping bar always occurs in a trend reversal as shown in Figure 6.22B. Look at the three bars following a non-overlapping bar for guidance. If the market is unable to rally back into the top bar within three bars, it shows supply and further downside action is possible. Use of this idea is helpful in determining the direction out of a congestion zone.

Markets tend to visit the same area two to three times. If market has a non-overlap day on the downside, the sell point is 1 to .5 range above the high of the non-overlap day. This works beautifully when a market first enters congestion. Be careful after about the third to fourth swing as the market may be preparing to leave congestion.

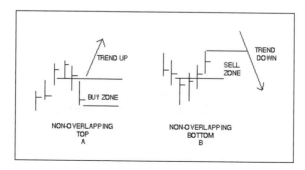

FIGURE 6.21 Nonoverlapping tops and bottoms.

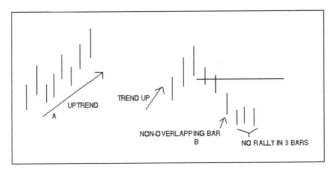

FIGURE 6.22   Trend continuation and change.

TWO-DAY INTERSECTION

Two wide-range bars to the upside that overlap only a small amount indicate aggressive demand for two bars in succession. The intersection of
these two bars is a zone of support/resistance as shown in Figure 6.23.
Orders placed around these points can let one get on board with a small
risk. Stops would be just outside the zone.

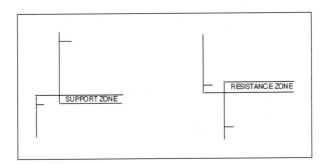

FIGURE 6.23   2 Wide range bars.

CHANNEL TRADING SYSTEMS

There are a number of channel systems commercially available that sell
in the range of $3,000 to $10,000. Some have shown good profits over the
years and are based on exact mathematical rules. Others involve some
judgment in trading and cannot be programmed. The three types are:

1. *Keltner channels.* This is a constant width channel based off a
   moving average such as a 10-day. The exact width is a percentage

of the price. One has to use different amounts depending on the time frame. One is looking for a channel width that encloses most but not all of the bars. The original Keltner used an average range above/below the channel.

2. *Bollinger bands.* This is a standard deviation from an average close.

3. *Donchian channels or Turtle system.* This is a breakout from a highest high or lowest low of a set number of days. The four-week breakout has been around for a long time as a trading system.

As markets are in a trading channel most of the time, the focus here will be on trading back and forth across these channels by using the tools presented in other chapters of this book. Some of these systems can be programmed. Others require some judgment. The basic method of trading these channels will be shown.

Keltner Channel

Chester Keltner was a noted technician who might be considered one of the earliest system traders. His book *How to Make Money in Commodities,* published in 1960, contained a system called the 10-day Moving Average Rule. This is a simple system that uses a constant width channel to time buy/sell signals. The rules are:

1. Compute the daily average price (high + low + close)/3.
2. Compute a 10-day average of the daily average price.
3. Compute a 10-day average of the daily range.
4. This daily average range is added or subtracted from the 10-day moving average to form a band or channel.
5. Buy when the market penetrates the upper band and sell when the market breaks the lower band.

It is always in the market. Computer testing shows this to be an ineffectual system. This system is buying on strength and selling on weakness. A number of people have expanded on this basic concept of trading the bands as follows:

1. Instead of buying at the upper band, you sell and vice versa. This makes good reasoning because markets are in a trading range most of the time. The disadvantage is that one may not be on board a strong move in the market.
2. The number of days are changed. A number of systems use a three-day average with bands around that average.

3. A number of systems use a lower time frame to time entry into the market. For instance, if the market reaches the upper band, you do not act until the next lower or higher time frame gives a signal.

Keltner Channel System Modified

Channel trading can be used in any market on any time frame depending on your style of trading (Figure 6.24). They also can be used as a day-trading vehicle in S&Ps. The rules are:

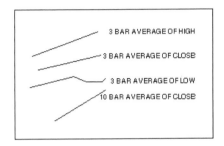

FIGURE 6.24   3 bar channels.

1. Three- and 10-bar moving averages of the closes are used. The averages are displaced forward by one bar. The longer-term average is the trend indicator. The shorter-term average with channels is used to detect short-term overbought/oversold conditions. Basic theory is to buy when the market is oversold or a short-term basis with the longer-term trend up and liquidate on market strength. Buy on weakness, sell on strength but trade in the direction of the longer term trend and vice versa.

2. Trend. The trend is determined by the slope of the 10-period average line, the pivot points, and thrust direction.

3. Channel width. The top channel line is the average of the last three highs and the reverse for the lower channel.

4. Support and resistance zones. Some subjectivity is required. If the low bar is wide range, the buy zone is the width of the most recent narrow range bar measured from the pivot point low.

5. Thrust and basic ABC corrections will be utilized.

Entry for Longs with Trend Up

Go long at one of the following as shown in Figure 6.25:

1. Buy in the support zone (Figure 6.25A).

2. Buy at the 10-bar average when it is below the lower three-day channel bar (Figure 6.25B).

3. Buy at the lower trend channel if it is below the 10-bar average (Figure 6.25C).

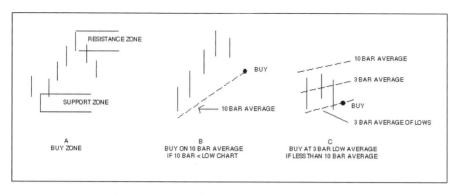

FIGURE 6.25 Action points for channel trading.

Taking profits requires judgment. Profits are taken as markets enter the resistance zone or by use of a trailing stop once a market enters the sell or resistance zone. The sell zone is:

1. In the range of the top bar.
2. At the top channel line if above the 10-bar average.
3. At the 10-bar average if it is above the channel top.

If a trailing stop is used, take profits on:

1. On re-entry into the channel if prior close was outside the channel.
2. On a close below the opening outside the top channel.
3. On a 50% opening range breakout to the downside.

The system requires use of some subjectivity on exactly which rule to use in a particular trading situation. This is where use of the big picture discussed in Chapter 1 comes into play. For instance, if the market is in the first part of a congestion phase, then profits are taken more quickly. However, if near the termination of the phase, then you might hold in anticipation of a breakout.

Stops

Enter a stop one entry bar range from point of entry, if stopped out on a long trade do not re-enter the market on the long side until the market has moved back up above the three- or 10-bar average and then back down to an oversold condition. If long and high of entry bar is taken out, move stop to just below entry bars low.

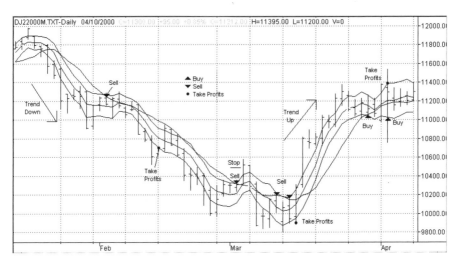

FIGURE 6.26 Bonds channel trading (June 2000). Created with TradeStation 2000i by Omega Research © 1999.

Figure 6.26 demonstrates these ideas. There may be some trades that were overlooked. This should give you the basic understanding of trading the Keltner Channels. Several courses are available that have different bells and whistles on this approach. They sell for $3,000 to $10,000. Some use indicators to determine trend. The use of pivot points, slope of the 10-day line, short-term patterns, and the big picture may be as effective as any method. You might examine the basic concept and develop your own techniques of entry and exit based on your comfort level of trading.

Bollinger Bands

Developed by John Bollinger, this method is based on using two standard deviations as a band above and below a moving average of say 14 or 20 days. The idea is to buy when the market penetrates the upper band and vice versa. As volatility increases, the bands increase and vice versa. One of the best long-terms systems using this basic idea was developed by Keith Fitschen called *Aberration*.

The Bollinger bands are great for immediately sizing up a market. We like to use a 20-day moving average with one and two standard deviations shown. A quick glance at a chart will tell you trend, volatility, and overbought/oversold conditions. A market above one standard deviation is overbought. If above two standard deviation, it is extremely overbought. Look at any chart and you will note that most of them will pullback to the average even in strongly trending markets. The market might be traded in this manner:

1. If the market is oversold, look for patterns on which to buy on both the current time frame and the next lower time frame. If short, be alert for taking profit at a sign of a selling climax or demand overcoming supply.

2. If the market is overbought, do the exact opposite.

3. If the bands are narrow, then look to buy puts and calls.

4. If the bands are widening, then sell calls and puts.

You should trade with the trend. This does not hold true at market turning points. A number of patterns such as a spring or upthrust are counter trend signals and frequently yield the most profit.

Figure 6.27 shows a few of the patterns that stand out with the one and two standard deviation bands shown.

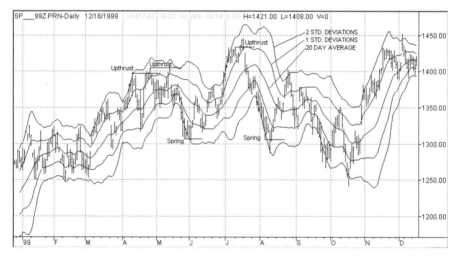

FIGURE 6.27 Bollinger Bands S&Ps daily (December 1999). Created with TradeStation 2000i by Omega Research © 1999.

THE PULLBACK

Buying on a pullback after a sign of strength will enable you to get on board a move with lower risk of being stopped out of the trade. A one-range stop might be used by buying on a pull back on short-term weakness. A larger stop is necessary if you buy on strength.

Most thrusts will have a pullback of about 50%. Figure 6.28 shows several types of pullbacks or corrections. You are buying on short-term weakness in anticipation of a turning point. A trade may be safer if you

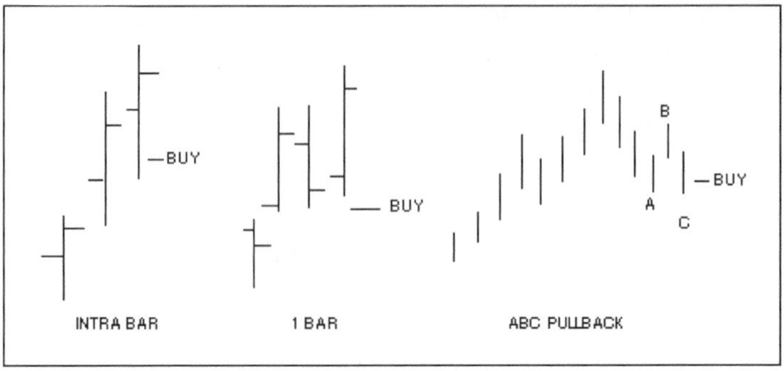

FIGURE 6.28   Types of pullbacks

enter the markets on the pullback rather then entering on the thrusts. True, you will miss some big moves, but a stop can be entered with less risk. The pullbacks provide information on whether the thrust was exhaustion or the beginning of a significant move.

Disadvantages include:

- Some big moves may be missed by waiting for the pullback to enter the market.
- You never knows at what level on the pullback to enter the market. Some techniques have been described earlier in this book. One possible answer to the problem is to look at the lower time frames. Minor reversal patterns in the lower time frames should take place

FIGURE 6.29   Yahoo—The pullback. Created with TradeStation 2000i by Omega Research © 1999.

prior to entry. Also the higher time frame shows areas of support or resistance. This may reduce the number of whipsaws.

- The pullback just might be a reversal of trend and one is faced with a loss.

The chart on Yahoo (Figure 6.29 on page 122) identifies some obvious thrusts followed by the pull back. The pullback failures are also noted.

HIGH OF LOW BAR FOR BUYING/LOW OF HIGH BAR FOR SELLING

Figure 6.30 identifies the buy zone and sell zone. The obvious method of trading this pattern is to buy when market enters the buy zone and vice versa. You can place orders in these zones with a stop below them or look at a lower time frame and wait for some evidence of demand/ supply prior to taking a position.

If the market decisively penetrates the zone, then it is no longer an area for action as support or resistance did not hold. The chart of Royal Dutch (Figure 6.31) illustrates this technique. Buy/sell

FIGURE 6.30   Buy at low bar, sell at high bar.

FIGURE 6.31   Royal Dutch Petroleum high/low bars for market entry. Created with TradeStation 2000i by Omega Research © 1999.

points have not been identified, but you can see the basic approach to this methodology.

THREE BARS UP/DOWN

A two- or three-day bar movement with thrusts above each bars high is frequently an action point (Figure 6.32). This is an area where the market is stretched and perhaps exhausted. A small amount of selling can and often does lead to a retracement or a resumption of a downtrend (vice versa). Most markets will at least have a pull-back after such action.

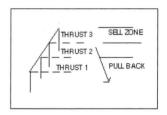

FIGURE 6.32   Three bars up.

The basic theory is that thrusts two and three will equal thrust one. Inside days are ignored. The following rules are (for sell side only):

1. Liquidate and perhaps reverse a position on the three relatively strong up bars in succession. Ignore inside days. Enter order at target points or on a close below opening on third day.
2. Targets for the third bar are: (a) Thrust method as shown above and (b) 0.5–1.0 range of bar one added to the high of bar one.
3. Use a 1.0 range stop above entry point. Move to high of third day when the low of entry bar is penetrated.
4. Take profit point (if short position taken) is in the lower ¼ range of the first bar of the three bar thrust if a short-term trader.

This is not a system by itself. It enables you to take profits or enter a trade under stretched conditions. The chart of Yahoo, Figure 6.33, demonstrates this thrust method.

Profit Protection

If market makes a three-day up swing in your favor giving quick large potential profits, they may be protected by:

- Liquidate on any three-day up.
- If the high on three-day up is penetrated, enter stop one tick below the low on the third day.

FIGURE 6.33   Yahoo—two to three bar thrusts as action point. Created with TradeStation 2000i by Omega Research © 1999.

- If the market closes below mid-range on third day, get out. Ignore inside days.
- Enter stop below each day's low.

DYNAMITE TRIANGLE

A powerful tool in your arsenal is the dynamite triangle. It enables you to get on board a fast-moving market and exit with a close stop if wrong (Figure 6.34).

The setup is several bars of relatively tight formation. The bar prior to breakout usually closes in the direction of the breakout. Movement may go either way out of this formation but usually goes in the same

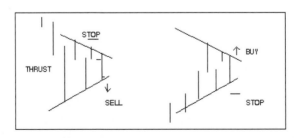

FIGURE 6.34   Dynamite triangles.

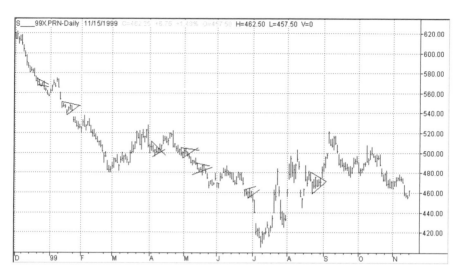

FIGURE 6.35 Soybeans (November 1999). Created with TradeStation 2000i by Omega Research © 1999.

direction as it entered. Entry may be made on the bar prior to breakout or on penetration of the tight trendline. Stop is immediately entered on the other side of the formation. Immediate failure does occur but that is why stops must be in place. Set up conditions are:

1. Market makes a strong movement out of congestion.
2. Market remains in a tight formation with small ranges for two to four bars.
3. Market continues its movement in the direction of the thrust by penetration of a tight trendline or close in direction of thrust.
4. Your entry point is to take action following the setup conditions.

Review Figure 6.35 and then look for this formation on additional charts. You may be surprised at the beauty and simplicity of this simple formation.

NARROW RANGE/WIDE RANGE

A narrow-range bar (NR) followed by a wide-range bar (WR) is often a signal at market turning points. It is movement away from a period of rest. Entry taken at these levels frequently leads to immediate profits or getting you on board for the bigger move.

Entry for buy (sell opposite) is:

1. Enter on close of wide-range bar or
2. Enter on the pullback to mid-range of the wide-range bar or at high of narrow-range bar.

Stop should be on the other side of the narrow-range bar.

This is not a stand alone pattern, but it is great when other filters suggest a possible turning point area. Figure 6.36 shows a number of narrow-range/wide-range signals. Although not totally inclusive, this chart should give you a basic understanding of this powerful little idea. Exits are not shown, but they are every bit as important as the entry.

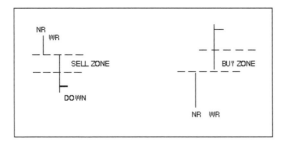

FIGURE 6.36 Narrow range–wide range.

TWO-DAY FLIP (2DF)

This pattern occurs after a strong thrust bar in one direction which gives the appearance of strong demand (if up) but opens lower the next morning with sell off all day (Figure 6.37). The abortive demand is over and supply is the dominant force. Two-day flips are frequently seen at market tops or bottoms. Both bars should have above average ranges. Figure 6.38 shows some two-day flips on Cisco Systems.

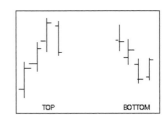

FIGURE 6.37 Two bar flip.

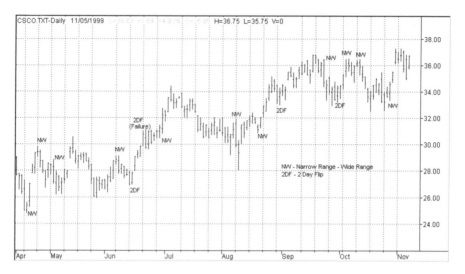

FIGURE 6.38 Cisco Systems narrow range–wide range reversal. Created with TradeStation 2000i by Omega Research © 1999.

TIGHT FORMATION BREAKOUT

A wide-range breakout where the breakout bar has a wider range day than several previous bars is generally a valid signal. You should go with it, provided it is in the direction of the trend. The prior days should be overlapping or in a tight range. It may be as many as seven to 10 bars or as few as two where it then becomes a simple narrow-range/wide-range formation. This is frequently called a breakout from a tight formation (Figure 6.39).

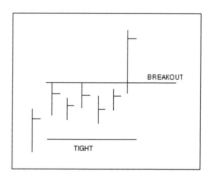

FIGURE 6.39 Breakout from a tight formation.

THE IMPORTANCE OF EXITS

Entering a trade is far easier than exiting a trade because this is when your mind is clearest. When you are in a trade, your emotions are totally involved. That is why you should determine under what conditions and where you will exit a trade *before* it is made.

Considerable emphasis is always placed on how you enter the market. Exiting a trade is of equal importance. The entry and exit from a trade must be designed to work in harmony because they are closely related. For instance, entering a trade on an 80-day breakout and exiting the trade through a four-day breakout are not compatible.

One entry technique is shown in Table 6.1. Six different methods of coming out of the trade were then tested against this constant entry method. This demonstrates the importance of exits from a trade. Tests were run on 24 different futures over the period from January 1984 through June 1999. One contract was traded per signal. No commission or slippage was included.

- *Entry method:* Opening range breakout, two patterns, and one trend filter. (Same entry for all examples.)
- *Exit methods:* Six methods of getting out of the trade are shown. This includes a reversal technique, four filter methods, and day trade.

TABLE 6.1   Exit Techniques with Same Entry Rules for All 6 Cases

6 DIFFERENT EXIT METHODS WITH SAME ENTRY RULES
TESTED ON 24 FUTURES, 1/1/84–6/30/99
SAME ENTRY AND EXIT FOR ALL FUTURES, ONE CONTRACT PER SIGNAL
$0 ALLOWED FOR COMMISSION AND SLIPPAGE

Exit Techniques	1	2	3	4	5	6
Filters	Reversal Exit**					Day Trade
ORBO	X	X	X	X	X	
Pattern 1	X					
Pattern 2	X	X	X			
Pattern 3				X		
Trend	X	X				

Results Summary						
Profit/Yr ($)	38,422	50,353	58,163	59,941	60,958	29,641
Maximum Drawdown ($):	150,068	107,346	39,128	31,421	24,599	20,803
Return on Capital (%)	5.00	9.4	29.4	38.2	49.6	28.5
Required Capital ($)*	750,340	536,730	195,640	157,105	122,995	104,015
Trades/Year on 24 Futures	205	205	377	421	431	545

Notes: Pattern 1—Range of 4 Closes <30 Day Average Range; Pattern 2—Highest of Last 4 Closes for Buy and Vice Versa; ORBO—Opening Range Breakout of 62% of Prior Days Range; Trend—Close of Prior Day > Close 50 Days Ago for Buy and Vice Versa.

*Required capital is the amount required to limit max drawdown to 20%.

**These are the same signals used for entry.

Profits vary from $30,000 per year to $60,000. Maximum draw down is from a low of $20,000 to $150,000. Return on capital required is 5.0% to 49%. This example is not recommended as a trading system and is represented merely to show the importance that your exit has in your trading.

Conclusions from Table 6.1 emphasize the importance of protecting profits once they are achieved by relatively close stops rather than waiting for the reverse signal to take place. As an example of how to use these tools, a hypothetical study of two people trading Yahoo is shown in Figures 6.40 through 6.43. Figure 6.40 shows one year of trading Yahoo with various market principles.

Investor Bob bought 300 shares of Yahoo at 58, when his broker told him it was making new highs. He is a long-term investor and does not believe in all this chart mumbo-jumbo. His investment was $17,400. He still owns his 300 shares which are now at 178. This gives him a profit of $120 per share or a net profit of $36,000 over a one-year period. This is a return of about 200%. Not bad.

Trader Bill is an avid chartist and believes the forces of supply/demand are shown on the chart. His philosophy is to trade a maximum of 300 shares with no pyramid trading. His trades were as follows (see Figure 6.41):

Point 1: The long-term trend is up when the market hit 50 and he began looking for a point of entry. He bought 300 shares at 45 upon

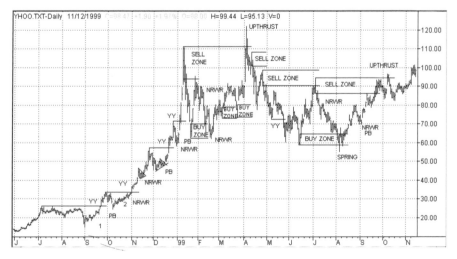

FIGURE 6.40 Yahoo—Demonstration of market principles (November 12, 1999). Created with TradeStation 2000i by Omega Research © 1999.

FIGURE 6.41 Yahoo—Demonstration of market principles (December 31, 1998). Created with TradeStation 2000i by Omega Research © 1999.

seeing the trading tools of trend up, trend up confirmed and penetration of the 04 line.

Point 2: He had another chance to buy at point 2, but did not as he had his 300 shares (Figure 6.41).

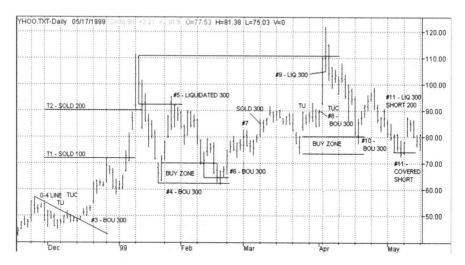

FIGURE 6.42 Yahoo—Demonstration of market principles (May 17, 1999). Created with TradeStation 2000i by Omega Research © 1999.

FIGURE 6.43 Yahoo—Demonstration of market principles (November 10, 1999). Created with TradeStation 2000i by Omega Research © 1999.

Target 1: Sold 100 shares at 84 for a profit of 39 or $3,900 (Figure 6.41).

Target 2: Sold the remaining 200 shares at 100 as the market had reached the second target and had penetrated a three-day low. Profit of $55 on the 200 shares or $11,000. Total profit of $14,900 (Figure 6.41).

Point 3: Purchased 300 shares at 102 based on the long-term trend remaining up and seeing the short-term filters of trend up, trend up confirmed, non-overlapping bars and 0–4 lines penetration. Stop loss was entered at 88. Sold 100 shares at 145 for 43 points profit or $4,300 (Figure 6.42).

Target 2: Sold the remaining 200 shares at 180 on the downside penetration of the second target. Profit of 78 on 200 shares or $15,600. Total profit now stands at $34,800 (Figure 6.42).

Point 4: Bought 300 shares on the reversal day at 143 for a possible move back toward the top. Stop at 119 (Figure 6.42).

Point 5: Sold all at 184 as this was the low of the high bar. The deep A leg forecast that the high would not be broken. Profit of 41 or $12,300. Total profit stands at $47,100. He did not sell short as trend was up (Figure 6.42).

Point 6: Bought the spring at 136 for a possible move back to 170–180. Stop at 116 (Figure 6.42).

Point 7: Sold all at 169 in the sell zone. Market could retrace back to 140. Profit of 36 or $10,800. Total profit stands at $57,900 (Figure 6.42).

Point 8: Bought 300 shares at 180 on trend up, trend up confirmed, non-overlapping bars and sharp recovery from the dip that implied aggressive demand and possible new highs (Figure 6.42).

Point 9: Upthrust. Sold at 210 on the close. Sharp reversal after reaching a new high implies heavy supply. Profit of 30 points or $9,000. Total profit stands at $66,900 (Figure 6.42).

Point 10: Bought 300 shares at 160 with a stop at 139. This was the high of the low bar of a previous dip that showed aggressive demand. Target of 200–210.

Point 11: Dumped all at 182 on the sharp reversal day and went short 200 shares as A-leg failed to reach the 50% point which implied a new low or a possible move back to the 120–140 area. The Target price is 110. Covered the 200 shares at 130 on penetration of the pivot point low at 145 at a half range below the YY day. Market was in the potential buy zone and he did not want to press his luck. Profit of 52 points or $10,400. Total profit stands at $77,300 (Figure 6.42).

Point 12: Went short at 172 on the sharp reversal day in the sell zone. Stop at 201. Downside target is back to test the lows at 120. Covered 100 shares at 144 on the ABC down for 28 points profit.

Point 13: Covered the other 200 shares at 130 (the high of the low day). Went long here with a stop at 110. This trade was stopped out for a loss of 20 points. Net results was a profit of $5,600. Total stands at $82,900. Bought 300 shares again at 130 on the trend up, trend up confirmed and minute double bottom for a possible trip back to the sell zone.

Point 14: Dumped 100 shares at 158 on the ABC up. Liquidated the remaining 200 shares at 170 (low of high bar in sell zone). Net profit of $10,800. Total profit stands at $93,700.

This gives trader Bob a return of over 600% on his initial investment of $13,500 (Figure 6.43). Can anyone duplicate this hypothetical study? It is possible. However, one must have complete control of his emotions and be ready to pull the trigger on short notice. You must trade a stock that is moving. The principles are clearly there for you to act on. The results would have been much higher if reinvestment plans were used. This study merely shows that the possibilities exist with clearly defined principles to act on.

USE OF TOOLS IN TRADING THE S&PS

This section will show how some of the various technical tools previously presented are used in a coherent fashion to produce profits by trading the S&Ps (Figure 6.44). These are *hypothetical* studies. The study has the benefit of hindsight. Read the hypothetical disclaimer.

The primary consideration is to look for buy signals when market is in the support zone and sell signals when market is in the resistance zone. Entry into a position may be done on the close or on an opening range breakout. Exit the trade when market is stretched. The tools and abbreviations used are:

Opening range breakout (BO)

Narrow-range day followed by wide-range bar (NRWR)

Upthrust (UT)

Spring (SP)

Three-day or bar equilibrium reverse (3DE)

Pullback after a thrust (PB)

Non-overlapping bar (NOL)

High of a low bar at a prior pivot point low (HLB)

Low of a high bar at a prior pivot point high (LHB)

Target (T)

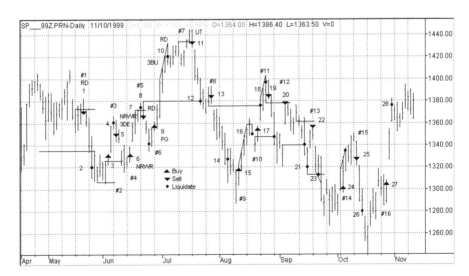

FIGURE 6.44 S&Ps futures trading. Created with TradeStation 2000i by Omega Research © 1999.

Trade 1

1. Sold short on reversal day at 1370 for a target of 1320. Stop above 1405 above PG. Moved to 1385 upon penetration of low of sell day. Other factors were:
   - Zone of distribution—two rallies into a bed of accumulation.
   - Three-bar upthrust—market cleared out all stops above three bars.
   - Pattern gap four bars earlier.
2. Covered short at 1320 at prior major pivot point low. This was also three bars down. 50 points profit.

Trade 2

3. Bought on close at 1330 for a possible trip back to 1360. Stop below five bar low. Moved below buy bar upon penetration of high on buy day.
4. Liquidated at 1380 on close of NR bar which was below opening. 50 points profit.

Trade 3

5. Sold at 1350 on close for a swing back to HLB at 1325. Stop above NR bar. 25 points profit.

Trade 4

6. Buy at 1332 on close in the buy zone and above the NR day high. Stop below the four-day low. Target of 1360–1380.
7. Liquidated at 1372 for 40 points profit. This was the fourth day up in the sell zone.

Trade 5

8. Sold the upthrust in the sell zone at 1365. Look for a possible quick move back to the high of low bar or 1340. Covered at 1340 for quick profit of 25.

Trade 6

9. Bought on close at 1359 for a possible move back to high around 1400. Note that pattern gap in buy zone, third dip into possible bed of accumulation, 3DE and non-overlapping bars.

10. Liquidated position at 1420 on reversal day. Stop had been moved in tight in anticipation of an upthrust. Note reversal bar after fourth bar up. Profit of 61 points.

Trade 7

11. Sold the upthrust at 1435 for a possible move back to support area of 1380. Note the island reversal on day following entry—very bearish.

12. Covered short at 1380 on fourth day down for 55 points profit. Looks like more downside is possible but when quick large profits come this quickly, take them. One never knows what the next rally may bring.

Trade 8

13. Sold at 1385 on close. Note the two tails and inability to rally in four days. Target is the low of 1310 made back in June. Note the gap on day following trade—bearish.

14. Covered short on reversal day at 1330 for 55 points profit.

Trade 9

15. Bought at 1318 for possible move back to resistance area of 1360–1380. Note the spring, opening range breakout, and close above prior days high in buy zone.

16. Liquidates at 1350 on close below opening after a five-day run for a profit of 32 points.

Trade 10

17. Bought at 1355 for a 50% swing above the pivot point high. This was a 3DE and spring type action as no supply was below the lows of days two and three back.

18. Liquidated at either 1378 at low of high bar or at 1396 which was the three-bar thrust target. Profit was 23–41 points.

Trade 11

19. Sold at 1383 on the reversal down day that reversed two prior closes. Market was in the sell zone. Target is 1350 which is high

of low bar. Stop above the three-day high. Target reached two days later for a profit of 33 points.

Trade 12

20. Sold at 1378 which was the low of high bar for a target zone of 1320–1340. There was a 3DE up four days after entry but trade was not taken as market was in sell zone. Stop maintained above the high of the day short was entered.
21. Covered short at 1320–1340. 1320 was the three-bar thrust target and a prior support point. Profit was 38–58 points.

Trade 13

22. Sold short at 1356 at the LHB. Target at three day low. Target reached three days later at point 23 for a profit of about 20 points.

Trade 14

23. Bought at 1305 on the pull back to the HLB for a target on 1340–1350 which is LHB. Liquidated at 1336. On 3BU for a profit of 35 points.

Trade 15

25. Sold short at 1325 on 3DE in sell zone for a target of 1305–1270.
26. Covered short at 1280 at prior support on and below low of wide range day.

Trade 16

27. Bought at 1306 on close of wide range reversal bar. Target is 1340. Market went screaming through that point with a wide range day. Liquidated above the wide range day at 1373 for a profit of 67 points at point 28.

Is the above hypothetical trading possible in real time with real money? We seriously doubt it. However, if even half is achieved then results are spectacular. The key to successful trading in this manner is to look for multiple signals to buy when you are in the buy zone and vice versa. Liquidating a position should be easier then entering a new position. Don't get married to a position and don't fret when you only get 10% of a possible move because you came out too early. Try to make trading as mechanical as possible. Also, there is no substitute for hard work in your studies.

Good trading and remember:

A trader who dies rich, dies before his time.

—John Hill

7

DRUMMOND GEOMETRY AND THE PLDOT: AN INTRODUCTION TO THE FUNDAMENTALS

The short-term movements have captured the imagination of traders for a long time. It is believed in some circles that the greatest profit potential exists in trading for the three-bar moves be it hourly, daily, weekly, or other periods. Many have tried to put these patterns into a coherent systematic approach. The leaders in this endeavor are Ted Hearne and Charles Drummond who wrote this chapter.

WHAT IS DRUMMOND GEOMETRY?

It is a unique form of market analysis developed over a 30-year period by Charles Drummond, a Canadian trader. Drummond Geometry is both a trend-following and a congestion-action methodology. It leads rather than lags the market, and uses projected charts to map future market activity. It foretells the most likely scenario that shows the highest probability of occurring in the immediate future and can be custom fitted to one's personality and trading style.

The key elements of Drummond Geometry include a combination of the following three basic categories of trading tools and techniques:

Ted Hearne is a Chicago-based trader. The material in this chapter is adapted from the *30 Lessons of the P&L School of Drummond Geometry* (Copyright © 1999, Ted Hearne and Charles Drummond). Contact Hearne via the web sites www.tedtick.com and www.pldot.com.

1. A series of short-term moving averages.

2. Short-term trend lines.

3. Multiple time-period overlays.

The fundamental concepts of this methodology are simple, but have been worked out to a high degree of sophistication. In this introduction, we will look at the PLdot, the first major building block of Drummond Geometry. PL stands for Point and Line, two of the main techniques of Drummond Geometry.

The concept of flow is central to Drummond Geometry. This methodology reflects how all of life moves from one extreme to another, flowing back and forth in a cyclical or wave-like manner. The markets also move with a rhythmic flow that traders can learn to see. By discovering the flow's underlying form through visualization, traders can monitor the market's flow and utilize that information to realize a profit. This is one important function of the PLdot.

The PLdot can be applied to any commodity, future, or stock and is a short-term moving average based on three bars of data that capture the trend/nontrend activity of the time frame that is being charted. The PLdot from the last three bars is plotted as a dot or line on the next bar to appear. The formula for the PLdot is the average of the high, low, and close of the last three bars.

$$PLdot = \frac{\{Avg[H(1),L(1),C(1)] + Avg[H(2),L(2),C(2)] + Avg[H(3),L(3),C(3)]\}}{3}$$

The PLdot is a series of points which describe the consensus of market activity in a mathematical sense. The first thing to note is that the dot bears a constant relationship to the immediate past—something that captures the recent energy of the hour, of the day, or of whatever time period the trader is looking at.

Think for a moment about the human activity that lies behind the charted record of trading. The PLdot is a short-term average and it represents the collective activity of the three latest bars (or time periods). One could say it is the center, the gut, the solar plexus or the heart of all this activity. One can say that it represents the collective opinion, expressed in action, of the current group, crowd, or mob as you may prefer to call it (depending on the intensity of market activity). This is important, because the concept of the crowd is one of the key elements of trading, market psychology, and market activity.

We all know that a crowd can be incredibly powerful. When it moves, the crowd wants to move everything and everyone with it. When it stops, it wants to make everything around it stop as well. The crowd is collective energy and manifests attractive energy. It is built out of the need to belong; the need for protection; the need for safety; and the need to feed, reproduce, and continue in its existence. The crowd has momentum and it has power. If a trader follows the crowd, or "goes with the flow," he will not be hurt, because the nature of the crowd is to protect its members.

The crowd does not always go in the same direction—it stops and it changes direction. But the crowd is always overshooting its goal, because in its wild rush it does not realize that it has gone too far until it sweeps past the target.

The key point in Drummond Geometry is that the crowd momentum does not stop at some random point in time and space—it is forced to stop at certain specific areas dictated by larger or smaller energy flows. All energy forces are wave-like in nature and in their various configurations; energy flows are the root cause of economic conditions, emotional states, and all collective and most individual actions.

These energy flows can be monitored and acted upon in a wide range of human endeavors, including trading for profit. But the energy flows that are reflected in the charts of market activity are not exclusive to the market itself. Similar wave-like energy flows exist throughout the natural universe and can be witnessed in a wide range of phenomena, from the easily observed waves of ocean surf, to large-scale patterns such as sunspot activity to the wave-like cycles of history.

The PLdot moving average has been empirically arrived at and has proven its usefulness in a multitude of markets. The PLdot moves in a straight line when the market is in a trend, but moves horizontally across the page in congestions. It is extraordinarily sensitive to trending markets, and is very quick to register the change of a market out of congestion into trend. But it is sensitive to a trend that is ending as well.

Figure 7.1 is a chart of the weekly S&P 500 Index, we see the PLdot move in a relatively straight line horizontally across the page on bars 3,4,5,6,7, and 8. Then we see a short down trend and following that the dots move in a straight line upward for the last 5 bars of the chart. The tendency of the PLdot to move in a straight line can be very helpful in monitoring a trend.

Many traders find that just one simple observation—trade with the trend if the market is on one side of the dot and in congestion if the market closes on both sides of the dot—is enough to bring profitable participation in the markets. In Figure 7.1, we see the close of the bar first on one side of the PLdot and then on the other side of the PLdot in bars 4,5, and 6. This is a sign of the market in congestion. In bars 6,7,8, and 9, we see closes below the PLdot, indicating trending activity to the downside. In bars 10 through 14 we see each bar close above the PLdot, indicating a trend to the upside.

In Figure 7.2 of the daily T-Bond futures, we see two trend reversals. On March 29th through April 1st we saw the market in a down-trend and

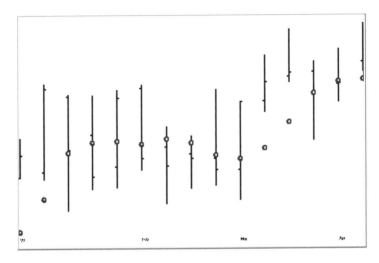

FIGURE 7.1 The PLdot is a key building block of Drummond Geometry. Created with Omega Research ProSuite 2000i © 1999.

the PLdots were above the close of each bar. The trading strategy would be to sell resistance. But on the 2nd of April, we saw the market close above the PLdot and this marked the end of the down-trend. As the market moved into the up-trend the PLdot switched sides and we do not see a close on the under side of the dot until April 13th, when the close moved decisively under the PLdot and the trend is over. From April 2 until April 12 the strategy is to buy support. Note that the dots move in a straight line until the trend is over, and then immediately stop moving in a

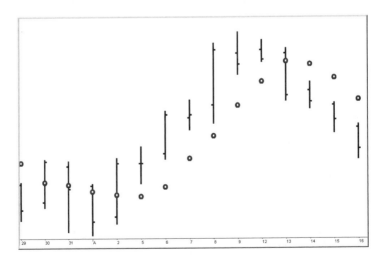

FIGURE 7.2 The PLdot is a sensitive indicator of trend/congestion activity. Created with Omega Research ProSuite 2000i © 1999.

straight line. When the new trend resumes to the downside, the dots again move in a straight line on April 14, 15, and 16th.

As you examine market activity through the lens of the PLdot, we see that prices will often veer away from the PLdot, but then come back to it. The pattern in Figure 7.2 is called the Return to the PLdot. It is a very simple, tradable pattern. When prices get a long way away from the PLdot, it is likely that they will return to the PLdot to check out the warmth, safety, and acceptance of the center of the crowd. The trick is to know exactly when and where "a long way away from the dot" actually is. The action of the PLdot along with short-term trend lines, time frame analysis and many other Drummond Geometry tools and techniques can help traders determine when that point is likely to be occurring with a high degree of certainty. The art of Drummond Geometry as a method of technical analysis comes in the application of these tools in various combinations under various market conditions.

In Figure 7.3 we see a number of bars marked with the Return to the PLdot pattern. When prices move far away from the dot, the trader would be alert to signs that the market will turn and return to the PLdot. Thus in the fourth full bar we see that the market is far away from the PLdot and moves back to it. The market continued through the PLdot and in the next nine bars we see good examples of this tendency for price to return to the vicinity of the PLdot. In each of these situations the trader would take a position against the trend by going short at the apex of the bar. The exact price at which to take a position would be marked by other Drummond Geometry tools such as the short-term trend lines and the time frame overlays. But the tendency of the market to turn and retrace its path when it is far away from the PLdot and move back to the PLdot is a constant in the market that is enormously helpful to the trader as he or she attempts to anticipate direction.

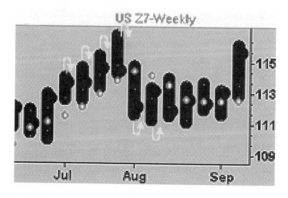

FIGURE 7.3 The "PLdot refresh." When the market is a long way away from the PLdot, Drummond Geometry says it will return to it to "refresh" its energy. Created with Omega Research ProSuite 2000i © 1999.

Another observation based on the PLdot is the PLdot Push. In this pattern, when a trend is underway, the PLdots seem to be pushing the bars in the direction of the trend, either upwards or downwards, depending on the direction of the move. You can imagine that the dots are doing the work, that they are pushing the market up. In fact, in Drummond Geometry the trader generally envisions that the dots contain a lot of energy, and that their energy waxes and wanes depending on the circumstances. If the dots push strongly, they create a very strong trend; if they sometimes lose energy, the trend weakens. This methodology has created a metaphor for market energy that can reap rich rewards as these techniques are further developed.

In Figure 7.4 of quarterly S&P we see the PLdot Push pattern at work in a strong up-trend. The PLdot gives traders a great deal of support in trending markets. When an up-trending market retraces to the area of the PLdot (or the "live PLdot," which is "tomorrow's dot today"), the trader goes long or adds to his long position. When in a down-trending market the trader goes short or adds to his short position. When the market moves to a position far away from the dots, the trader takes partial profits or reverses position, depending on his or her trading style. Thus in Figure 7.4, we can see that the trader could initiate or add to a long position at any time that the market retraced to the PLdot. The concept also holds for the *live dot* as well, as shown in the last two bars on the chart. (The live dot is an advanced concept in Drummond Geometry that indicates the point on the current bar where the PLdot for the next bar is forming.)

Once these first concepts are grasped, then the trader applies these in multiple time frames—another big concept of Drummond Geometry.

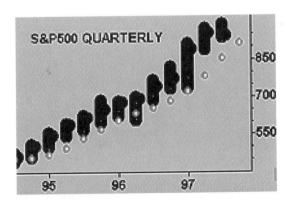

FIGURE 7.4 The "PLdot Push." In a trending market, Drummond Geometry says the PLdots tend to "push" the price bars in the direction of the trend. Created with Omega Research ProSuite 2000i © 1999.

Let's pause and review for a moment. We have seen that there are three fundamental elements to Drummond Geometry. The first is the use of short-term moving averages such as the PLdot. The second fundamental element is the use of short-term, two-bar trend lines. Like the PLdot, these short-term trend lines are projected into the future, where they indicate points of interest on the first upcoming bar, the future bar that has yet to trade. The Drummond Lines indicate areas of energy termination, where the market it likely to stop its movement. There are a number of these lines and in the world of Drummond Geometry they are drawn in various configurations under different market conditions.

When used by a trader knowledgeable in Drummond Geometry, these two main sets of tools—the short-term moving averages and the short-term termination trend lines—can establish support and resistance areas in the near-term future with surprising accuracy.

In Figure 7.5, these two tools are shown in action. The trend is defined and supported by the PLdots, and the Drummond termination lines forecast the extremes of the bars. The green areas above and below the last bar to the right show the support and resistance zones. These zones are defined by the Drummond Lines.

Although it is obviously very helpful to know where support and resistance will form in the upcoming bar, the bar that has not yet traded, this information alone is not enough to trade successfully.

Success in trading depends not just on knowing where support and resistance is located, but whether or not that support or resistance will be strong or weak. Strong resistance will hold, and drive the market back down, whereas weak resistance will break and permit the market to rise higher. Similarly, strong support will hold, and send the market higher,

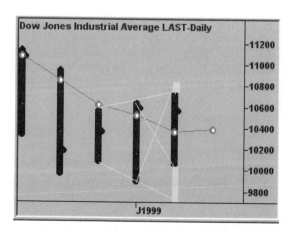

FIGURE 7.5 Dow Jones Industrial average LAST—Daily. Created with Omega Research ProSuite 2000i © 1999.

while weak support will break, and let the market move lower. Knowing when support or resistance is strong and when it will be weak is the name of the game in trading. Once a trader can reliably make that determination, then it is possible to trade with confidence.

This challenge has perplexed traders for many decades. The problem is especially thorny because there is often little if anything on any single time frame chart that will tell a trader if support or resistance will hold. And yet without question this is the fundamental problem of trading— will the support or resistance hold, or will it break?

The trader who wishes to make progress in resolving this question must learn to look at the market in context. Establishing market context, and showing how market context can be used to determine if support or resistance will be strong or weak, is accomplished through time frame coordination. The coordination of support and resistance in different time frames is the third major tool of Drummond Geometry.

In principle, the concept of time frame coordination is simple and clear. Basically, it is this: If you can align support and resistance levels on various time frames and take action when they coincide, and avoid action when they do not reinforce each other, your success ratio will be much better than if you rely on a single time frame alone.

Charles Drummond came to his understanding of time period interaction empirically, some 30 years ago, as he was establishing for himself the ways that chart patterns played out in a single time frame chart. As he was looking at the short-term moving average and some of the short-term, two-bar trend lines that form the basis of his methodology, he realized that these patterns existed on any chart. It did not matter if they were hourly, daily, weekly, monthly, or yearly.

Reflecting on this simple observation, Drummond realized that it would be interesting to see what happened when the charts were superimposed onto one another. And furthermore, he thought it might be relevant to see when the support of one time frame would line up with the support of a higher time frame. Thus he would look at the daily support or resistance in the area of weekly support or resistance, and weekly resistance in the area of monthly resistance, and so forth. When this was done, viola!

The multiple time frame approach has proven to be a fundamental advance in the field of technical analysis and one that can significantly improve trading results.

Today we find many traders looking at more than one time frame chart when they analyze the market. But few have developed the approach into a comprehensive, effective, trading methodology that combines analytical sophistication with tradable rules and principles. Some technicians have experimented with time frames, others have not. Yet this area is most probably the most important new direction in contemporary technical analysis, and will likely be the most fertile ground for exploration in the next few years. The current popular approaches related to fractals, chaos, complexity theory, and the like, are all fiddling with the fundamental concept of time frame analysis.

Let's look at the concept in detail. What is meant by the word *time frame* anyway? A time frame is any regular sampling of prices in a time series, from the smallest such as one minute up to the longest, which might for practical purposes be capped out at in a ten-year bar chart (each bar representing ten years), although there is no theoretical limit. A single time frame chart might commonly be hourly, daily, weekly, or monthly.

There is no magic in selecting one time frame over another as a starting point. All time frames are somewhat arbitrary and are set more by custom than by science. With the advent of 24-hour global trading even the common sense division into daily and weekly charts can be called more arbitrary than not. In purely theoretical terms, there is no difference in validity between a weekly chart and a nine-day chart, nor any intrinsic superiority of a 16-hour chart over a daily. In practical terms, however, Drummond Geometry analysts generally stick with conventional customary divisions into hourly, daily, weekly, and the like.

The essential starting point for time frame coordination is to note that the Drummond support and resistance tools are valid for any chart based on any time frame. Minute, hour, day, week, month—it does not matter, the patterns formed and the termination points indicated flagged by the tools of Drummond Geometry lines will appear and can be followed on bar charts in any time frame. Consider:

- The Drummond dot and the Drummond Geometry support and resistance lines appear on any time frame (e.g., daily, hourly, and 15 minute).

- If market analysis is coordinated to show the interaction of these time frames, then the trader can monitor what happens when the support and resistance lines of the different time frames coincide. This is an extremely powerful concept, because support or resistance on one time period has a much higher likelihood of holding when it is backed up by support or resistance on a higher time period.

How does Drummond Geometry approach time period coordination? First, the trader must decide what he or she is trying to do, for that will determine the arrangement of time frames. If the trader is trying to take as much as is possible out of a weekly bar (i.e., to sell the weekly high and buy the weekly low), then the trader has a "weekly focus" and the weekly chart would be the trader's "focus time period." The focus time frame creates that bar chart on which the trader is trying to place his or her trades.

If the trader is trying to pick off the daily highs and lows, then he has a "daily focus." If he is trying to sell the monthly high and buy the monthly low, then he has a "monthly focus."

Second, to see the market in context, the trader would then select a higher time period. If the focus time period is daily, then the higher time period would be weekly. If the focus time period is weekly, then the higher time period would be monthly.

Third, the trader would select a lower time frame. The lower time frame would be used to monitor the market at key decision points and to determine at the earliest possible moment exactly what is occurring at those areas where the market is encountering significant support or resistance levels.

Let's say that you wish to trade a weekly focus. If this is so, and you would like to see if the integration of time frames holds potential, then you need to look at both a higher time frame and a lower time frame. The next higher time frame would be the monthly and the next lower time frame would be daily.

Figure 7.6 shows an example of a coordinated look at three time periods. Now what can be observed? On the monthly chart we see the PLdot pushing the trend up, and providing support. On the weekly chart during the first week in June (the last bar to the right) we see a Drummond Line establishing support for the weekly bar. On the daily chart for June 2nd (the last bar to the right) we see support areas set up by the Drummond Lines. This coordination of monthly, weekly, daily support means that the support will likely be strong.

Note that this powerful technique of time frame coordination combined with the projection of support and resistance areas permits the trader to accurately and confidently make a hypothesis in advance about

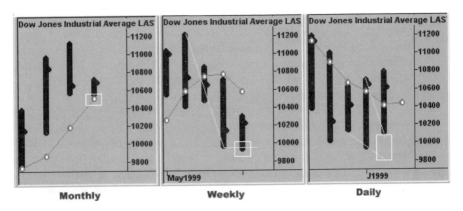

FIGURE 7.6 Dow Jones: Monthly-weekly-daily. Created with Omega Research ProSuite 2000i © 1999.

where the market would react to predicted resistance. This ability to predict an event and then to monitor it as it occurs is very powerful.

Figure 7.7 presents another example. The same principle is in evidence here but it is shown in much faster time frames. The focus is the
daily, the higher time frame is the weekly, and the lower time frame is
the hourly.

The situation is very similar to the previous example although the
time frames are different. Support is established on the Weekly Chart,
and in the same area on the daily chart. On the 60-minute chart we see
support from the daily area represented by the large rectangle as well
as support from the 60-minute chart. This coordination of multiperiod
support gives the trader a clear indication of a good place to buy.

Note that in these examples the technique works regardless of the
time frames used.

Another example, Figure 7.8, uses yearly bars. Yes, you read correctly, yearly bars! These longer time frames can be very valuable. Imagine how effective your trading could become if you knew that the yearly
high was in place!

In Figure 7.4 the yearly time frame shows support from the live dot
and the Drummond Line. This support area is carried over to the quarterly chart and shown as a rectangle. Support in that area on the quarterly chart is similarly carried over to the monthly chart and shown as
a rectangle. Support is likely to be strong and hold when it is backed up
by support from higher time periods.

This multitime period of analysis is very helpful. When combined
with other elements of Geometry or other technical analysis tools,
traders develop an understanding of how support and resistance reinforce

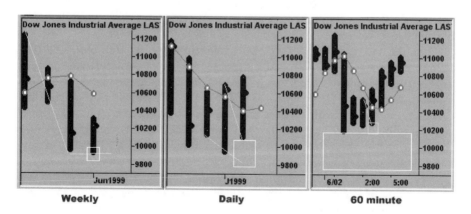

Weekly   **Daily**   **60 minute**

FIGURE 7.7 Dow Jones: Weekly–daily–60 minute. Created with Omega Research
ProSuite 2000i © 1999.

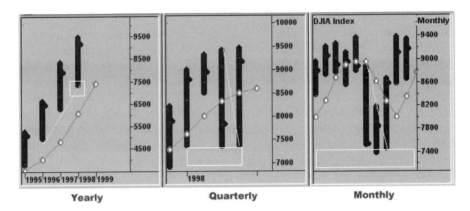

FIGURE 7.8 Dow Jones: Yearly–quarterly–monthly. Created with Omega Research ProSuite 2000i © 1999.

each other and weave together into a coordinated approach to market analysis that helps them approach the market with confidence.

The question arises: how many time frames should a trader try to monitor? If three time frames are better than one, then shouldn't twelve time frames be four times better still?

In theory, there are an infinite number of different time frames, beginning with one-tick bars, moving from there up to one-minute bars, and so on up to infinity. We can't possibly monitor all of these. Fortunately, we don't have to.

Bear in mind that if two time frames are very close together, then they will be nearly identical. Although traders may not know which time period is exactly optimal, when they are very close together then the information one gets from each time period will be very similar, and hence of less value.

Should one use the 60 tick chart? Would not a 65 tick chart be better? Why not a 67 tick? What if everyone used the 60 tick, then maybe a different time period chart would be better? There is no end to the speculation, and all of these questions are valid. However, one thing that can be said for certain, is that it is helpful to have time period charts separated by a significant amount of time as opposed to being very close to one another. The useful information comes from the major differences and major similarities in support and resistance as the energy of different time frames is mapped.

The *factor-of-five* rule helps determine which time frames to select for this type of analysis. This rule states that the first higher time frame should be roughly five times as long as the focus time frame. The second higher time frame should be five times as long as the first higher time frame, and so on. Similarly the first lower time frame would ideally be five times lower than the focus time frame, and so forth.

This is a rule-of-thumb; there is nothing "magical" about the ratio of five to one. But if the ratio is nearly 1:1, the trader will see only the fine-tuning of a single energy wave; if the ratio is 10:1 or 25:1, the trader runs the risk of missing important information.

The intraday minimum can be a factor of two; and when looking at long time frames on the yearly chart we often look at the 2.5-year chart to establish context.

Here is a representative set of time frames that have worked well empirically over time:

5 minute	Quarterly
30 minute	Yearly
One hour	Two-and-a-half year
Daily	Five year
Weekly	Ten year
Monthly	

Many contemporary charting packages permit the trader to construct price bars based on ticks rather than the amount of time that has passed. Each bar is formed after a certain number of ticks or minimum price changes occur. These tick bars are very helpful as they tend to smooth out periods of slow market activity and result in charts that clearly show the full range of market energy playing out, and can account for the tick volume geometrically. A 60-tick chart in T-Bonds is usually about equivalent to a conventional fifteen-minute chart; a 360-tick chart in T-Bonds is usually equivalent to about an hourly chart. Tick charts are particularly helpful in revealing the underlying market structure in markets that have periods of very thin trading, such as during the overnight hours. A ten-minute chart might show many periods with little or no activity, where as a 100-tick chart would collect all of that activity into a bar that would be filled with all of the actual market activity, independent of the time elapsed.

If you have charting software that permits this kind of data manipulation, by all means experiment with it and see if you find it of value for your trading style. To get an idea of the number of ticks to use, set up a one-tick bar chart and count the number of ticks in an hour. Bonds might have 360 ticks per hour on average, and Soybean Oil 60 per hour, and so on.

CONCLUSION

Traders who analyze support and resistance will have much greater success if they coordinate these support and resistance levels on several time periods. Daily resistance sold in the area of weekly and/or monthly resistance has up to three times the likelihood of being strong and holding than does daily resistance taken in places where it exists by itself. The determination of whether or not resistance is strong or weak can be seen at the earliest by monitoring the trade on a time frame that is lower than the time frame in which the trade is taken. A trader who understands the context of a market will always be better off than one who trades by looking only at a single time frame. Drummond Geometry offers a comprehensive methodology of establishing support and resistance areas in multiple time frames, and then coordinating their locations to determine their strength or weakness.

8

INTRODUCTION TO MECHANICAL TRADING SYSTEMS

The foundation of all mechanical trading systems is technical analysis. The basic tenet of technical analysis is that history will somewhat repeat itself. System traders and market technicians will always be tied together in this one belief.

> Many people reject the notion that market activity is repeatable or ordered, because they feel whatever pattern occurred before is random or without precedent. They believe present trading conditions are too unlike anything that happened in the past to make any type of valid comparison. The market has no memory and every situation is unique. There is a fallacy in this way of thinking. Every day and market situation is unique, but there are common patterns which may be generalized, just as every person is unique, but generalities exist for all humans. Everyone may not have the same likes and dislikes, but everyone has likes and dislikes. (Robert Rotella, *The Elements of Successful Trading* New York Institute of Finance 1992)

A mechanical trading system is a mathematically defined algorithm (step-by-step instructions) that is designed to help the user make objective trading decisions. These instructions are based on historically reoccurring events. With the use of a trading system, a small amount of money, and a telephone, a person can open an account and start trading commodities and/or stocks. How successful that person is depends on several factors:

- Amount of starting capital.
- The person's trading psychology.
- Validity and robustness of the trading system.

Most beginning commodity traders fail. This failure rate can be attributed to the amount of money that a trader begins with. All systems, even good ones, can go through draw-down periods. If a beginning trader (1) starts with a small amount of money and right off the bat has a significant draw down, that trader will usually quit. Unfortunately, most traders quit right before a system turns around. If another trader (2) has more starting capital and experiences the same draw down, that person is more likely to continue trading.

	Trader A	Trader B
Starting capital ($)	5,000	10,000
Drawdown ($)	5,000	5,000
Drawdown (% of starting capital)	100	50
Effect	Quits	Continues

A person's trading psychology can make or break a trading plan. One advantage of a trading system is the elimination of human emotion. The computer makes all of the decisions and the trader is along for the ride. When a trader overrides a system trade, he loses that advantage. How many traders will follow a system trade after it has issued five losers. To reap the benefits of system trading, all system traders should take the sixth trade.

The most important thing to a system trader is the validity of the system that he has built his trading plan around. If the system is garbage, then the whole trading plan will fail. The rest of this book is designed to guide the reader through the pitfalls and obstacles presented by trading systems. We can't control how much money you start with, nor can we change your psychology, but we can help you design and/or buy decent trading systems that may have a good chance of being profitable in the future.

Example of a mechanical trading system: Buy if the 9-day moving average crosses above the 13-day moving average. Sell if the 9-day moving average crosses below the 13-day moving average. If the buy/sell order is filled then place a $1500 protective stop. If the open profit exceeds $2000 then use a $500 trailing stop. This is a precisely defined algorithm. If two different traders were to trade this system, their overall results would and should be similar.

Example of a trading tool: When the stochastic enters the overbought region and begins to hook down and a head and shoulder pattern comes to an end then short the market on the open. Place a protective stop at the nearest support level. This is a loosely defined algorithm; there are no exact parameters. Unlike the mechanical trading system, if two traders were to follow this approach, their overall result would probably be quite different. Many traders don't believe the markets can be traded with a mechanical approach and therefore use tools to help in their trading decisions. This type of trader feels that the markets are so complex, that a simple mathematical formula cannot interpret all of the parameters and nuances that are involved with market movement.

Mechanical trading systems and technical analysis have been proven to make money in the markets. Not all systems have made money, but a few have and this has given rise to a multimillion dollar industry. As with any type of "get rich if you follow my instructions" scheme, this industry has developed a somewhat bad reputation. There are many self-appointed experts and gurus selling $3000 systems to people who have never heard of technical analysis. You can turn your television on late at night and for $95 you can learn how to become a successful trader. You don't need experience, a lot of money (other than the $95), time nor an education in technical analysis. Who would believe this? A lot of people would, including lawyers, doctors, scientists, financial engineers, CEOs, and maybe even yourself. The Commodity Futures Trade Commission (CFTC) is trying to crack down on these rainbow merchants (we have attached this label to system vendors who paint trading as a pretty and colorful picture), by requiring them to register as informational commodity trading advisors (CTA). If system vendors are registered, they have to be careful and conscientious of the literature they distribute. Not all system vendors are snake oil salesmen, we have dealt with some of the most responsible, intelligent, and conscientious people in the industry. Some of these vendors even trade their own money and/or have clients that have positive real time results using their systems.

WHY USE A TRADING SYSTEM?

There are several different reasons why a trader should use a trading system:

- Continuous and simultaneous multimarket analysis.
- Elimination of human emotions.
- Back test and verification capabilities.

Mechanical system traders believe that the trending nature of the markets can be understood through the use of mathematical formulas. With the correct filtration, the noise (congestion) can be removed from the music (trend). We believe that the markets, be it soy beans or currencies, are continuously in this state of flux; trending or congesting. Accepting this premise, we have discovered that a single system can profitably trade many markets. This is a tremendous benefit because traders can trade all kinds of different markets without having to fully understand the nuances of all of the individual markets. On any given day, a system trader can be trading 50 markets simultaneously with great ease. Through the use of a system, a trader can also take advantage of the non-emotion factor: With the computer making all of the decisions, there are no human emotions involved. Human traders can wake up on the wrong side of the bed or be suffering from the flu and this can have a tremendous impact on their trading decisions. Trading systems don't care how we humans are feeling, they continually monitor the markets and make their objective trading decisions.

Mechanical trading systems (MTS) can be verified and analyzed with accuracy. With the use of data and a computer (or pencil, note pad, and calculator), this type of system can be back tested over decades of historical data. The back testing and verification attributes of MTS are probably the main reason that this approach is so popular. Through the use of back testing, traders can get a sense of a trading plan's viability. Unfortunately in a lot of cases, a historical track record of a MTS can be misleading. Some system vendors over optimize a system's parameters to look favorably when tested on historical data. (This is known as curve fitting and will be described in greater detail in the next few pages.) Historical back testing has the benefit of hindsight and must be looked on with a certain level of skepticism. On a positive note, a verified walk forward test of a MTS can be highly enlightening. A walk forward analysis is a test on market data that was not available when the system's parameters were derived. This type of analysis is by far the most revealing when evaluating a system's performance. The longer the walk forward test, the better.

Of monies under management of commodity trading advisors, 80% was traded by systems. Commodity Trading Advisors (CTA) use systems due to their ease of use, non-emotion factor, and their ability to be used as a foundation for an entire trading platform. The trading system is but a mere beginning, the tip of an iceberg, for a serious money manager. With the use of a mechanical trading plan, money management and portfolio analysis, today's CTAs systematically manage billions of dollars. Since everything is mathematically defined, a CTA can demonstrate a hypothetical track record based on the different needs of his clients. In doing so, he can customize a specific trading plan. Without a mechanical approach to the market, he could not do this; he could not look back over decades of data and accurately demonstrate his subjective analysis.

MTS can give somebody, who has no idea of the soybean market, the ability to trade this market and at the same time trade many different markets.

THROW THOSE ADS AWAY

MTS sounds like the greatest thing since sliced bread. Why doesn't everybody buy a system and make a lot of money and then retire? Unfortunately, it's not that easy. The only thing a valid system can give its user is a slight technical edge. This edge will hopefully make a little money over the long run. Many seasoned traders have commented that this is the hardest business in which to make an easy buck. However, for the educated trader there does exist a Holy Grail. The Holy Grail is the knowledge that a Holy Grail does not exist. This is why all potential system buyers should throw away any ad, sales literature, and any other type of propaganda that looks to good to be true. And all system developers should do the same if they devise a trading system that looks to good to be true. Figure 8.1 is fictitious but it is similar in content to many ads that can be found in different periodicals and/or on the World Wide Web.

The equity curve shown in Figure 8.1 looks too good to be true and it is. This equity curve was created by a mechanical system that was curve fitted to the nth degree. The track record covers sixteen different markets over an eleven-year test period. A lot of people would look at

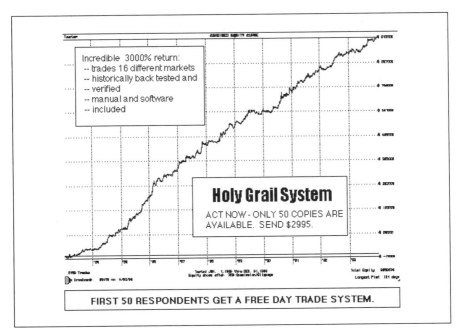

FIGURE 8.1 Typical Holy Grail ad. Sample track record of an overly curve-fitted system.

the length of time and the different markets involved with this test and say that there is no way a person could curve fit that much data. Herein lies the trap. With the computer power and ample data that is available today, any type of equity curve can be generated. Figure 8.1 was built from 1983 through 1993 data. We only used this amount of historical data so that we could reserve some data for a suitable out of sample test. Figure 8.2 shows how the exact same system performed in a walk forward test from January 1, 1994, through August of 1999.

The unknowing system purchaser was expecting approximately $82,000 in profit a year and $25,970 in maximum draw down, when in fact he only averaged $6,245 a year and suffered through a maximum draw down of $62,808. That is a decrease of 76% in profit and an increase of 151% in maximum draw down.

Is the system vendor that shows this type of hypothetical performance lying? No, he is not. Is he misleading the public? Yes, because he should know better. The vendor of this type of system knows that for this type of performance to continue, history must repeat itself almost exactly.

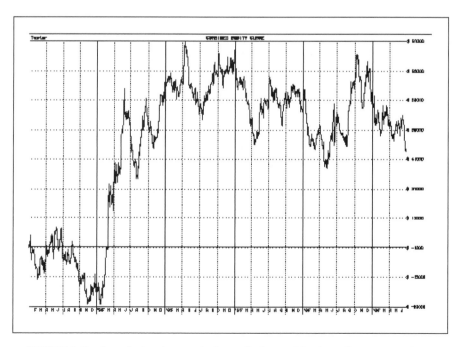

FIGURE 8.2 Sample track record of a walk forward test on the same system.

SHOULD I BUY A TRADING SYSTEM?

We have painted a gloomy picture of the MTS industry. However, we believe that good research can be purchased and successfully used at the retail level. System buyers must do their homework before purchasing a new system or they will be victimized. As a potential system purchaser, you must understand that hypothetical track records only give the best case scenario. Hypothetical or simulated performance results have certain inherent limitations. Unlike actual performance records, simulated results *do not* represent actual trading. Also, since the trades have *not* actually been executed, the results may have under-or-over compensated for the impact, if any, of certain market factors, such as lack of liquidity. Simulated trading programs in general are also subject to the fact that they are designed with the benefit of hindsight. As a rule of thumb, you should expect only one half the total profit and twice the maximum draw down of a hypothetical track record. You should only use this rule of thumb, if you are confident that the system being back tested has robust parameters (parameters that weren't curve fitted to historical data—if you don't understand what robustness means, don't worry we will discuss it in full detail later). Unfortunately, the only way to determine a system's robustness is to understand the logic and mathematics behind the system, and to do that you usually have to buy it. In some cases, with black boxes, you never see the logic, so beware. If you want to purchase a trading system and don't want to get burned, propose the following questions to the system vendor. If you can't answer yes to most of the questions, then move onto another system.

Pre-System Purchase Questions:

1. Does the hypothetical historic record look good over a ten-year test period?

     You would be amazed how often a system vendor shows performance of a system for less time than this. They use the excuse that the markets have evolved and that data ten years ago has no relevance to today's markets. Many times, if a certain market is trending like the recent moves in the S&P 500, vendors will only show performance over the most recent time period

2. Does the hypothetical historic record look realistic? Average annual returns less than 150% on 3*margin. (Margin is the amount of deposit necessary to trade a certain market.)

     Systems that generate consistent performance greater than this are usually overly optimized and are doomed to fail in the future. Let's get real! If a system performed this well, then there would be no markets.

3. If it is a multiple market system, are the parameters the same or similar for all markets?

Another indication of over optimization and curve fitting. If parameter A is 25 for the Japanese Yen and 102 for the Swiss Franc and 56 for the Deutsche Mark, then there is a good chance that the parameters were curve fit. Parameters should be similar for different markets especially if the markets are in similar sectors.

4. Is there a real time track record for a minimum of 18 months? If so, is it respectable?

The only true test is the test of time. If a system performs well after it is released to the public (or after the vendor has stopped tweaking the parameters), it has demonstrated the ability to trade on unknown data. The system doesn't have to duplicate historical performance to be considered good. If it performs half as good as the historical performance, then it probably has a fair chance of future success.

5. Does the system seem logically sound and not overly complex?

Systems should be simple and based on price movement. I have never seen verified systems that based trades off of astrology, numerology, day of month, astronomy, and so on. Overly complex approaches usually get bogged down and confused.

6. Does the system vendor seem more like a technician than a salesman?

After initially contacting a system vendor, does he call frequently pressuring you to buy his system? Does he boast of his system's performance or does he let his real time track record speak for itself?

7. Has the system been tested by a third party?

Third party verification is the best objective analysis that you will receive. A person other than the vendor or paid by the vendor that can share his experience with either real time tracking or trading of the system can solidify your buying decision.

MYTHS AND FACTS CONCERNING TRADING SYSTEMS

Many myths have been created since the genesis of trading systems in the mid-1970s. The following list will give you some of the misconceptions that are running wild in this industry. We will elaborate more on these topics throughout the rest of the chapters in this book.

- *Myth: Only good trading systems cost thousands of dollars.*

- *Fact:* We have seen systems that cost less than $100 out perform ones that cost $10,000. A holy grail does not exist. We personally don't think you should pay more than $3000 for a trading system.

- *Myth: The markets are too chaotic for a simple approach to work.*

- *Fact:* The markets aren't really that complex. They are either trending or not. When you make a system too smart, it tries to capture every possible market move. We have seen simple systems catch a trend and hold it, while more complex systems try to capture every sub movement and end up missing the trend.

- *Myth: Markets are too different for a single approach to work.*

- *Fact:* Personally, we have never seen a single approach work in all markets. However, we have seen systems that work in a majority of markets. If a system works well in the Swiss Franc it should work in the other currencies without modifications. Usually if a system works in currencies, it will also work well in the financials (excluding stock market indexes), again without modifications. A lot of the systems that perform well in these markets can carry over to the energies, grains and meats. The metals are another story.

- *Myth: If a system trades multiple markets, then the parameters need to be optimized for each individual market.*

- *Fact:* If a system is based off of sound market principles then it should be robust enough to work with similar parameters for all markets. Of course there are certain types of parameters that may need to be different. A $1500 stop in the S&P is totally different than a $1500 stop in corn. Instead of fixed parameters you should use market defined parameters (e.g., instead of $1500 why not use 40% of the average range). By doing this, you can eliminate market by market optimization.

- *Myth: All the good systems are under the control of multimillion $ CTAs (commodity trading advisors).*

- *Fact:* Most successful CTAs do use trading systems. The systems they use are the same systems available to anybody. Many well-known CTAs use the very simple n-week channel breakout method. The reasons that they are generally more successful than individual traders are: (a) they have a lot more money to capitalize their trading and (b) they trade at such a higher volume that they can utilize portfolio and money management analysis.

- *Myth: Markets are constantly changing, therefore systems need to be reoptimized periodically.*

- *Fact:* If a system is designed well and based of sound market principles it should be able to trade any market evolution. Remember, the market is either trending or not. No system will be profitable all of the time. There will be times when a market won't have any direction and during this time all systems will have draw downs. Reoptimizing a system will curve fit the most recent historical data. Who knows how long the market will continue to act in the same manner.

- *Myth: I should expect the same return and maximum draw down that was portrayed when I historically back tested my system.*

- *Fact:* I wish this were true. In my experience, you should expect ½ the profit and twice maximum draw down. There are two reasons for this: (1) a computer simulation cannot exactly duplicate market conditions and (2) any historical back test has some level of optimization. Let's further expand on these two reasons.

  1. Computers cannot simulate exact market conditions.

     When testing systems we usually levy a $100 commission/slippage charge for each trade. Traders slipped anywhere from $100 up to $1000 on a one contract basis.

  2. Any historical back test has some level of optimization.

     When a person applies an idea to some historical data and analyses the performance numbers, I guarantee that they will change or tweak something and rerun the test. A trader will not put his money on something that doesn't perform well historically. This optimization is fine, if the trader/developer doesn't get carried away. If too many optimizations are done, then the system has been perfectly fit to the historical data. The only way this type of system will perform well is for history to exactly repeat itself. Unfortunately, optimization is a necessary evil, for without it nobody could develop and test trading systems.

- *Myth: I can make 100% a year trading futures.*

- *Fact:* If someone could consistently do this, then there would be no markets. In my ten years of experience, I have never seen a system do this. I have seen systems do this on a couple of occasions, but never consistently. Most large CTAs aim for 20% to 25% return with a minimum of 10% to 15% draw down. Futures trading should be considered as another asset class. It is a great way to diversify your portfolio.

- *Myth: I only need to capitalize my account by the amount required to cover margin.*
- *Fact:* This is a recipe for disaster. Your worst case draw down is usually ahead of you. Without a buffer, you could be knocked out of the game within a couple of days of trading. Let's assume you want to trade the Japanese Yen and you send your broker a check for the initial margin ($3000). The next day you get a signal, and you buy a Japanese Yen contract and by the end of the day your account is up $250. You really feel great about yourself and the system. The next morning, unfortunately, something occurs in the far east and the Japanese Yen gaps down 250 points (February 16, 1999 and April 3, 2000). Your account is down $3125. The next thing you know, your broker is calling you for more money or he is liquidating your account.

CONCLUSION

We touched upon some keenly important topics in this chapter. The most important to remember are:

- Don't trade commodity systems unless you have enough risk capital.
- To receive the benefits of a trading system, you must trade it religiously.
- Realize the limitations of hypothetical track records.
- Don't believe all of those trading system ads or brochures.
- Propose the "right" questions to a system vendor.
- Educate yourself in the areas of trading systems and technical analysis.

Read the rest of this book. We hope this chapter hasn't scared you off from mechanical trading systems. Sometimes the truth initially hurts, but in the end it will pay for itself several times over. The truth is most systems will not live up to their billing. If the consumer understands this, then hopefully the ninety percent failure rate of beginning traders will dramatically decrease.

9

WHERE TO START

After you have decided to trade the markets with a mechanical approach, there are several decisions you must make before you can place your initial trade. All mechanical systems need daily, weekly, or monthly input before they can generate a trading decision. Some systems need more input than others. Several basic tools are required to process this input and generate actual trading signals.

HARDWARE

A computer is a necessity for any system trader. It is not that good trading systems are highly computational or need millions of instructions carried out in a matter of seconds, but tasks that could take a trader several hours a day can be accomplished in a matter of minutes with the aid of a computer. A computer with the following specifications should be more than sufficient: 300+mhz processor, 4 gigabyte hard drive, 64 megabytes of ram, 56k modem, color monitor, and internet access. An Apple Macintosh or IBM PC with these specifications would work fine. Trading programs used today are engineered for both platforms, but as in most arenas, the PC platform will have more programs available.

SOFTWARE

Charting, testing, and database management software make a system trader's life much easier. The day-to-day maintenance of a mechanical system can only be done with a computer and software. The chores involved with system trading are: data collection, data update, signal calculation, and position and equity accounting. The number of chores are multiplied by the number of different markets that are being traded. A computer and software allows traders to do other things throughout the day. There is a vast array of software packages sold today to assist people in their trading. The computer decision is simple compared to the decision of which software package to buy. The price of these packages range from only a few dollars to thousands of dollars. The price of the software usually depends on the number of built-in functions. TradeStation™ by Omega Research does just about everything you could possibly need to trade a mechanical system: you can download data on all markets, update your database, design and implement your trading system, monitor your system's progress, chart different indicators, and receive real time quotes. This type of software is relatively expensive (more than $2000) and is not absolutely necessary. With a little bit of daily elbow grease, you can trade a system with a much less expensive software package. In fact, a good portion of the systems that are available at the retail level can be programmed into a simple spreadsheet. It is up to you, do you spend more money and less effort or less money and more effort. Whatever software package you decide to purchase, it should at minimum have the following features:

- Display bar charts over different time periods (daily, weekly, monthly).
- Database management (update and maintain price data).
- Display different indicators.
- Display data in tabular form.

Optional features include:

- Display intraday bar charts.
- Drawing capabilities (trend lines, Fibonacci retracements, etc.).
- Historical back testing capabilities.
- Real time system monitoring capabilities.

For further information, we would point you to *Futures Magazine's Guide to Computerized Trading*. This guide gives a brief description of the different software packages and contact information.

The two largest software providers for the Apple Macintosh and PC platform are:

Apple Macintosh Platform	PC Platform
ProTA Gold	TradeStation™
BeeSoft	Omega Research
311 Summerdale Lane	8700 W. Flagler Street Suite 250
Algonquin, IL 60102	Miami, FL 33174
support@beesoft.net	www.omegaresearch.com
(847) 854-3960	(305) 485-7000
Trendsetter Software	Metastock
2024 N. Broadway, Suite 310	Equis International Inc.
Santa Anna, CA 92706	3950 South 700 East, Suite 100
(800) 825-1852	Salt Lake City, UT 84107
	www.equis.com
	(800) 882-3040

DATA

It doesn't matter how fast your computer is or how robust your trading system is, your trading is not going to go anywhere without good data. Data is the fuel to your system just as gas is to your car. Data basically comes in two different formats: real time or historical. Real time data is available within seconds from the action in the pit on the exchange floor. Historical data is all data that is not real time—Fifteen-minute delayed, end-of-day, end-of-week, and so on. As with anything, timeliness and speed comes with a premium. End-of-day data will typically cost $30 a month, whereas real time data can cost up to $800 a month. End-of-day data is sufficient to profitably trade a system. In many cases, real time data can lead to information overload. We have seen traders with real time data quotes make a sound and logical trade, and then prematurely exit because the market goes quickly against them. In the end, their first decision ends up being profitable. The end-of-day data trader, would not have known about the initial adverse move, and would have stayed with the trade. Figure 9.1 shows the difference between what the end-of-day trader sees and what a real time trader sees.

If you plan to day trade (enter and exit a trade in the same day), then real time data is required. When day trading markets such as the S&P 500, you only have small windows of opportunity. Real time data is necessary to capitalize on those opportunities and to protect yourself from adverse market movements.

The search for good data can be as difficult as the search for a good trading system. Two different traders trading the same market with the same system, but with data from different vendors, can end up with completely different results. How can that be if the data comes from one

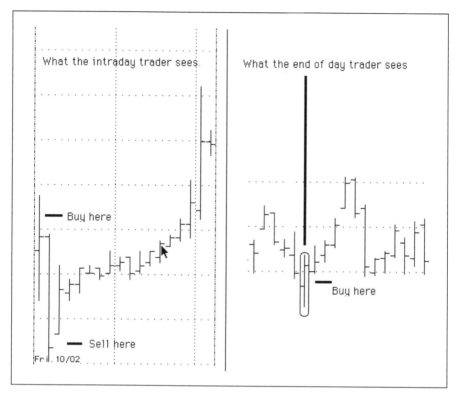

FIGURE 9.1   Different view points. Intraday view versus end-of-day view.

source, the exchange? Sheldon Knight did an extensive analysis of different data vendors in the September 1999 issue of *Futures* magazine. In this article, Mr. Knight answered that question, "To understand how data differences happen, we first have to look at how different vendors process activity on the exchange floor to get end-of-day open, high, low, and closing prices. During the trading day, some traders in the pit are bidding to buy futures contracts while others are offering to sell the same contracts at slightly higher prices. An actual trade occurs when a bid or an offer is accept by another trader. . . . When exchanges report the high and low prices, they use the highest bid and lowest offer even if no trade actually took place at those prices. This convention is used partly because a stop order is triggered by a bid or offer at the stop price, and a limit order will be filled if a bid or offer occurs at the limit price. So a system test will miss some trades unless bids and offers are included in the test data. On the other hand, discretionary traders prefer to study actual trades on their charts.

These conflicting requirements of different traders lead some end-of-day data vendors to include bids and offers in their reported highs

TABLE 9.1 How Clean Is Your Data

	Bridge/ CRB*	CSI	Dial/ Data*	Omega
Soybeans				
Days Tested	748	748	748	723
Days missing in vendor database	0	0	0	25
No. of errors in open, high or low	26	18	64	68
S&P 500				
Days Tested	759	758	759	758
Days missing in vendor database	0	0	0	0
No. of errors in open, high or low	86	9	257	38

*Bridge/CRB, Dial/Data, and Reuters/Equis comparisons are for combined overnight and day sessions. Others are for day sessions only. Data cover 1996–1998. Reprinted with permission from *Futures Magazine,* September 1997.

Bridge/CRB
30 S. Wacker Dr., Suite 1810
Chicago, Il 60606
(312) 454-1801

Commodity Systems Inc. (CSI)
200 W. Palmetto Park Rd.
Boca Raton, FL 33432
(561) 392-8663

Dial/Data division of Tract Data Corp
95 Rockwell Place
Brooklyn, NY 11217
(212) 422-4300

Omega Research Inc.
8700 W. Flagler St., Suite 250
Miami, FL 33174
(305) 485-7000

Reuters DataLink (Marketed by
    Equis in Glance Market Data
    Service, Inc.)
3950 South 700 East, Suite 100
Salt Lake City, UT 84107
(801) 265-8886

340 Brooksbank Ave., Suite 208
North Vancouver, B.C.
Canada V7T 2C1
(604) 983-0200

MJK Associates
1289 Park Victoria Dr., Suite 205
Milpitas, CA 95035
(408) 941-3400

Genesis Financial Data Services
425 E. Woodmen Rd.
Colorado Springs, CO 80919
(719) 260-6111

Pinnacle Data Corp.
1016 Plank Rd.
Webster, NY 14580
(716) 872-0845

Prophet Financial Systems, Inc.
430 Cambridge Ave.
Palo Alto, CA 94306
(650) 322-4183

Reuters/ Equis*	MJL	Genesis	Glance	Pinnacle	Prophet
748	748	706	746	748	748
0	0	0	2	0	0
67	24	38	23	24	24
758	758	750	755	758	758
0	0	0	3	0	0
9	42	44	199	45	42

and lows, while others try to include only actual trades. However, vendors are not consistent in applying their own rules. Some days include bids and offers while other days from the same vendor do not."

Similar problems, like the ones described by Mr. Knight, are also found in the opening and closing prices. Table 9.1 gives information about 10 of the more prominent data vendors and their respective data reporting accuracy.

Continuous versus Individual Contracts

Faulty and/or inconsistent reporting is not the only problem with data. Futures data, unlike cash or equity data, expires every few months and this causes problems for most testing software. The most widely used testing software cannot handle rolling out of an existing position in one contract, and rolling into the same position in another contract. Because of this limitation, data vendors offer their subscribers continuous contracts of the various markets. A continuous contract is one long flow of data made up of the individual contracts while they are the front month. Due to the nature of futures, there are usually large gaps in price between the new and expiring contracts. Since you can't accurately test data with large price gaps, most data vendors offer software that allows the price gaps to be smoothed out. The end result is an artificial continuous contract. This type of contract includes prices that may have never existed. The debate between continuous contracts versus actual contracts has been going on for years. On one hand, most software packages will only test continuous data. On the other hand, most traders only trade the individual contracts. What is a trader to do? There are three solutions to this conundrum.

The first solution is to test with continuous contracts and trade with actual contracts. The majority of system traders trade in this manner (not necessarily the best way) because they don't believe that it makes that much of a difference; they believe that historical analysis of trading systems gives only a ballpark view of a system's potential. If a few trades are off, so be it. Everything should wash out in the end.

A second solution is to test with continuous contracts and trade with continuous contracts. More traders (especially long termers) are trading in this manner for two reasons.

Testing long-term systems on individual contracts can sometimes give somewhat erroneous information. If you want to test a 100-day moving average system on a Value Line contract, you would find that there simply is not 100 days of historical data. A futures contract is considered top step or front month when it is the most actively traded contract for that particular market. Most futures contracts are front month for less than sixty days. Many times you will find that there simply isn't 100 days of data to load or the data that you are loading is so thin in the early stages that the output of your system has no relation to the current actual market. Creating trade signals on a continuous contract, in some cases, can give more accurate results.

The second reason to trade and test in this manner is the security in knowing that you are trading a system the exact way that you tested it. If you decide on this solution, you have one more problem to overcome; not all continuous data contracts are created equal. The different data vendors use different smoothing formulas and algorithms to remove the price gaps between contracts. In Mr. Knight's article, he tested a simple system on three S&P 500 continuous contracts from different vendors. Even though the data came from different vendors, you would think that since the tests used the same system and same market, you would get somewhat similar results. We were surprised by Mr. Knight's findings:

	Total Profit ($)	Maximum Drawdown ($)
Test 1	127,500	25,375
Test 2	95,275	27,000
Test 3	95,500	45,475

You may think that this throws a monkey wrench into the works, but really it doesn't. Consistency is the key. If you test with a certain vendor's continuous data, then trade with that same vendor's data. By doing this, you hopefully won't have any unexpected surprises.

Finally, the third solution is to test on actual contract data and trade on actual contract data. We believe that this is the best solution; it solves the problem of testing systems on artificial data and you trade exactly what you have tested and developed. We know it sounds like we are contradicting ourselves due to our discussion on generating long term trading signals on actual contract data, but the majority of trading systems don't have such a long term view. If your trading system needs less than forty days of historical data, there shouldn't be a great difference between signals generated on actual versus continuous data. However, if your system needs more historical data, then by all means use continuous contracts. As with anything dealing with accuracy, testing with actual contracts is very difficult. We know of only one software package that can test in this manner and that is our own Excalibur™. Excalibur can test over long periods of time and rollover from one contract to another. This type of testing is very accurate, because as in real trading, rollover costs are incorporated into the system performance accounting. If you don't have Excalibur, you can still test individual contracts with your software package; it just requires a lot more work. Instead of one big test over the entire time period, you have many small tests over each contract. In addition, it is up to you to keep track of the systems performance statistics, such as total profit, maximum draw down, percent wins, average win, and so on. All the tests that were carried out in this book were done with Excalibur testing on individual contracts.

When you decide on a data vendor and a format, it is very important that you know exactly what you are getting. Does your vendor include bid and ask prices in the highs and lows? What is the smoothing formulas used to create continuous contracts? Once you have educated yourself on your data, then their should be no surprise when you start real time trading.

INDICATORS

Any mechanical trading system must have some consistent method for entering and exiting the market. Most of the time this method or trigger is based on some type of indicator or mathematically based statistic that has price forecasting capability. Anything that indicates what the future may hold is an indicator. Some of the more popular indicators today include moving average, rate of change, momentum, stochastic, rsi, Donchian breakout, Bollinger bands, Keltner bands. Most charting software has more than 50 built in indicators. Of all of the indicators that are out there, only a handful are worth more than a grain of salt. Indicators cannot stand alone; they should be used in concert with other ideas and logic. To demonstrate the viability of pure indicator based systems, we have tested a few of the more popular indicators and show the results on the following pages.

Stochastics

This oscillator type indicator was developed by George Lane in the 1950s and compares the current market close to the range of prices over a specified time period. Stochastics try to indicate when a market is either overbought or oversold. It is based on the assumption that when an up trend/downtrend approaches a turning point, the closing prices start to move away from the high/low price of a specific range.

The overall purpose of the stochastic oscillator is to give warning to supply overtaking demand in an up trend and demand overtaking supply in a downtrend. The number that is generated by this indicator comes in the form of a percentage oscillating between 100 and 0. A reading of 70 or more indicates the close is near the high of the range. On the other side of the scale, a reading of 30 or less indicates the close is near the low of the range. The "raw" stochastic values oscillate so quickly that they aren't of much value, therefore most of the time these values are smoothed with a moving average. In most cases, traders take these smoothed values and smooth them even further by applying another moving average. These end values are called slow stochastics.

The most widely used stochastic based system is to buy when the 14-day slow stochastic reaches the oversold territory (30% or less) and then retraces back and to sell when the overbought territory (70% or greater) is reached and then retraces back. (See Table 9.2.)

Relative Strength Index

Welles Wilder introduced this oscillator indicator in his 1978 book, *New Concepts in Technical Trading Systems* (Greensboro, NC: Trend Research). Similarly to stochastics, RSI oscillates between 0 and 100 and tries to determine overbought and oversold situations. The RSI calculates the ratio of up closes to down closes over a specified range of prices. The more up closes or stronger up closes the higher the ratio and vise versa. Usually a reading of 70 or more indicates overbought and a reading of 30 or less indicates oversold.

Most traders like to buy when the RSI enters the overbought zone of 70 or more and then retraces and sell when the RSI enters the oversold zone of 30 or less and then retraces. Table 9.3 shows if the RSI had any better luck than the stochastic.

MACD

Moving average convergence divergence (MACD) was developed by Gerald Appel in 1979. MACD, another price oscillator, is derived from three different exponentially smoothed moving averages. This indicator

TABLE 9.2   Stochastic Test

ONE CONTRACT PER TRADE
TEST PERIOD 1/1/83–8/31/99
$75 ALLOWED FOR COMMISSION AND SLIPPAGE

Individual Market	Total PL ($)	Avg PL/ Yr ($)	Max DrawDn ($)	Trds/ Yr	Win (%)	W:L	Gain/Mr +DD (%)
Soybeans	−7,455	−447	41,475	13	45	0.9	−1
Pork Bellies	−832	−50	43,524	13	48.1	1	−0.1
Euro $	−6,950	−417	16,125	11	43.8	0.9	−2.5
Crude Oil	−58,300	−3,644	61,070	12	39.1	0.6	−5.8
Cotton	−47,625	−2,858	64,700	12	45.6	0.7	−4.4
Gold	−3,600	−216	19,530	12	44.2	1	−1
Treasury Note	−58,340	−3,500	72,600	11	44.3	0.6	−4.7
Japanese Yen	−22,775	−1,367	74,475	10	51.5	0.9	−1.8
Swiss Franc	−44,575	−2,675	57,713	11	46.3	0.8	−4.5
Muni Bonds	2,480	177	35,550	12	49.1	1	0.5
Natural Gas	9,370	1,004	27,140	11	43.8	1.1	3.2
Heating Oil	−50,513	−3,031	58,724	12	46.5	0.7	−5
Unleaded Gas	5,590	379	26,258	13	52.7	1	1.3
Deutsche Mark	−24,375	−1,463	31,275	10	44.5	0.8	−4.5
British Pd.	856	51	55,356	10	47.9	1	0.1
US Bonds	−51,350	−3,081	87,960	11	45.1	0.8	−3.4

Summary Performance

Net Profit ($):	−359,203
Maximum Drawdown ($):	393,753

is usually plotted as two different lines. The first line (MACD line) being the difference between the two moving averages (long-term ma— short-term ma), and the second line (signal or trigger line) being an exponentially smoothed moving average of the MACD line.

The purpose of the MACD is to try and eliminate the lag that is associated with moving average type systems. This is accomplished by anticipating the moving average crossover and taking action before the actual crossover. Unlike the stochastic and RSI, this oscillator doesn't have fixed upper and lower extremes.

The typical MACD system buys when the MACD line crosses the signal line from below and sell when the MACD line crosses the signal line from above. We haven't had much luck with pure indicator based systems, but let's see how MACD works out in Table 9.4.

TABLE 9.3 Relative Strength Index

ONE CONTRACT PER TRADE
TEST PERIOD 1/1/83–8/31/99
$75 ALLOWED FOR COMMISSION AND SLIPPAGE

Individual Market	Total PL ($)	Avg PL/ Yr ($)	Max DrawDn ($)	Trds/ Yr	Win (%)	W:L	Gain/Mr +DD (%)
Soybeans	−17,555	−1,053	24,420	12	53.8	0.9	−4.1
Pork Bellies	−4,592	−276	39,700	11	57.1	1	−0.7
Euro $	−72,800	−4,368	77,450	35	31.1	0.4	−5.6
Crude Oil	−57,880	−3,618	61,720	15	50.9	0.6	−5.7
Cotton	−100,875	−6,053	108,285	10	48.5	0.5	−5.5
Gold	−1,510	−91	22,900	17	46.3	1	−0.4
Treasury Note	−79,450	−4,767	86,850	11	50.8	0.6	−5.4
Japanese Yen	−116,375	−6,983	131,675	11	49.2	0.5	−5.2
Swiss Franc	−78,738	−4,724	104,925	10	51.8	0.7	−4.4
Muni Bonds	−26,910	−1,922	41,720	11	53.5	0.8	−4.4
Natural Gas	−51,800	−5,550	60,670	13	46.3	0.6	−8.6
Heating Oil	−33,285	−1,997	41,639	11	53.2	0.8	−4.6
Unleaded Gas	−44,541	−3,020	50,534	12	52.3	0.7	−5.7
Deutsche Mark	−22,200	−1,332	38,038	11	53.3	0.9	−3.4
British Pd.	−71,488	−4,289	105,813	10	59.1	0.7	−4
US Bonds	−84,470	−5,068	105,670	10	49.1	0.6	−4.7

Summary Performance

Net Profit ($):	−865,218
Maximum Drawdown ($):	908,516

Commodity Channel Index

Donald Lambert introduced this oscillator type indicator in 1980. Unlike the RSI and stochastics, CCI is a trend following indicator. In addition to this major difference, the formula for this indicator is much more complex. CCI expresses how far current prices have deviated from a moving average. If prices have deviated considerably, then there is a good chance a new trend has developed. This indicator sounds in part like the standard deviation based bollinger bands, but it is different. First off, it uses the typical price ((high + low + close)/3) in its moving averages, instead of just the close. Secondly, the author added a constant multiplier (.015) to the formula so that 70–80% of the values would fall between the values of +100% and −100%.

Donald Lambert suggested that long positions should be initiated when the CCI exceeded +100 and then liquidated when the CCI retraced

TABLE 9.4   Moving Average Convergence Divergence

ONE CONTRACT PER TRADE
TEST PERIOD 1/1/83–8/31/99
$75 ALLOWED FOR COMMISSION AND SLIPPAGE

Individual Market	Total PL ($)	Avg PL/ Yr ($)	Max DrawDn ($)	Trds/ Yr	Win (%)	W:L	Gain/Mr +DD (%)
US Bonds	−45,560	−2,734	71,910	25	38.3	0.9	−3.7
Treasury Note	−61,080	−3,665	73,730	25	37.1	0.8	−4.9
Muni Bonds	−47,790	−3,414	61,360	25	33.8	0.8	−5.4
British Pd.	24,731	1,484	34,763	24	39.3	1.1	4.1
Deutsche Mark	14,675	881	18,388	23	38.8	1.1	4.5
Japanese Yen	35,113	2,107	34,850	23	37.6	1.1	5.6
Swiss Franc	−10,500	−630	32,150	24	37.7	1	−1.9
Crude Oil	−38,970	−2,436	45,960	26	38.5	0.8	−5.1
Heating Oil	−23,755	−1,425	54,230	26	38.4	0.9	−2.5
Natural Gas	39,590	4,242	14,260	22	42.6	1.4	23.2
Cotton	−40,505	−2,430	56,075	25	32.9	0.8	−4.3
Coffee	98,888	5,933	50,738	24	39.2	1.2	10.7
Sugar	−25,435	−1,526	29,770	24	34	0.8	−5
Soybeans	13,860	832	33,145	25	41.1	1.1	2.4
Corn	88	5	12,475	24	33.4	1	0
Wheat	−8,538	−512	22,688	24	37.7	0.9	−2.2
Silver	45,490	2,729	63,985	25	36.1	1.2	4.1
Gold	−9,970	−598	23,900	25	34.7	0.9	−2.4
Live Cattle	−37,444	−2,247	44,568	25	35.1	0.7	−5
Pork Bellies	−6,880	−413	29,740	24	39.4	1	−1.3
Live Hogs	19,268	1,156	13,868	23	40.6	1.2	7.7

Summary Performance

Net Profit ($):	−67,471
Maximum Drawdown ($):	290,555

back to this point. Short positions are initiated and liquidated in a similar manner except the trigger value is −100.

As with the other indicators, we put this one to the test. You may see a pattern evolving as you look at Table 9.5.

In their book *The New Technical Trader* (New York: John Wiley & Sons), Tushar Chande and Stanley Kroll explain how most traders try to overcome the failure rate of indicators:

Even the best indicator does not work 100 percent of the time; hence, using indicators is a game of percentages. Since each indicator has a significant

TABLE 9.5   Commodity Channel Index

ONE CONTRACT PER TRADE
TEST PERIOD 1/1/83–8/31/99
$75 ALLOWED FOR COMMISSION AND SLIPPAGE

Individual Market	Total PL ($)	Avg PL/ Yr ($)	Max DrawDn ($)	Trds/ Yr	Win (%)	W:L	Gain/Mr +DD (%)
US Bonds	−99,980	−5,999	104,310	34	32.8	0.6	−5.6
Treasury Note	−67,030	−4,022	70,280	32	35.9	0.6	−5.6
Muni Bonds	−50,610	−3,615	58,610	32	35	0.7	−6
British Pd.	−15,756	−945	25,513	31	37.6	0.9	−3.5
Deutsche Mark	−12,400	−744	24,563	31	39.4	0.9	−2.9
Japanese Yen	3,525	212	36,600	32	38.7	1	0.5
Swiss Franc	−27,850	−1,671	33,688	33	38.8	0.9	−4.7
Crude Oil	−51,240	−3,203	54,930	31	33.8	0.6	−5.6
Heating Oil	−61,312	−3,679	66,692	33	34.7	0.7	−5.4
Natural Gas	−37,420	−4,009	38,490	34	34.8	0.7	−9.4
Cotton	−78,980	−4,739	82,840	34	28.8	0.6	−5.7
Coffee	−36,019	−2,161	50,569	31	36.1	0.9	−3.9
Sugar	−49,526	−2,972	53,245	31	27.6	0.5	−5.5
Soybeans	−47,615	−2,857	56,605	33	32.8	0.7	−4.9
Corn	−41,188	−2,471	42,225	33	24.7	0.5	−5.8
Wheat	−52,125	−3,128	54,175	33	27.4	0.5	−5.7
Silver	−28,845	−1,731	68,530	33	29	0.8	−2.4
Gold	−45,020	−2,701	52,850	32	31.8	0.7	−5
Live Cattle	−53,792	−3,228	54,388	34	27.8	0.5	−5.9
Pork Bellies	−100,936	−6,056	106,308	33	32.8	0.6	−5.6
Live Hogs	−63,892	−3,834	68,236	34	30.6	0.5	−5.5

Summary Performance

Net Profit ($):	−1,021,684
Maximum Drawdown ($):	1,057,508

failure rate, traders have developed many indicators to analyze prices, the random nature of price changes being one reason why indicators fail. Therefore, traders use multiple indicators to confirm the signal of one indicator with another. They believe that the consensus is more likely to be correct.

Chande and Kroll go on to explain that this is not a viable approach due to the strong similarities that exist between price based momentum indicators, using multiple ones simultaneously creates redundancy (Figure 9.2). A trader does not achieve diversification or confirmation by using different indicators that are basically first cousins.

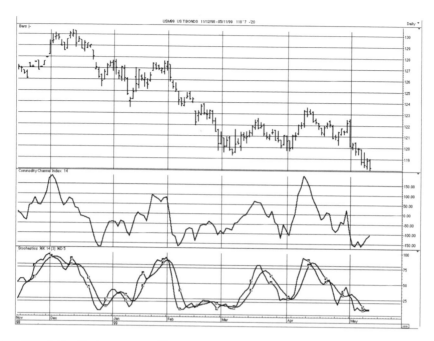

FIGURE 9.2 First cousins. Chart created with ProTA Gold™ software at www
.beesoft.net.

So far we have concentrated on momentum-based indicators. We
have basically proven that as pure systems, these indicators fail most of
the time. They seem to be based on sound market principles, so why do
they fail? I believe that Chande and Kroll summed this answer up best
in their book, *The New Technical Trader*.

- None of them is a "pure" momentum oscillator that measures momentum directly.
- The time period of the calculations is fixed, giving a different picture of market action for different time periods.
- They all mirror the price pattern; hence, you may benefit more directly trading prices themselves.
- They do not consistently show extremes in prices because they
  use a constant time period.
- The smoothing mechanism introduces lags and obscures short-
  term price extremes that are actually valuable for trading.

So far it probably seems that indicators are a waste of time. But before we drive the last nail into the indicator coffin, let's look at some
non oscillating longer term momentum indicators.

Bollinger Bands

John Bollinger, a leading analyst, has made this indicator famous. Bollinger bands are also known as alpha-beta bands. This indicator usually uses 20 or more days in it calculations and does not oscillate around a fixed point. Bollinger bands, when graphed, create an envelope usually above and below the current prices. Unlike the oscillator based indicators, this indicator and the other ones that we will discuss in the remainder of this chapter have the same scale as price charts.

Bollinger bands consists of three lines and are very simple to derive; the middle line is a simple moving average and the outside lines are plus 2 standard deviations above the moving average or minus 2 standard deviations below the moving average. The number of standard deviations can be varied.

A typical Bollinger band type system buys when price reaches the bottom band and liquidates as the price moves up past the moving average. The sell side is simply the opposite. Statistically speaking, when a price goes beyond two standard deviations it should work its way back to the moving average. In our testing, we used this logic and in addition we used a $1500 money management stop loss and instead of simply liquidating when the price moved to the moving average line, we forced the price to penetrate this line and them retrace back from it. Table 9.6 shows the results of the testing.

Overall we got the same results with this test as we did with the oscillators, but we noticed something promising with the results of the Bollinger band test. The system lost consistently across most markets and traded on average less than ten times a year per market. Sometimes traders come up with great ideas that don't initially work the way they were designed. In the case of the Bollinger band test, the performance numbers indicate a good idea applied incorrectly. Systems that are based seemingly on sound market principles and trades sparingly and loses consistently are occasionally considered good candidates for logic reversal. Instead of buying when prices reached the lower band, we decide to sell. We did the same thing for the upper band; instead of selling we bought. We used the same money management stop, but this time we eliminated the profit targets. Let's see how reversing a systems entry logic can sometimes create a winning system (Table 9.7).

We know what you're saying: Why not reverse the logic on the previous indicator tests? We could have but we didn't have the correct recipe. Systems that trade frequently and lose consistently are not good candidates for logic reversal. The problem with such systems is they can't overcome the commission and slippage that is levied against each trade. They may be profitable before execution costs, but when commission and slippage is taken into account, each trade is usually a net loss.

TABLE 9.6 Bollinger Band (Test A)

ONE CONTRACT PER TRADE
TEST PERIOD 1/1/83–8/31/99
$75 ALLOWED FOR COMMISSION AND SLIPPAGE

Individual Market	Total PL ($)	Avg PL/ Yr ($)	Max DrawDn ($)	Trds/ Yr	Win (%)	W:L	Gain/Mr +DD (%)
US Bonds	−29,940	−1,796	44,010	10	37.4	0.8	−3.8
Treasury Note	−59,340	−3,560	66,210	9	35.8	0.5	−5.3
Muni Bonds	−27,960	−1,997	39,920	9	40	0.8	−4.8
British Pd.	−26,994	−1,620	43,500	9	38.7	0.8	−3.6
Deutsche Mark	−12,925	−776	25,438	9	44.3	0.9	−2.9
Japanese Yen	−76,038	−4,562	79,388	10	34.6	0.6	−5.6
Swiss Franc	−60,588	−3,635	74,838	10	30.9	0.6	−4.7
Crude Oil	−43,730	−2,733	44,100	10	42.4	0.6	−5.9
Heating Oil	−47,006	−2,820	54,541	9	42.6	0.6	−5
Natural Gas	−43,460	−4,656	49,240	12	38	0.5	−8.7
Cotton	−41,330	−2,480	49,930	10	43.3	0.7	−4.9
Coffee	−78,150	−4,689	97,463	10	31.7	0.6	−4.6
Sugar	−14,470	−868	19,174	9	52.7	0.8	−4.4
Soybeans	−16,510	−991	24,590	9	50	0.8	−3.8
Corn	−26,350	−1,581	27,125	9	44.9	0.5	−5.7
Wheat	8,713	523	10,013	8	63.3	1.2	4.9
Silver	−26,680	−1,601	33,370	8	44.5	0.7	−4.5
Gold	1,980	119	16,510	9	53.7	1	0.7
Live Cattle	−13,500	−810	18,892	11	52.5	0.8	−4.2
Pork Bellies	14,252	855	20,112	10	50.9	1.1	3.8
Live Hogs	−8,916	−535	17,640	10	47.3	0.9	−2.9

Summary Performance

Net Profit ($):	−630,043
Maximum Drawdown ($):	640,540

Instead of using the Bollinger bands to determine overbought/oversold situations, we used them to determine trend. In the long run, the trend-following type systems will outperform the counter trend and short-term oscillator based system. The next two tests will involve trend following indicators.

Moving Average Crossover

This is probably the most utilized indicator out there. It is very simple, and as you will see, quite effective. The calculation for a simple moving

TABLE 9.7　Bollinger Band (Test B)

ONE CONTRACT PER TRADE
TEST PERIOD 1/1/83–8/31/99
$75 ALLOWED FOR COMMISSION AND SLIPPAGE

Individual Market	Total PL ($)	Avg PL/ Yr ($)	Max DrawDn ($)	Trds/ Yr	Win (%)	W:L	Gain/Mr +DD (%)
US Bonds	61,780	3,707	19,130	6	44.4	1.5	17
Treasury Note	44,630	2,678	15,830	7	45	1.5	15.5
Muni Bonds	9,730	695	20,700	7	44.4	1.1	3.1
British Pd.	11,669	700	47,113	7	33.1	1.1	1.4
Deutsche Mark	47,075	2,825	13,725	6	49.5	1.5	18.7
Japanese Yen	135,525	8,132	21,225	6	51.4	2.6	34.2
Swiss Franc	72,763	4,366	13,825	7	50.9	1.6	28.1
Crude Oil	35,450	2,216	17,220	9	50	1.4	11.5
Heating Oil	−14,360	−862	30,517	9	39.2	0.9	−2.6
Natural Gas	25,870	2,772	16,610	9	46	1.4	13.4
Cotton	51,660	3,100	17,255	8	44.7	1.5	17
Coffee	86,850	5,211	63,094	8	34.6	1.5	7.7
Sugar	7,874	472	15,949	7	47	1.1	2.8
Soybeans	−9,640	−578	37,045	9	38.7	0.9	−1.5
Corn	8,513	511	13,825	8	41.8	1.2	3.6
Wheat	−20,325	−1,220	26,913	8	36.9	0.7	−4.4
Silver	−26,835	−1,610	50,895	8	38.1	0.8	−3
Gold	−39,010	−2,341	45,010	8	37.6	0.7	−5
Live Cattle	−6,268	−376	19,612	10	39.6	0.9	−1.9
Pork Bellies	−31,264	−1,876	41,096	8	33.3	0.8	−4.3
Live Hogs	−27,320	−1,639	34,864	10	32.9	0.7	−4.6

Summary Performance

Net Profit ($):	423,396
Maximum Drawdown ($):	78,195

average is simply to sum up the closes (opens, highs, lows or midpoints) for the past x days and divide by x. Do this every day and soon you will have a moving average line or curve. A cross-over system involves two or more moving averages usually consisting of a longer-term and shorter-term average. When the short-term moving average crosses from below the long-term moving average, this usually indicates a buying opportunity. Selling opportunities occur when the shorter-term moving average crosses from above the longer-term moving average. Moving averages can be calculated in basically three different manners: simple (as described earlier), exponential, and weighted. Exponential and weighted

TABLE 9.8 Simple Moving Average

ONE CONTRACT PER TRADE
TEST PERIOD 1/1/83–8/31/99
$75 ALLOWED FOR COMMISSION AND SLIPPAGE

Individual Market	Total PL ($)	Avg PL/ Yr ($)	Max DrawDn ($)	Trds/ Yr	Win (%)	W:L	Gain/Mr +DD (%)
US Bonds	55,940	3,356	14,950	5	53.9	1.6	19
Treasury Note	18,760	1,126	17,540	5	42.1	1.3	5.9
Muni Bonds	44,330	3,166	14,910	6	46.8	1.7	18.9
British Pd.	281	17	22,244	5	39.8	1	0.1
Deutsche Mark	52,200	3,132	15,938	6	50	1.6	18.1
Japanese Yen	73,913	4,435	26,913	5	53.9	2	15
Swiss Franc	40,363	2,422	18,513	5	52.3	1.4	12
Crude Oil	19,530	1,221	8,370	6	41.5	1.4	11.7
Heating Oil	10,828	650	22,411	7	42.7	1.1	2.7
Natural Gas	41,500	4,446	13,990	7	53.6	1.9	24.7
Cotton	12,170	730	33,520	7	41.3	1.1	2.1
Coffee	32,944	1,977	81,338	6	36.7	1.2	2.3
Sugar	7,269	436	12,925	6	43.5	1.2	3.2
Soybeans	−19,995	−1,200	43,970	8	36.4	0.8	−2.6
Corn	4,363	262	10,100	6	42.6	1.1	2.5
Wheat	−15,163	−910	18,025	6	29.6	0.7	−4.8
Silver	−595	−36	24,575	7	40.4	1	−0.1
Gold	−3,820	−229	18,220	6	43.8	0.9	−1.2
Live Cattle	8,984	539	16,108	8	41.9	1.2	3.2
Pork Bellies	−17,740	−1,064	34,636	6	40.4	0.8	−2.9
Live Hogs	−9,680	−581	31,524	7	38.2	0.9	−1.8

Summary Performance

Net Profit ($):	355,638
Maximum Drawdown ($):	61,425

moving averages tend to skew the moving averages toward the most recent prices. In our testing, we will demonstrate the effectiveness of moving average crossovers and in addition show that there really isn't that much difference between the three different types of moving averages (Tables 9.8, 9.9, 9.10).

The overall net results from the three different moving average tests were quite similar. Each moving average made more money in some markets and loss more in others. Each moving average is as good as the others, and research time should not be spent on trying to determine which is best. One thing should stand out in our testing, however. This was the

TABLE 9.9 Exponential Moving Average

ONE CONTRACT PER TRADE
TEST PERIOD 1/1/83–8/31/99
$75 ALLOWED FOR COMMISSION AND SLIPPAGE

Individual Market	Total PL ($)	Avg PL/ Yr ($)	Max DrawDn ($)	Trds/ Yr	Win (%)	W:L	Gain/Mr +DD (%)
US Bonds	28,750	1,725	35,250	10	39.3	1.2	4.5
Treasury Note	39,160	2,350	13,850	10	41.2	1.3	15.3
Muni Bonds	−18,460	−1,319	49,940	11	31.2	0.9	−2.5
British Pd.	15,050	903	58,763	11	34.3	1.1	1.5
Deutsche Mark	58,638	3,518	14,763	10	45.5	1.5	21.8
Japanese Yen	133,475	8,009	28,550	9	48.4	2.1	25.7
Swiss Franc	71,038	4,262	23,663	10	44.8	1.4	16.8
Crude Oil	44,910	2,807	11,500	12	41.4	1.5	20.8
Heating Oil	7,568	454	22,562	13	40.7	1.1	1.8
Natural Gas	33,330	3,571	19,410	12	44	1.4	15.3
Cotton	34,325	2,060	44,300	12	38.2	1.2	4.5
Coffee	34,819	2,089	107,813	13	33.3	1.1	1.9
Sugar	10,685	641	10,819	10	40.6	1.2	5.6
Soybeans	−25,605	−1,536	57,805	12	33.5	0.8	−2.6
Corn	6,838	410	14,125	12	34.9	1.1	2.8
Wheat	1,888	113	24,225	12	33.8	1	0.5
Silver	−30,795	−1,848	34,595	12	33.8	0.8	−5
Gold	−18,430	−1,106	21,160	13	35.7	0.8	−4.9
Live Cattle	−16,380	−983	25,752	13	42.5	0.8	−3.7
Pork Bellies	−44,160	−2,650	58,536	12	36.1	0.8	−4.3
Live Hogs	9,316	559	24,080	12	39.9	1.1	2.2

Summary Performance

Net Profit ($):	374,641
Maximum Drawdown ($):	119,598

second test that actually made money and it was based on trend following logic. Another pattern is developing.

Donchian Breakout

If you approach the market from a long-term standpoint, this envelope indicator should be right up your alley. Richard Donchian popularized this method back in the 1960s. This indicator involves two lines that are plotted above and below the market, similarly to Bollinger bands. The top line represents the highest high of n days back (or weeks) and

TABLE 9.10   Weighted Moving Average

ONE CONTRACT PER TRADE
TEST PERIOD 1/1/83–8/31/99
$75 ALLOWED FOR COMMISSION AND SLIPPAGE

Individual Market	Total PL ($)	Avg PL/ Yr ($)	Max DrawDn ($)	Trds/ Yr	Win (%)	W:L	Gain/Mr +DD (%)
US Bonds	45,340	2,720	26,120	−15,050	40.2	1.2	9.4
Treasury Note	49,410	2,965	11,980	−4,530	46.1	1.4	22
Muni Bonds	15,140	1,081	20,900	−6,360	40.1	1.1	4.8
British Pd.	24,175	1,451	49,650	−8,638	36.6	1.1	2.8
Deutsche Mark	40,563	2,434	22,825	5,100	40.6	1.3	10.1
Japanese Yen	149,175	8,951	17,275	9,513	48.5	2.1	45.1
Swiss Franc	43,325	2,600	27,200	5,413	43.1	1.2	9
Crude Oil	15,540	971	20,830	7,300	37.6	1.1	4.2
Heating Oil	−24,196	−1,452	52,387	7,090	37.3	0.9	−2.7
Natural Gas	44,030	4,718	17,310	−9,670	44.8	1.6	22.1
Cotton	10,165	610	30,175	1,590	36.3	1.1	2
Coffee	−11,063	−664	95,756	−5,625	33.3	1	−0.7
Sugar	−5,275	−317	21,862	−470	33.2	0.9	−1.4
Soybeans	−20,020	−1,201	43,960	−1,755	35.6	0.9	−2.7
Corn	−988	−59	13,613	−5,263	34	1	−0.4
Wheat	−7,563	−454	26,100	−2,600	33.5	0.9	−1.7
Silver	−33,445	−2,007	42,090	−9,965	36.6	0.8	−4.5
Gold	−1,740	−104	21,010	−4,960	37.9	1	−0.5
Live Cattle	−14,608	−876	19,592	−1,512	35.6	0.8	−4.4
Pork Bellies	−28,508	−1,710	47,464	−4,664	38.2	0.9	−3.4
Live Hogs	1,452	87	26,588	5,604	39.4	1	0.3

Summary Performance

Net Profit ($):	289,256
Maximum Drawdown ($):	87,515

conversely the bottom line represents the lowest low of n days back (or weeks). Richard Donchian felt if price penetrated either band then a trend was fully underway; buy on strength and sell on weakness.

Let's test the idea of buying when the day's high penetrates the highest high of four weeks back and selling when the day's low penetrates the lowest low of four weeks back (Table 9.11).

Again, we have a winning approach. It seems as if the trend following indicators are by far superior to the overbought/oversold type indicators. Because systematic trading has no room for subjectivity, we feel that trend following type systems are hard to beat. The advantages of a trend

TABLE 9.11 Donchian Breakout

ONE CONTRACT PER TRADE
TEST PERIOD 1/1/83–8/31/99
$75 ALLOWED FOR COMMISSION AND SLIPPAGE

Individual Market	Total PL ($)	Avg PL/ Yr ($)	Max DrawDn ($)	Trds/ Yr	Win (%)	W:L	Gain/Mr +DD (%)
US Bonds	50,130	3,008	25,610	11	44	1.3	10.6
Treasury Note	37,910	2,275	14,200	11	46.3	1.3	14.5
Muni Bonds	−15,010	−1,072	39,820	12	38.1	0.9	−2.6
British Pd.	44,906	2,694	47,475	11	41.1	1.2	5.5
Deutsche Mark	48,350	2,901	26,500	10	44.3	1.4	10.4
Japanese Yen	130,988	7,859	30,563	10	47.9	1.8	23.7
Swiss Franc	59,188	3,551	21,613	11	42.9	1.3	15.2
Crude Oil	49,910	3,119	14,910	12	44.7	1.5	18.4
Heating Oil	25,532	1,532	25,393	13	40.9	1.2	5.6
Natural Gas	44,990	4,820	16,080	13	45.6	1.6	24
Cotton	13,180	791	47,650	13	37.4	1.1	1.6
Coffee	33,581	2,015	50,850	13	38.4	1.1	3.6
Sugar	−12,163	−730	21,627	12	37.6	0.9	−3.3
Soybeans	−7,175	−431	37,225	13	37.5	1	−1.1
Corn	5,138	308	7,538	12	36.9	1.1	3.8
Wheat	850	51	26,563	13	33.3	1	0.2
Silver	−60,140	−3,608	76,385	13	36.1	0.7	−4.6
Gold	−13,450	−807	25,190	13	37.7	0.9	−3
Live Cattle	−2,164	−130	14,964	14	38.4	1	−0.8
Pork Bellies	−15,208	−912	36,496	13	39.9	0.9	−2.3
Live Hogs	688	41	28,512	15	38.8	1	0.1

Summary Performance

Net Profit ($):	418,545
Maximum Drawdown ($):	85,970

following systems are: (1) 100% objective. (2) Trading infrequently reduces execution costs. (3) Captures the big swings where most of the big money is. The disadvantages are: (1) Whipsaws are inevitable. Most trend following systems have less than 50% wins. (2) Signals are usually late because they are not issued until a trend has developed. (3) If a market is in a trading range, there is a good chance of having a high number of consecutive losers before a trend is initiated.

Weighing the advantages and the disadvantages, we still feel that the systematic trader will have a better chance with a trend following methodology. We have only scratched the surface on the subject of indicators, but feel that further research on the hundreds of different indicators (overbought/oversold and trend following) would be a waste of your time and ours. The testing that we have shown exemplifies what we have found over the past 15 years.

FIVE APPROACHES USED BY THE BEST TRADING SYSTEMS

The top winning trading systems that we track basically fall into five different categories. That's it! All of the profitable trading systems that we have analyzed, has evolved from five basic approaches. And they are:

1. Donchian channel.
2. Moving average cross over.
3. Short-term volatility based open range breakout.
4. S&P day trade.
5. Pattern recognition.

In this section we are going to present complete turnkey systems based on these five approaches. The logic of these systems as well as the performance numbers will be fully discussed.

ANATOMY OF A TRADING SYSTEM

All trading systems are basically identical when it comes to their over all make up and objectives; all systems enter the market and exit the market and all systems strive to be profitable. Most system traders and developers spend 90% of their time developing entry techniques and the rest of their time is dedicated to the decision that ultimately determines profitability. It doesn't seem rational that traders spend much more time with an entry technique when it is the exit that determines the entry's effectiveness. We feel that research time should be split 50/50 between the entry and exit technique.

One of the great things about futures and stocks is that you can make as much money when the market goes down as when it goes up. All systems should have a long and short entry technique to cover the only two directions the market can go. When we discuss long and short entry techniques with traders, the one question that seems to always come up is: Should my short signal be the complete opposite of my buy signal? At first, this question my seem simple to answer. If all markets go up and down, then you should enter the market long and short based on the same premise. Ultimately, we feel that this is the right answer, but the fact is all markets don't go up and down in the same manner. We have never seen an extended bear market in the S&P futures for example. Why should you bang your head against the wall by shorting a bull market? Also, any system designed and tested with historical S&P futures data automatically has a bullish bias. In most cases, if you look at the profit distribution between long and short positions on a S&P system, you will find that long profits out number short profits two to one. If markets seem to have a bias, then why shouldn't we enter a long position differently than we do a short position. There are two basic answers to this question: (1) A lot of markets don't have a bias and those that do can shift their bias and systems should be prepared for this. Most systems have a short term memory (i.e., look back over a very short term history) and don't know what the overall long term trend is. (2) Having different long and short entry techniques increases the number of parameters and therefore increases the likelihood of over optimization. As an overall rule of thumb, the short entry should be the complete opposite of the long entry. All of the top systems that we track follow this guideline.

After a position has been entered, there are three different ways a system can get out of that position: reverse and take an opposite position with a loss or a profit, liquidate the position with a loss, liquidate the position with a profit (break even trades are considered profitable). A system can incorporate one of these types of exits or all of them.

Types of Exits

Reversal: This type of exit occurs when the system has determined that the market is headed in the opposite direction of its original intent. The system then exits the current trade and self corrects itself by entering a new trade in the opposite direction. This type of stop can be profitable or not. The problem with this type of exit/reentry is whipsaws. Whipsaws occur when a system chases the market; the system initiates a position and the market goes against it, so the system reverses and tries to go in the same direction of the market, but as it does the market then reverses and goes back in the original direction. Reversal stop based systems are in the market 100% of the time and are ready and waiting for the long-term trend. It doesn't use protective stops or profit objectives; it allows the market to determine entries and exits.

Protective stop: The system was wrong and wants to get out with a minimal loss. This stop is always a loss. The problem with protective stop exits is premature trade termination. Let's say we are willing to risk $1,000 on a trade and we initiate a long position. Immediately the trade turns ugly and we are stopped out with a $1,000 loss. The next day the market goes down another $500; we feel confident about our decision to terminate the losing trade. The next five days the market goes back up in the initial direction $8,000. If we had only used a wider stop, then we would have stayed with the trade and would have been up $8,000. Determining the optimal protective stop amount is very difficult.

Profit objective: The system has made a predetermined profit and the possibility to make more money is extremely low. This stop is always a winner. Everybody would have to love this exit technique. Let's assume we are trading a system that has an average win of $2,000 and we have initiated a long position. A few days later we are pleasantly informed that we are in the profit $2,000. Based on historical statistics, this is the optimal amount the system will make on any given trade. Why should we stick with the trade if the probability of making more money is minimal and the probability of giving back some of the profit is high. The problem with this stop, similar to the protective stop, is premature trade termination. In certain situations, this stop will take $2,000 out of the market and leave $3,000 on the table. Most systems make all of their money on a small handful of big winners. If you limit the big winners, then you won't have enough money to cover the more frequent small losers.

To reiterate, the exit technique, be it a reversal, protective stop, or profit objective, requires much thought and research. For this reason, we will emphasize this aspect when we discuss the five turnkey trading systems.

Donchian Channel

Three systems that are currently in our top ten have some type of Donchian variation. As you saw with the indicator, this is a longer term trend following system that buys on strength and sells on weakness. Let's start with the basic entry technique: Buy when today's high exceeds the highest high of 30 days back and sell when today's low exceeds the lowest low of 30 days back. This is a simple technique that will buy on strength, sell on weakness, trade infrequently and hopefully capture some longer term trends.

How do we get out of the market? Let's utilize a money management stop and some type of profit objective in addition to the system's reversal signal (we will use the full gambit of exit techniques). We feel that longer term systems need more room to work when a trade is initially put on and most of the time a pure money management stop isn't universal; a $2,000 move in the Japanese Yen is quite different than a $2,000 move in sugar. All markets trend and congest, but they trend and congest in different magnitudes and manners. We like to normalize our protective stops so that they are a function of the market. By doing so, the protective stop or any type of parameter becomes a characteristic of that particular market. Our stop will be the midpoint between the highest high and lowest low of thirty days back. This type of stop is predetermined, dynamic and a reflection of current market conditions. Through past experience we have discovered that pure profit targets do not work on longer term systems, unless they are huge. We like to lock in profits on longer term systems with a trailing stop. A trailing stop is a stop that follows the market as it goes in your favor. When the market starts to turn back against you, the trailing stop locks itself in and waits for the market to come to it, hence locking in some profit. Trailing stops work better than profit targets because they give an existing trend room to fluctuate. In a lot of instances, a long-term trend will show exhaustion and retrace a good percentage then take off back in the direction of the trend. We have seen profit targets prematurely exit a trend with a $4,000 profit when a trailing stop holds on for $10,000. Similarly to the protective stop, a dynamic trailing stop seems to work better. Our trailing stop will be based on the amount of time the system is in the market. Our initial trailing stop will simply be the highest high of the past 30 days if we are long and the lowest low of the past 30 days if we are short. For every 5 days that we are in a trade, we will decrement the number of days by two that we look back to attain the highest highs and lowest lows. (For example, if we are long and we have been in a trade for 5 days, our trailing stop will change from being the lowest low for the past 30 days to the lowest low for the past 28.) As you can tell, we have given as much thought to our exits as we have our entries, if not more (Table 9.12).

Now that we have the entry and exits of our system figured out, let's see how it works on a portfolio of different markets. The exact rules are:

- Go long when the highest high of the past 30 days has been penetrated.
- Go short when the lowest low of the past 30 days has been penetrated.
- Place a protective stop at the mid point between the highest high of 30 days and the lowest low of 30 days.
- Initialize your trailing stop to be the lowest low of 30 days back if you are long and the highest high of 30 days back if you are short.
- For every 5 days that you are in a trade, decrement the number of days that you look back to calculate your trailing stop by two. Never let this number go below six.
- Always use the stop that is currently closer to the market by comparing the protective stop and the trailing stop.

Moving Average Cross Over and Back to the Classics

Several of the top rated system utilize moving averages in the entry and/or exit techniques. We feel that the crossover method gives good

TABLE 9.12   Modified Donchian Breakout

ONE CONTRACT PER TRADE
TEST PERIOD 1/1/83–8/31/99
$75 ALLOWED FOR COMMISSION AND SLIPPAGE

Individual Market	Total PL ($)	Avg PL/ Yr ($)	Max DrawDn ($)	Trds/ Yr	Win (%)	W:L	Gain/Mr +DD (%)
US Bonds	45,720	2,743	25,940	10	43.6	1.3	9.6
Treasury Note	35,810	2,149	12,220	10	43.6	1.3	15.7
Muni Bonds	4,260	304	25,210	10	38.3	1	1.1
British Pd.	75,975	4,559	26,200	9	41.3	1.5	16.5
Deutsche Mark	27,025	1,622	17,700	10	43.4	1.2	8.5
Japanese Yen	98,188	5,891	20,800	9	49	1.8	25.2
Swiss Franc	88,975	5,339	11,400	9	49.4	1.8	40.7
Crude Oil	27,270	1,704	15,850	12	44.3	1.3	9.5
Heating Oil	−6,976	−419	45,364	12	39.1	1	−0.9
Natural Gas	39,690	4,253	15,910	12	47.3	1.7	21.4
Cotton	16,915	1,015	33,555	12	34.3	1.1	2.9
Coffee	118,894	7,134	49,369	11	40.6	1.5	13.1
Sugar	14,179	851	8,366	10	42.9	1.3	9.4
Soybeans	−4,035	−242	33,740	11	34	1	−0.7
Corn	8,500	510	9,250	10	36.8	1.2	5.2
Wheat	−10,738	−644	21,100	11	33.2	0.9	−2.9
Silver	−35,010	−2,101	62,150	12	35.8	0.8	−3.3
Gold	−28,090	−1,685	36,040	12	33.2	0.8	−4.5
Live Cattle	−10,604	−636	20,872	13	36.7	0.9	−3
Pork Bellies	−19,948	−1,197	34,432	12	38.4	0.9	−3.2
Live Hogs	−1,096	−66	23,040	12	40.4	1	−0.3

Summary Performance

Net Profit ($):	483,604
Maximum Drawdown ($):	67,200

trend confirmations. Moving averages have been ridiculed and criticized ever since the dawn of trading systems. Why? One reason is that they are perceived as an over simplified approach. Another, is in the fact that they lag the current market condition and price. Bleeding edge technology and instantaneous information distribution has pushed traders away from the classical approaches to the markets. If a strategy or a system doesn't mention chaos theory, neural network, genetic algorithm, or game theory then new traders don't want anything to do with it. It is unfathomable for many traders to believe that a simple moving average system will outperform the majority of the new buzz word techniques. We have known a few of the world's largest banks and CTAs, who spent millions of dollars to research these new age techniques, abandon them for the simplified classic approaches. Don't get us wrong, we are more than willing to embrace any idea or technology that proves itself. We simply haven't heard of anything that can outperform the moving average and Donchian systems of the world. Let's get back to our second system. Again, through experience, we have discovered that an intermediate term moving average crossing a longer term moving average seems to work best over a broad spectrum of different markets. We will enter the market long when the 13-day moving average of closes crosses from below the 39-day moving average and yesterday's close is greater than the close of 40 days back. We will use just the opposite approach to enter short; the 13-day moving averages must cross the 39-day moving average from above and yesterday's close must be less than the close of 40 days back.

Again, let's use the full gambit of exit techniques that we have at our disposal. Since our entry signals will be indicating longer term trends, we need to have a good size protective stop to prevent premature trade termination. In addition, the stop should be made a function of the market as is our entry technique. An average true range calculation is a good indication of market risk. The average true range for the past x days is calculated by summing up the true ranges (not actual ranges—true range differs from actual range in that the previous days close figures in when calculating the range—true range = max(close[1] or high) − min(close[1] or low)) and then dividing by the x. This calculation basically states that for the past x days the market has moved an average of y amount on a daily basis. Daily risk is defined by the amount the market can move against you on a daily basis. We know that in certain market conditions, there is unlimited risk, but for the majority of time we can closely approximate how much the market may move against our position. If we are trading a moving average crossover with longer term averages, then we must accept the fact that the market will most likely go against us more than one average true range. Even though we are willing to take some heat, we still need to define our threshold of pain. For this example, lets assume a protective stop in the amount of five times the average true range for the past 20 days. Why five times and 20 days? First, we know the market is going to move more than one or two ATRs against us, so let's use a stop that won't get us out on every trade and one that will limit extreme market losses. Second, the last 20 days usually gives a good indication of the current market's psychology. We could have optimized over past data and come up with different values for different markets, but why kid ourselves. We will discuss the dangers of over optimization in the next chapter. To lock in profits, let's trail our stop whenever we get five ATRs in profit. In other words, when the market has gone in our favor in the amount of five times the average true range for the past 20

TABLE 9.13   Simple Moving Average Crossover System

ONE CONTRACT PER TRADE
TEST PERIOD 1/1/83–8/31/99
$75 ALLOWED FOR COMMISSION AND SLIPPAGE

Individual Market	Total PL ($)	Avg PL/ Yr ($)	Max DrawDn ($)	Trds/ Yr	Win (%)	W:L	Gain/Mr +DD (%)
US Bonds	55,940	3,356	14,950	5	53.9	1.6	19
Treasury Note	18,760	1,126	17,540	5	42.1	1.3	5.9
Muni Bonds	44,330	3,166	14,910	6	46.8	1.7	18.9
British Pd.	281	17	22,244	5	39.8	1	0.1
Deutsche Mark	52,200	3,132	15,938	6	50	1.6	18.1
Japanese Yen	73,913	4,435	26,913	5	53.9	2	15
Swiss Franc	40,363	2,422	18,513	5	52.3	1.4	12
Crude Oil	19,530	1,221	8,370	6	41.5	1.4	11.7
Heating Oil	10,828	650	22,411	7	42.7	1.1	2.7
Natural Gas	41,500	4,446	13,990	7	53.6	1.9	24.7
Cotton	12,170	730	33,520	7	41.3	1.1	2.1
Coffee	32,944	1,977	81,338	6	36.7	1.2	2.3
Sugar	7,269	436	12,925	6	43.5	1.2	3.2
Soybeans	−19,995	−1,200	43,970	8	36.4	0.8	−2.6
Corn	4,363	262	10,100	6	42.6	1.1	2.5
Wheat	−15,163	−910	18,025	6	29.6	0.7	−4.8
Silver	−595	−36	24,575	7	40.4	1	−0.1
Gold	−3,820	−229	18,220	6	43.8	0.9	−1.2
Live Cattle	8,984	539	16,108	8	41.9	1.2	3.2
Pork Bellies	−17,740	−1,064	34,636	6	40.4	0.8	−2.9
Live Hogs	−9,680	−581	31,524	7	38.2	0.9	−1.8

Summary Performance

Net Profit ($):	355,638
Maximum Drawdown ($):	61,425

days, our stop will trail the high of the day that penetrated this point by five times the current ATR. In addition to our protective and trailing stop, we can exit and reverse our position if the opposite entry technique sets up (Table 9.13). The exact rules for our moving average cross over system are:

- Buy on the open when the 13-day moving average of closes crosses from below the 39-day moving average and yesterday's close is greater than the close of 40 days back.

- Sell on the open when the 13-day moving average of closes crosses from above the 39-day moving average and yesterday's close is less than the close of 40 days back.
- Calculate the average true range for the past twenty days.
- Use five times the average true range as our initial protective stop.
- Every time we move five ATRs in the profit place a trailing stop five ATRs from the high of the day that penetrated that point.
- Always use the stop that is currently closer to the market by comparing the protective stop and the trailing stop to the reversal stop.

Short-Term Volatility Based Open Range Breakout

The title of this system sounds complicated, but it is quite simple in concept and calculation. Popularized by Larry Williams, this little system is being used to manage billions of dollars. The incorporation of the opening is what makes this system so successful. The opening price usually gives an indication of price direction for the day and many times for the next few days to come. The volatility aspect of the system gives the magnitude of potential market movement in that direction.

As with the other systems that have been presented, we will incorporate a trailing stop. Since we are dealing with a system that holds onto a trade for an average of less than 12 days and can possibly trade frequently, the trailing stop should be designed around these facts. Entry and exit techniques are related and should be designed with each other in mind. You wouldn't have system exit a trade after three days if its entry was based on an eighty day breakout. Our opening range breakout system will succeed less than 50% of the time due to the fact that a trade can be easily triggered in congestive markets and result in whipsaw trades. Since we are going to win less than 50% of the time, we need to let our winners run as long as they can and cut our losses before they get too big. We will utilize a protective stop in the amount of three times the average ten day true range and pull our stop to break even when we attain a profit equal to three times the ten day average true range. This may seem to be a wide protective stop for such a short-term system, but it is a necessary evil. We will demonstrate the ineffectiveness of using tight protective stops when system trading in the next chapter. A trailing break even stop is one that gets us out at our entry price after a certain amount of profit is attained. In cases where a trade only lasts for a short period of time, this type of stop seems to work better than one that tries to lock in more profit.

Opening range breakout systems buy or sell when the market moves a certain amount from the open. With some luck, the market will break from the open and continue in that direction for several days. However, most of the time the market will move a certain amount from the open and then reverse and either congest for awhile or go strong in the new direction. The problem with this type of system is in the determination of how far must the market move from the open to indicate a further move in that direction. If the distance is too close, then you will suffer from whipsaw mania. If too far, then you will be missing a large portion of the move on every trade.

With this system we will buy/sell off of the open a certain percentage of the difference between the highest high and lowest low for the past three days. The difference between the highest high and lowest low provides us a measurement of short-term volatility. Volatility is a good indication of market indecision. High volatility usually indicates a nontrending market, because the market is swinging from high levels to low levels. While working with open range breakout systems, we discovered chart patterns that helped indicate short-term market direction. With these patterns we were able to determine days when a trade should be triggered quicker than normal. This led us to the concept of the buy easier/sell easier day. Based on pattern recognition, if a market closes lower than the previous day, the following day or days usually trend upward. If a market closes higher than the previous day, the following day or days usually trend downward. If the market closes down from the previous day, then we have a buy easier day. If the market closes up from the previous day, then we have a sell easier day. On buy easier days, we will buy when the market moves up 50% of the range between the highest high and lowest low for the past three days from the open price and sell when the market moves down 100% of the same range from the opening. On sell easier days, we will sell when the market moves down 50% of the range between the highest high and lowest low of the past three days from the open price and buy when the market moves up 100% of the same range from the opening (Table 9.14). To summarize our opening range breakout system, here are the rules:

- Calculate the highest high and lowest low for the past three days and define the difference between the two as our volatility measure.

- Determine if tomorrow is a buy easier or sell easier day. If today's close is greater than or equal to yesterday's close, then tomorrow is a sell easier day. If today's close is less than yesterday's close, then tomorrow is a buy easier day.

- If today is a buy easier day, the buy stop is calculated by dividing the volatility measure by two and adding the quotient to the open

TABLE 9.14   Short-Term Volatility Based Breakout System

ONE CONTRACT PER TRADE
TEST PERIOD 1/1/83–8/31/99
$75 ALLOWED FOR COMMISSION AND SLIPPAGE

Individual Market	Total PL ($)	Avg PL/ Yr ($)	Max DrawDn ($)	Trds/ Yr	Win (%)	W:L	Gain/Mr +DD (%)
US Bonds	68,560	4,114	23,270	32	42.9	1.2	15.8
Treasury Note	32,620	1,957	24,880	31	42.7	1.2	7.4
Muni Bonds	68,110	4,865	31,490	31	43.2	1.4	14.6
British Pd.	16,538	992	33,069	28	39.7	1.1	2.9
Deutsche Mark	39,313	2,359	36,925	29	41.4	1.2	6.2
Japanese Yen	55,900	3,354	25,813	26	41.1	1.2	11.8
Swiss Franc	49,688	2,981	22,675	29	42.4	1.2	12.2
US$ Index	20,210	1,470	35,860	35	39.1	1.1	4
Crude Oil	41,210	2,576	9,590	32	43.9	1.3	22.2
Heating Oil	−41,332	−2,480	47,657	32	37.5	0.8	−5
Natural Gas	44,780	4,798	12,660	36	41.2	1.4	28.8
Cotton	−9,250	−555	55,185	35	37	1	−1
Coffee	178,350	10,701	51,525	36	40.3	1.4	19
Sugar	−11,962	−718	33,163	38	35.9	0.9	−2.1
Soybeans	30,400	1,824	29,435	35	38.7	1.2	5.9
Corn	16,875	1,013	8,288	29	39.4	1.2	11.5
Wheat	−14,088	−845	21,538	34	39.1	0.9	−3.8
Silver	39,900	2,394	40,145	38	38.1	1.2	5.6
Gold	−28,150	−1,689	44,460	36	36.5	0.8	−3.7
Live Cattle	−16,100	−966	22,636	38	38	0.9	−4.2
Pork Bellies	5,100	306	27,984	36	42.1	1	1
Live Hogs	5,544	333	16,516	34	40.9	1	1.9

Summary Performance

Net Profit ($):	588,204
Maximum Drawdown ($):	84,129

price. The sell stop on a buy easier day is calculated by simply subtracting our volatility measure from the open price.

- If today is a sell easier, the sell stop is calculated by dividing the volatility measure by two and subtracting the quotient from the open price. The buy stop on a sell easier day is calculated by adding our volatility measure to the open price.
- Calculate the average true range for the past 10 days.
- Use three times the average true range as our initial protective stop.

- Once we move three ATRs in the profit pull our protective stop to the break even point.
- Always use the stop that is currently closer to the market by comparing the protective stop or break even stop to the reversal stop.

How important is our pattern and the concept of the buy easier and sell easier day? Tables 9.15 and 9.16 show the exact system without the buy easier/sell easier setup. Table 9.15 buys and sells 50% off of the open and Table 9.16 buys and sells 100% off of the open.

TABLE 9.15   Short-Term Volatility Based Breakout System (Test A)

ONE CONTRACT PER TRADE
TEST PERIOD 1/1/83–8/31/99
$75 ALLOWED FOR COMMISSION AND SLIPPAGE

Individual Market	Total PL ($)	Avg PL/ Yr ($)	Max DrawDn ($)	Trds/ Yr	Win (%)	W:L	Gain/Mr +DD (%)
US Bonds	81,890	4,913	19,380	44	43.2	1.2	22.3
Treasury Note	23,530	1,412	20,080	43	43	1.1	6.5
Muni Bonds	77,620	5,544	18,030	44	44.9	1.3	28
British Pd.	40,838	2,450	37,575	40	38.6	1.1	6.3
Deutsche Mark	33,425	2,006	24,363	41	40.6	1.1	7.8
Japanese Yen	15,138	908	46,163	36	37.3	1	1.9
Swiss Franc	31,688	1,901	31,725	41	41.2	1.1	5.7
US$ Index	−13,030	−948	34,200	47	39	1	−2.7
Crude Oil	26,650	1,666	22,990	46	40.2	1.1	6.7
Heating Oil	−57,204	−3,432	71,371	47	36.4	0.8	−4.7
Natural Gas	74,110	7,940	10,060	47	43.3	1.6	56.5
Cotton	−22,010	−1,321	51,290	49	35.1	0.9	−2.5
Coffee	192,094	11,526	47,063	50	39.5	1.3	22.2
Sugar	−15,994	−960	28,594	50	33.6	0.9	−3.3
Soybeans	38,565	2,314	19,630	48	37.9	1.2	11
Corn	2,288	137	11,775	41	34.6	1	1.1
Wheat	9,025	542	8,988	48	38.1	1.1	5.6
Silver	49,120	2,947	41,775	50	35.6	1.2	6.7
Gold	−29,670	−1,780	43,650	46	36	0.9	−4
Live Cattle	−7,580	−455	16,964	51	38.1	1	−2.6
Pork Bellies	−12,520	−751	44,796	49	40.2	1	−1.6
Live Hogs	8,560	514	22,072	46	38.6	1.1	2.2

Summary Performance

Net Profit ($):	541,105
Maximum Drawdown ($):	129,233

TABLE 9.16   Short-Term Volatility Based Breakout System (Test B)

ONE CONTRACT PER TRADE
TEST PERIOD 1/1/83–8/31/99
$75 ALLOWED FOR COMMISSION AND SLIPPAGE

Individual Market	Total PL ($)	Avg PL/ Yr ($)	Max DrawDn ($)	Trds/ Yr	Win (%)	W:L	Gain/Mr +DD (%)
US Bonds	6,990	419	37,880	13	39.8	1	1
Treasury Note	14,690	881	26,810	12	39.3	1.1	3.1
Muni Bonds	−400	−29	22,400	12	39.9	1	−0.1
British Pd.	39,663	2,380	22,225	12	41.7	1.2	10
Deutsche Mark	29,150	1,749	28,325	11	41.1	1.2	5.9
Japanese Yen	91,838	5,510	24,163	11	45.5	1.6	20.6
Swiss Franc	39,950	2,397	23,550	11	43.2	1.2	9.5
US$ Index	11,480	835	33,220	14	44	1.1	2.4
Crude Oil	53,690	3,356	11,600	12	44.1	1.7	24.6
Heating Oil	25,129	1,508	28,505	11	41.3	1.2	4.9
Natural Gas	45,240	4,847	18,140	13	51.3	1.7	21.9
Cotton	−8,825	−530	26,370	13	34.6	0.9	−1.9
Coffee	104,494	6,270	72,206	13	44.1	1.4	8.1
Sugar	−5,947	−357	21,291	16	37.6	0.9	−1.6
Soybeans	30,450	1,827	18,890	14	44.1	1.3	9
Corn	−12,213	−733	17,838	12	33	0.8	−4
Wheat	−7,300	−438	17,650	13	34.9	0.9	−2.4
Silver	−31,815	−1,909	65,240	17	34.4	0.8	−2.8
Gold	−8,680	−521	27,580	17	36.8	0.9	−1.8
Live Cattle	964	58	12,576	13	35.3	1	0.4
Pork Bellies	−2,876	−173	25,312	11	38.4	1	−0.6
Live Hogs	−17,040	−1,022	31,376	13	35.9	0.8	−3.1

Summary Performance

Net Profit ($):	397,126
Maximum Drawdown ($):	114,267

S&P Day Trade

The S&P day trade system is by far the most popular system out there. In almost every Top Ten list that we have published an S&P day trade system has been included. People are constantly drawn to the idea of day trading. They like the idea of closing out all positions at the end of the day and not exposing themselves to overnight risk. By the end of the day, day traders know exactly how much they made or lost and can go home and not worry about any adverse news that may affect the markets.

Sounds to us like this is the way go, but unfortunately with most utopian type plans, there are extensive drawbacks and obstacles involved with day trading.

Only a small handful of markets trade with enough intraday range to make good day trading vehicles. Day traders can only capture a small portion of a market's daily range and if that daily range is not large enough, then there isn't enough profit potential to cover execution costs. The only markets that offer sufficient daily ranges are the stock index futures and the new internet stocks. The rest of the markets are best traded on a position basis. Figure 9.3 shows a 30-day moving average of daily ranges on several different markets.

The S&P 500 offers the most profit potential when compared to the other markets. The stock future indexes mirror the U.S. economy and are highly susceptible to rumors and reports. These markets can easily move $10,000 in a day and have extended periods of illiquidity. We have known traders that were slipped more than $2000 trading the S&P 500. With this type of risk the margin requirements for the stock index futures are usually very high. These markets are usually out of reach for the average trader or should we say should be out of reach for the average trader. Traders that only have $20,000 to trade can either trade a small portfolio of anti correlated markets or one contract of the S&P 500. Most traders unwisely risk their entire capital on trying to day

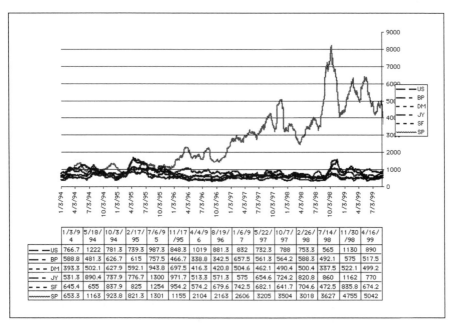

	1/3/94	5/18/94	10/3/94	2/17/95	7/6/95	11/17/95	4/4/96	8/19/96	1/6/97	5/22/97	10/7/97	2/26/98	7/14/98	11/30/98	4/16/99
US	766.7	1222	781.3	739.3	987.3	848.3	1019	881.3	832	732.3	788	753.3	565	1130	890
BP	588.8	481.3	626.7	615	757.5	466.7	338.8	342.5	657.5	561.3	564.2	588.3	492.1	575	517.5
DM	393.3	502.1	627.9	592.1	943.8	697.5	416.3	420.8	504.6	462.1	490.4	500.4	337.5	522.1	499.2
JY	531.3	890.4	737.9	776.7	1300	971.7	513.3	571.3	575	654.6	724.2	820.8	860	1162	770
SF	645.4	655	837.9	825	1254	954.2	574.2	679.6	742.5	682.1	641.7	704.6	472.5	835.8	674.2
SP	653.3	1163	923.8	821.3	1301	1155	2104	2163	2606	3205	3504	3018	3627	4755	5042

FIGURE 9.3   Where's the volatility? (Price is vertical and time is horizontal.)

trade the stock index futures. They place more importance on profit than on risk, which is the main recipe for self-destruction.

Over the years, several different system vendors, sensing the demand for day trade systems, have tried to come up with a successful approach to day trading the S&P 500 futures. Most of their ideas failed, but there is one concept that has shown consistent performance and can be found in the top five S&P day trade systems. This concept is actually a combination of two different entry techniques: open range breakout and a counter trend setup. All of the successful S&P day trade systems have a open range breakout entry similar to the system we last discussed. In addition to this entry technique, they also can enter the market on a counter trend move or a retracement. As we discussed with the last system, the number one nemesis to breakout systems is the false breakout. This occurs when the market moves in one direction and triggers a trade and then retraces back in the opposite direction. The retracement entry technique tries to take advantage of the market when the initial breakout fails. The combination of these two entry techniques have shown extraordinary performance over the past three years. The breakout is there to capture the big trending days and the retracement is there to capture the false breakouts.

The S&P day trade system that is presented here has the same overall approach to the market as systems that cost thousands of dollars. There are other key components in this system other than the breakout and counter trend entry techniques. First off, this system will not take a trade unless it determines that there is enough profit potential. It does this by calculating the average range for the past 10 days and the average open to close range for the past 10 days and dividing the latter calculation by the former. If the quotient is not greater than .5 then a trade is not allowed to take place. Since the majority of the trades and profit will probably come from the breakout from the open entry technique, there would be no use in trading if the range from the open to the close is less than ½ of the actual range. On days where the average open to close range is less than ½ of the average actual range, the majority of market movement is found between the open and low and between the high and close. These areas are known as dead zones for open range breakout systems.

The second interesting component of our system is the concept of buy easier and sell easier days. This system, similar to the one we discussed previously, can buy or sell easier on specific days. Once again the determination of these easier days are based off of a chart pattern. This pattern involves the "key of the day" which is calculated by adding the high, low, and close together and then dividing by three. This key of the day boils the three most important statistics down to one. If the closing price is above the key, this usually indicates upward momentum and the opposite is true if the closing price falls below the key. With this in mind, we defined a buy easier day when the closing price is greater than the key of the day and defined a sell easier day when the closing price is less than the key.

The breakout buy and sell stops are a function of market volatility and are similar in calculation to the open range breakout system that we discussed earlier. In this system, our volatility measure is defined as the average actual range for the past ten days (note: actual range is simply the high of the day minus the low of the day). On buy easier days, the buy stop is calculated by multiplying the volatility measure by thirty percent and adding this amount to the open price. Conversely the sell stop is calculated by multiplying the volatility measure by sixty percent and subtracting this amount from the open price. On sell easier days, the buy and sell stops are calculated in the same manner, but the percentages are switched. The buy stop uses 60% and the sell stop uses 30%.

The counter trend or retrace entries are functions of yesterday's actual range and the key price of yesterday and do not use the buy/sell easier day concept. The counter trend buy stop is set up when the market trends down from the open to the buy trigger point. The buy trigger point is calculated by subtracting 75% of yesterday's actual range from the key price of yesterday (remember the key price is calculated by adding the high, low, and close together and dividing by three). Once this point is penetrated a buy stop is placed at the key price of yesterday minus 25% of yesterdays actual range. The counter trend sell stop is set up in a similar fashion; first the market must trend up to or past the key price of yesterday plus 75% of yesterday's actual range and then trend down to the same key price plus 25% of yesterday's actual range. As you can see, the counter trend entries are trying to take advantage of failed breakouts.

There are no trades allowed before 10:00 A.M. eastern or after 3:30 P.M. eastern. Only one trade is allowed in one direction on a daily basis. A buy and a sell is allowed in the same day, but two buys or two sells are not; you can have up to two trade signals a day and the signals must be doing the opposite (buying and selling).

In an attempt to keep things a little less confusing, a simple money management stop of 300 points is used. In addition, there aren't any trailing stops or break even stops. All trades are exited at the end of the day. These are definite areas for further research. This is the most complicated system you will find in this book, so let's summarize the system (Table 9.17):

- Calculate the average actual range for the past 10 days and define this as our volatility measure.
- Calculate the average open to close range for the past 10 days.

TABLE 9.17   S&P Day Trade System

ONE CONTRACT PER TRADE
TEST PERIOD 1/1/90–2/29/00
$100 ALLOWED FOR COMMISSION AND SLIPPAGE

Total Net P/L ($)	90,075	Avg. Net/Year ($)	8,860
Winning Months (%)	47	Avg. Ret. MaxDD/Yr (%)	30
		Avg. Ret. with Time (%)	127
Max DrawDn ClsTrd ($)	23,895		
Max DrawDn w/OTE ($)	23,895		
Best Trade ($)	18,650	Worst Trade ($)	−2,150
Average Trade ($)	71	Net Prof:Loss Ratio	1.2
Average Win ($)	998	Average Loss ($)	−568
Long Net P/L ($)	48,815	Short Net P/L ($)	41,260
No. of Trades	1,269	Avg. Trades/Year	125
No. of Winning Trades	518	Percent Winners (%)	40.80
No. of Losing Trades	751	Most Cons. Losses	17
Avg. Days Per Trade	0.5	Longest Flat Time (Days)	1,092
Time in the Market (%)	23	Sharpe Ratio	0.16

	Net P/L ($)	Max ClsTrd ($)	No. of Trades	Win (%)	Avg Win	Cons Loss	Flat No. of Days
Last 6 months	11,985	12,723	68	25.0	3,401	11	47
Last 12 months	22,945	12,723	107	27.1	3,163	11	83
This year	13,638	6,358	30	26.9	3,840	19	12
Last year	−4,458	19,608	106	29.5	2,849	10	215
Total	90,075	23,895	1,269	40.8	998	17	1,092

- Divide the average open to close range by the average actual range and if this quotient is less than 0.5 then no trades can be placed.
- Calculate the key price of today by adding the high, low, and close together and divide by three.
- Determine if tomorrow is a buy easier or sell easier day. If today's close is greater than today's key price, then tomorrow is a buy easier day. If today's close is less than today's key price, then tomorrow is a sell easier day.
- If tomorrow is a buy easier day, the buy stop is calculated by multiplying the volatility measure by 30% and adding the product to the open price. The sell stop on a buy easier day is calculated by multiply the volatility measure by 60% and subtracting the product from the open.

- If tomorrow is a sell easier day, the sell stop is calculated by multiplying the volatility measure by 30% and subtracting the product from the open price. The buy stop on a sell easier day is calculated by multiplying the volatility measure by 60% and adding it to the open price.
- Determine the retrace buy trigger for tomorrow by subtracting 75% of today's actual range from the key price of today. The retrace buy price is the key price of today minus 25% of today's actual range. If at any time the market trades below the retrace buy trigger, a long position can be entered at the retrace buy price.
- Determine the retrace sell trigger for tomorrow by adding 75% of today's actual range to the key price of today. The retrace sell price is the key price of today plus 25% of today's actual range. If at any time the market trades above the retrace sell trigger, a short position can be entered at the retrace sell price.
- No trades allowed before 10:00 A.M. eastern or allowed after 3:30 P.M. eastern.
- A maximum of two trades are allowed on a daily basis and they must be doing the opposite (buying and selling). You can initiate one long position and one short position on a daily basis, but you can't initiate two position going in the same direction.
- Use a simple 300 point protective stop.
- Close out any open positions on the close of tomorrow.

Pattern Recognition

Pattern is defined as a predictable route or movement. Hence all trading systems are in some form or manner pattern recognition systems. A long-term moving average cross over system utilizes pattern recognition it its decision when to buy or sell. The crossover in this case is the pattern. An open range breakout is pattern recognition and the pattern in this case is the movement from the open to the breakout point. All systems look for some type of reoccurring event and try to capitalize on it. These reoccurring events are the patterns.

System vendors have been selling pattern recognition software for as long as trading systems have been around. This type of software looks for reoccurring visual chart patterns and analyses the immediate market action that follows. Japanese candlestick patterns are also of a visual pattern nature. Information concerning a day's market action can be seen easier and quicker with a candlestick chart than with a typical bar chart. A candlestick bar consists of a shadow and a body. The shadow is drawn from the high of the day to the low and the body is a rectangle drawn from the open price to the close price around the shadow. A light-colored candle body indicates the close was higher than the open. A dark body indicates the close was lower than the open. Candlestick or other types of visual patterns are usually quite simple and can be recognized with the naked eye. Three candlestick chart patterns, Doji Star, Big Bullish Candle, and Hammer are shown in Figure 9.4:

- Big Candle—An unusually long body with a wide range between high and low.
- Doji—The open is the same as the close.
- Hammer (Bullish)—A small body (either color) near the high with a long lower shadow and a short or no upper shadow.
- Hammer (Bearish)—A small black body near the low with a long upper shadow and a short or no lower shadow.

Other visual chart patterns can be described in language also:

- IF HIGH(1) > HIGH(2) AND OPEN < HIGH(1) THEN BUY AT HIGH(1).

FIGURE 9.4   A sample of candlestick chart patterns.

A few system vendors have misused pattern recognition and misled their clients into believing that reoccurring simple visual patterns, by themselves, can foretell future market action. Some vendors have scanned historical data and found occurrences of visual patterns that seemed to have prophetic powers. They then bundle these patterns up with a piece of software and sell the whole thing as a system. Absolutely nothing is wrong with this if all of the performance numbers are fully disclosed. In most cases, the vendor has found a bunch of different patterns that when added together creates a great looking equity curve. The problem is that most of these patterns occurred less than 30 times in history. A sample of less than 30 is considered statistically insignificant. The whole pattern system may add up to over 30 trades, but the important thing to remember is the number of occurrences of each individual pattern. We know of another system vendor that scanned history and developed a calendar system (another form of pattern recognition) based on probabilities of success. His research revealed that if one were to buy or sell on certain days of the year, then those trades would have a high historical probability of being profitable. These calendar systems look phenomenal in historical analysis, but this type of system does not take into consideration current market levels, recent market action, or any events leading up to the trade day. Would you buy the S&P 500 on every March 14, if history states that this action has proven to be 75% accurate. We wouldn't, unless we knew what had happened in the market over the prior days leading up to the trade date. This type of pattern recognition is a beautiful study in how to curve fit a system to historical data.

The correct way to use pattern recognition is to incorporate it into a system that utilizes other entry techniques. Certain visual patterns do offer a small glimpse of the future and when used in concert with other techniques can create profitable systems. The system that is shown here was created by John Hill and demonstrates the success of pattern recognition when used as a filter (a calculation or pattern that determines if a trade should take place). This system was developed around the idea of a pattern that consists of the last four days' closing prices. A buy or sell signal is not generated unless the range of the past four days' closes is less than the 30-day average true range. This pattern indicates that the market has reached a state of rest and any movement, up or down, from this state will most likely result in a significant move. The buy entry, if it is allowed, is calculated by adding 62% of yesterday's true range to the opening price and conversely the sell entry, again if allowed, is calculated by subtracting 62% of yesterday's true range from the opening. The protective stop for a long position is calculated by subtracting 62% of yesterday's range from the open price and is recalculated on a daily basis. This stop is either a reversal stop if a trade entry is allowed or a liquidation stop if an entry is not allowed. On the other side, the protective stop for a

short position is calculated by adding 62% of yesterday's true range to
the open price and is recalculated on a daily basis. Again, this stop is
either a reversal stop if a trade is allowed or a liquidation stop if one is
not. To demonstrate the importance of the four-day close pattern, we have
tested the system with and without the pattern filter. Before we show the
performance, let's summarize this pattern system:

- Calculate the average actual range for the past 30 days and define this as our volatility measure.

TABLE 9.18   Volatility Based Breakout with Pattern Recognition

ONE CONTRACT PER TRADE
TEST PERIOD 1/1/83–8/31/99
$75 ALLOWED FOR COMMISSION AND SLIPPAGE

Individual Market	Total PL ($)	Avg PL/ Yr ($)	Max DrawDn ($)	Trds/ Yr	Win (%)	W:L	Gain/Mr +DD (%)
US Bonds	103,330	6,200	13,330	49	47.2	1.4	38.7
Treasury Note	50,020	3,001	10,840	49	44.3	1.3	24.3
Muni Bonds	86,030	6,145	15,740	44	46.2	1.5	35
British Pd.	44,200	2,652	24,688	44	40.5	1.2	10.1
Deutsche Mark	1,813	109	32,475	42	39.3	1	0.3
Japanese Yen	−26,913	−1,615	44,850	40	36.1	0.9	−3.4
Swiss Franc	46,438	2,786	22,900	45	40	1.2	11.3
US$ Index	5,430	395	38,840	47	38.5	1	1
Crude Oil	34,370	2,148	10,660	41	44.5	1.3	16.9
Heating Oil	12,734	764	22,982	44	42.2	1.1	3.1
Natural Gas	50,080	5,366	5,550	41	43.8	1.6	56.2
Cotton	24,085	1,445	17,300	45	40.5	1.1	7.9
Coffee	187,294	11,238	51,806	50	45.4	1.5	19.8
Sugar	−2,834	−170	16,498	49	37.1	1	−1
Soybeans	42,610	2,557	11,740	50	43.1	1.3	19.5
Corn	−9,763	−586	14,963	44	33.4	0.9	−3.8
Wheat	−338	−20	10,538	47	38.9	1	−0.2
Silver	49,915	2,995	46,325	57	38.2	1.2	6.1
Gold	−11,270	−676	32,260	55	34.9	0.9	−2
Live Cattle	−10,652	−639	15,752	46	38.8	0.9	−3.9
Pork Bellies	36,376	2,183	19,788	42	44.9	1.2	9.8
Live Hogs	−692	−42	17,220	49	38.5	1	−0.2

Summary Performance

Net Profit ($):	707,044
Maximum Drawdown ($):	75,293

- Calculate the highest and lowest close for the past 4 days.
- Determine if a trade can take place tomorrow. The distance from the highest close to the lowest close for the past 4 days must be less than the 30-day average true range.
- If a trade is possible, calculate the buy and sell stop. The buy stop is calculated by adding 62% of yesterday's true range to the opening and the sell stop is calculated by subtracting 62% of yesterday's true range from the opening.

TABLE 9.19 Volatility Based Breakout without Pattern Recognition

ONE CONTRACT PER TRADE
TEST PERIOD 1/1/83–8/31/99
$75 ALLOWED FOR COMMISSION AND SLIPPAGE

Individual Market	Total PL ($)	Avg PL/ Yr ($)	Max DrawDn ($)	Trds/ Yr	Win (%)	W:L	Gain/Mr +DD (%)
US Bonds	146,980	8,819	24,130	80	45.6	1.3	32.9
Treasury Note	54,880	3,293	27,830	80	43.9	1.2	11.2
Muni Bonds	169,300	12,093	10,750	79	46.2	1.6	96.4
British Pd.	52,606	3,156	39,100	71	41.1	1.1	7.8
Deutsche Mark	−15,938	−956	67,488	75	37.2	1	−1.4
Japanese Yen	−37,788	−2,267	67,588	71	37.9	0.9	−3.2
Swiss Franc	44,000	2,640	34,650	75	40	1.1	7.3
US$ Index	620	45	49,410	78	38.2	1	0.1
Crude Oil	24,000	1,500	22,120	81	40.7	1.1	6.2
Heating Oil	32,655	1,959	36,767	80	41.9	1.1	5.1
Natural Gas	104,750	11,223	8,860	79	44.9	1.7	87.3
Cotton	12,620	757	23,805	82	39.8	1	3.1
Coffee	281,100	16,866	43,463	84	44.4	1.4	34.9
Sugar	−17,987	−1,079	23,766	84	35.6	0.9	−4.4
Soybeans	30,845	1,851	21,635	81	40.3	1.1	8.1
Corn	−21,338	−1,280	29,663	77	31.5	0.9	−4.2
Wheat	−20,075	−1,205	32,275	86	38.4	0.9	−3.6
Silver	23,225	1,394	86,745	84	36.5	1.1	1.6
Gold	−33,800	−2,028	48,690	81	35.5	0.9	−4.1
Live Cattle	−24,056	−1,443	32,636	87	37.8	0.9	−4.3
Pork Bellies	14,400	864	29,940	87	42.2	1	2.7
Live Hogs	−37,440	−2,246	51,920	86	35.9	0.8	−4.2

Summary Performance

Net Profit ($):	774,142
Maximum Drawdown ($):	168,930

- If a long position is initiated then place a protective stop. The protective stop for a long position is calculated by subtracting 62% of yesterday's true range from the open and is recalculated on a daily basis. This protective stop is either a reversal stop or a liquidation stop based on the ability to initiate new trades.
- If a short position is initiated then place a protective stop. The protective stop for a short position is calculated by adding 62% of yesterday's true range to the open and is recalculated on a daily basis. This protective stop is either a reversal stop or a liquidation stop based on the ability to initiate new trades.

Table 9.18 on page 204 shows the system with the pattern filter, and Table 9.19 on page 205 shows the same system without the pattern.

Did the pattern filter really help? We would have to definitely say yes. The overall maximum draw down was cut in half, and coffee went from being 36.3% of the total portfolio return to 26.8%.

CONCLUSION

We covered a lot of ground in this chapter, so don't worry if everything didn't sink in. The most important points to remember are:

- Get a computer, if you don't already have one.
- Base your research and actual trading on clean historical data.
- If you want your real time trades to mirror your hypothetical ones, then use the same data from the same vendor in the same format. Remember there are various data formats: actual, perpetual, and continuous. The different formats can be created in different manners; a back-adjusted continuous contract is different than a forward-adjusted continuous contract.
- Most systems based purely on popular indicators usually fail.
- Traders are always excited about leading edge technology, but inevitably fall back on the classical approaches. Most traders are not rocket scientists, thank goodness, and will tinker around with new age ideas, but most of them will trade only what they can fully understand.
- The most popular and successful approaches to trading the markets are:
  —Donchian breakout
  —Moving average crossover

—Short-term volatility open range breakout

—S&P and stock day trading

—Pattern recognition

• Exit techniques determine success of entry techniques and should be given equal research time.

10

HISTORICAL TESTING—A BLESSING OR A CURSE

Fast computers, historical data, and testing software are the greatest tools for system traders. With the use of these tools any conceivable mathematically defined idea can be evaluated. Before the advent of the computer, traders had to spend hours testing a simple system over a few months of historical data. Their tools consisted of a calculator; printouts of daily open, high, low, close data; and pencil and paper. In today's world, 20 years of data on 50 different markets can be tested in a matter of seconds. This is real power. Unfortunately, power can be used or abused. Knowledgeable system traders use this power to determine viable trading ideas, develop systems with robust parameters, and select portfolio composition. Naive beginning system traders abuse the power to fool themselves and unscrupulous system vendors abuse the power to fool others by developing trading systems that only work in the past.

Let's say you want to buy or develop a trading system. How can one differentiate between an honest and robust track record and one that has been optimized to only work in history. The only measures of a trading system's viability and potential profitability are found in its historical performance results. Through due diligence and research, the answer can be found. This chapter tries to point out the pitfalls and provide answers to problems that arise out of historical back testing.

SIMULATED ANALYSIS

When it comes to trading systems, the majority of historical performance data comes in the form of simulated analysis. Simulated analysis has several pitfalls, but the main two are insufficient slippage accounting due to hidden fast market conditions in historical daily data and analysis with the benefit of hindsight. Historical testing almost always gets the price that you want to buy or sell at. Most back testing software then levies a commission and slippage charge for each and every trade. The industry standard for commission and slippage charge ranges from $75 to $100. In the past few years, especially in the S&P and coffee, we have observed certain days that trades were slipped $500 or more. Slippage occurs when the market moves so fast that an order can't get filled because there are no buyers/sellers at the order price. Orders usually do get filled, but at a much less desirable price. Testing on daily bars, a person or a computer would not see nor reflect such high slippage amounts. Testing with intraday tick data could help alleviate the errors in slippage accounting, but unfortunately this type of data is very expensive, requires a lot of disk space, and is unreadable or impractical to use with today's testing software. A hypothetical simulated back test on daily bars is a study in best case scenarios. If you start your trading system analysis with this in mind, you will be starting out on the right foot. In the next section, we discuss the dangers of curve fitting with the benefit of hindsight.

CURVE FITTING

As we have mentioned before, a hypothetical track record is useless unless the underlying system is somewhat robust. With the benefit of hindsight, any historical track record can be manufactured; system parameters can be adjusted until all of the best historical trades are taken. Using hindsight and optimizing parameters and forcing a system to only take the best historical trades is known as *curve fitting*. Over optimizing and curve fitting guarantees two things: unbelievable historic performance and an extremely high probability of system meltdown in the future. How can the public determine if a system is overly curve fitted or not. This is a dead end question unless the logic to the system is fully disclosed. Forget trying to determine robustness (the lack of a system's performance sensitivity to changes in its parameters) of a black box system. If you are buying a black box system, you better know and have faith in the person you are buying from. And unfortunately, the logic of a white box system is usually not revealed until money has changed hands. Many times a vendor will disclose the number of parameters before he sells a system. As a system purchaser, you would have to ask whether the parameters are the same for all markets or are different for different markets. If the number of parameters is less than five and they are the same for all markets then there is a good chance that the system was not curve fitted to historical data. The opposite is true if there is a high parameter count and the parameters are commodity dependent. This rule of thumb is the first step in the hunt for a robust system. The second step occurs after the white box system has been purchased and you have the system programmed into a piece of software. You may think that this is putting the carriage before the horse, but remember that a full test can't be carried out unless the logic is fully revealed. The cost of the system could be minuscule compared to the potential losses that could be generated by an over-optimized system. In some cases, you may get the system vendor to demonstrate the robustness of his system by running different parameter sets on his system on individual markets. If the system vendor optimized the system originally, he may already have different runs with different parameter sets.

After you have attained either the system in software form or the optimization reports from the vendor, you can begin to determine robustness. Table 10.1 shows a typical optimization report. An optimization report will usually list the different parameters and the different results of those parameters tested over the same time period over the same market. A robust parameter is one that when changed (up or down) in incremental values does not result in drastic differences in overall performance.

TABLE 10.1 Typical Optimization Report

ONE CONTRACT PER TRADE
$75 ALLOWED FOR COMMISSION AND SLIPPAGE

Parameter 1	Parameter 2	Total PL ($)	Avg PL/ Yr ($)	Max DrawDn ($)	Trds/ Yr	Win (%)	W:L	Gain/Mr +DD (%)
20	20	−43,506	−5,675	63,569	130	37.6	0.9	−8.7
30	20	−46,738	−6,096	79,194	109	36.1	0.8	−7.6
40	20	−29,875	−3,897	70,813	85	34.5	0.9	−5.4
50	20	−27,106	−3,536	58,150	69	33.5	0.9	−5.9
60	20	−25,588	−3,338	50,431	56	31.5	0.9	−6.4
70	20	−11,806	−1,540	34,725	45	33	0.9	−4.3
80	20	−5,906	−770	35,863	38	33.7	1	−2.1
90	20	−8,675	−1,132	37,369	33	33.7	0.9	−2.9
100	20	−11,675	−1,523	36,294	31	32.1	0.9	−4
110	20	−13,106	−1,709	41,188	26	33.5	0.9	−4
120	20	−9,900	−1,291	35,750	23	33.5	0.9	−3.5
130	20	−5,506	−718	35,988	21	35	1	−1.9
140	20	−2,644	−345	36,956	18	35	1	−0.9
150	20	−4,569	−596	36,538	17	31.5	1	−1.6
20	30	−18,538	−2,418	41,238	101	37.6	0.9	−5.7
30	30	−32,513	−4,241	57,481	88	34.7	0.9	−7.2
40	30	−20,050	−2,615	51,563	70	33.1	0.9	−4.9
50	30	−18,525	−2,416	43,313	59	33.6	0.9	−5.4
60	30	−29,788	−3,885	44,975	50	33.4	0.8	−8.4

Figure 10.1 is a three-dimensional area graph that plots the profit that is generated by different combinations of two parameters. There are peaks, valleys and plateaus. It goes without saying that you don't want to pick the combination of parameters that falls in the valleys. At the same time, going against initial intuition, you don't want the combination that falls on the peaks either. The most robust parameter set is the one that falls on a high and level plateau. If you change this set of parameters up or down, the net result doesn't differ dramatically. You want this parameter set, because we all know that history does not repeat itself exactly and that the optimal parameters today may not be the optimal parameters tomorrow. We optimized a simple open range breakout system on the British Pound from 1983 through 1991. The rules for the system are to buy a certain percentage of the distance between the highest high and lowest low for the past three days off of the open. The sell side is just the opposite. In addition, we utilized a simple $1000 money management stop. In our optimization test, we were striving to find the best combination of percentages. Figure 10.2 shows the three-dimensional area graph

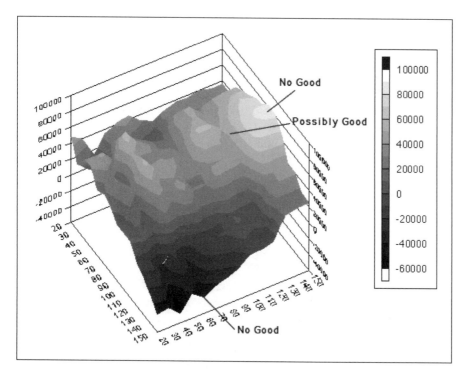

FIGURE 10.1 Three-dimensional area graph of a British Pound optimization (1983–1991). The x-axis = parameter 1; y-axis = parameter 2; z-axis = $ profit.

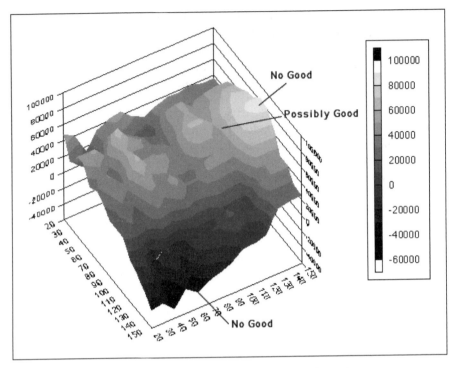

FIGURE 10.2   Same three-dimensional area graph as Figure 10.1.

of our optimization run. The x-axis represents parameter 1, the y-axis represents parameter 2 and the z-axis is net profit.

In this illustration, we picked three combinations of parameters: two that we thought were unreliable and one that showed potential. We chose the one good parameter set due to its placement on a high and level plateau. The parameter sets that we felt would be unreliable were found on peaks and in valleys. We walk-forward tested the three different sets of parameters on the British Pound from January 1992 through August 1999. Table 10.2 shows the performance of these walk-forward tests.

In this analysis, the valley parameters outperformed the peak and plateau parameters from a profit standpoint. The plateau parameters performed the best from a draw down standpoint. Figure 10.3 shows how parameters can shift through time. This three-dimensional area graph shows the profit generated by the same combination of parameters, but over the time period of January 1992 through August 1999. It is interesting to see how some peaks turned into valleys and how the optimal parameters shifted from one set of values to another.

The original "best" parameters were not optimal during the second optimization run. No markets repeat history exactly and if you don't

TABLE 10.2   Performance Using Three Different Sets of Parameters

ONE CONTRACT PER TRADE
TESTED FROM JANUARY 1992 THROUGH AUGUST 31, 1999
$75 ALLOWED FOR COMMISSION AND SLIPPAGE

Parameter Set	Total Net Profit ($)	Max DrawDn ($)	
Valley	−1,131	40,031	Best from profit stand point
Plateau	−4,738	19,588	Best from drawdown stand point
Peak	−18,175	35,838	Worst overall

choose a parameter set that works in most market conditions, you will be on the losing end of most trades. This analysis brings us to an interesting question: Does optimization really help?

There is but one use for optimization and that is for locating ballpark parameters. When you begin to develop a trading system, you have no idea of what your parameters should be. Through the use of optimization, you can rule out parameter ranges that don't make sense and

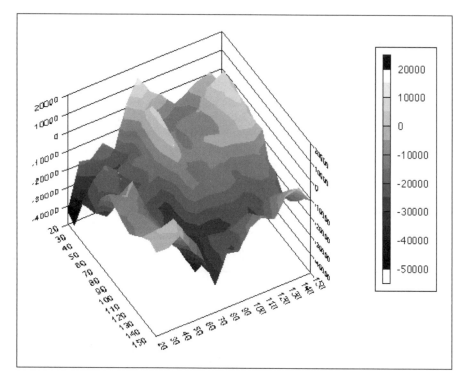

FIGURE 10.3   Three-dimensional area graph of a British Pound optimization (1992–1999). The x-axis = parameter 1; y-axis = parameter 2; z-axis = $ profit.

get a general idea of a systems overall effectiveness. If you optimize a system's parameters and nothing seems to work, then you know that you need to move onto another idea.

PERIODIC REOPTIMIZATION—DOES IT WORK?

Through our examples and studies, we have discovered that optimization is not always the best way to fine tune a trading system. Optimal parameters shift through time and this shift is impossible to foresee. Many traders and system developers feel that because of ever-changing markets, parameters should be reoptimized on a periodic basis. They also feel that the parameters need to be reoptimized over the most recent history. Reoptimization is not the answer. Markets evolve and may look different today than they did 5 or 10 years ago. However, if a system is logical and based on sound market principles, it should be able to cope with any curve balls the market may throw it. It may get beat up from time to time, but it should come out ahead over the long term. I'm not saying that a system should never be changed; a $500 stop in the S&P 5 years ago is not the same as it is in today's market. If a market demonstrates a totally different personality than what is historically portrayed, then a system's fixed parameters may need to be changed. One way to prevent the need to change fixed parameters, is to make all parameters a function of the market (e.g., instead of a $500 stop use 10% of the average range). We feel that reoptimization is a way to try and fix something that is broken.

We put our beliefs to the test and tested a simple Donchian system that is reoptimized on a rolling 2-year basis. (Remember Donchian type systems buy when the highest high of x days is penetrated and sell when the lowest low of x days is penetrated.) We optimized the channel

TABLE 10.3 Optimal Parameters over Several Markets and Time Periods

	British Pound L/S		Deutsche Mark L/S		Japanese Yen L/S		Coffee L/S		Soybeans L/S		Swiss Franc L/S		US Bonds L/S	
1983–1984	42	30	30	6	22	10	6	34	30	14	38	6	14	18
1985–1986	10	46	6	46	18	50	46	6	50	14	6	34	10	14
1987–1988	46	26	14	46	18	50	34	22	38	26	34	46	10	22
1989–1990	14	38	18	22	6	38	26	6	42	10	14	30	26	38
1991–1992	50	18	26	6	30	22	34	38	6	30	38	26	22	46
1993–1994	30	30	39	26	10	42	14	18	14	26	6	26	46	38
1995–1996	42	42	46	30	34	10	10	18	10	14	10	30	22	36

Example: In 1985 and 1986, we tested the BP with 42 days as the buy channel and 30 days as the sell channel.

TABLE 10.4 Performance Results Using Reoptimizing Parameters

ONE CONTRACT PER TRADE
TEST PERIOD 1/1/86–4/30/99
$75 ALLOWED FOR COMMISSION AND SLIPPAGE

Individual Market	Total PL ($)	Avg PL/ Yr ($)	Max DrawDn ($)	Trds/ Yr	Win (%)	W:L	Gain/Mr +DD (%)
US Bonds	58,370	4,169	18,610	11	44.7	1.4	19.6
British Pd.	2,813	201	46,725	9	33.6	1	0.4
Deutsche Mark	9,638	688	22,200	12	38.2	1.1	2.9
Japanese Yen	57,988	4,142	35,163	11	42.7	1.4	11
Swiss Franc	48,550	3,468	33,750	13	42.8	1.3	9.8
Coffee	129,866	9,276	53,554	13	45.3	1.5	15.9
Soybeans	−21,425	−1,530	26,560	15	35.1	0.8	−5.5

Summary Performance

Net Profit ($):	285,799
Maximum Drawdown ($):	65,423

TABLE 10.5 Performance Results Using Static Parameters

ONE CONTRACT PER TRADE
TEST PERIOD 1/1/86–4/30/99
$75 ALLOWED FOR COMMISSION AND SLIPPAGE

Individual Market	Total PL ($)	Avg PL/ Yr ($)	Max DrawDn ($)	Trds/ Yr	Win (%)	W:L	Gain/Mr +DD (%)
US Bonds	45,720	3,266	18,420	10	41.6	1.3	15.5
British Pd.	40,663	2,905	26,588	10	40	1.2	10.3
Deutsche Mark	16,513	1,180	29,238	10	43.7	1.1	3.9
Japanese Yen	128,588	9,185	18,213	9	52.5	2.2	44.2
Swiss Franc	91,100	6,507	20,275	9	50	1.7	29.6
Coffee	103,478	7,391	66,540	11	40.8	1.4	10.3
Soybeans	−26,745	−1,910	35,210	13	32.4	0.8	−5.2

Summary Performance

Net Profit ($):	399,310
Maximum Drawdown ($):	50,526

length to get into a long position and then into a short position. Every two years the parameters were reoptimized over the previous two years and the optimal parameters were selected and used for the following two years. Table 10.3 on page 214 shows the time periods and optimal parameters for those periods for seven different markets.

Table 10.4 on page 215 shows the overall performance of the seven markets with rolling the optimal parameters every two years. Table 10.5 on page 215 is similar to Table 10.4, but instead of using optimized or reoptimized parameters, the system uses a fixed parameter for all markets for all time periods.

The fixed parameter set easily outperformed the reoptimzed parameters. These results basically state that overoptimization and reoptimization simply does not work and you end up trying to out guess the markets.

ALTERNATIVE TO OPTIMIZATION—ADAPTIVE PARAMETERS

We have seen that optimization (one time or periodic) does not solve the problem of parameter shift. An optimal parameter may start out at a particular value, but through time that value may change; in 1983 the parameter may have the value of five and in 1987 the optimal parameter may have a value of ten. How can a trader keep up with the ever-changing optimal parameters? You can either ignore the shift and hope that your parameter selection and underlying system are robust enough to handle changing market conditions or you can have your parameters adapt to the market conditions.

Adaptive parameters are ones that change dynamically based on some function of the market. In 1996, we developed the *Dynamic Breakout* system. We started with a simple channel breakout system and optimized the channel lengths over several years of data over several different markets. We used the power of optimization in the correct manner; we wanted to eliminate the combinations of parameters that simply were out in left field and didn't apply. We found out that channel lengths that fell between 20 and 60 worked for most of the markets that we tested.

For parameters to dynamically change, they must be a function of the market. Something about the market must dictate what the parameters should be and how they should change. Because we are dealing with mechanized trading systems, we had to come up with a mathematical formula that in somehow reflected the state of the current market condition. The amount a market has moved up and down over the past few days usually gives a good indication of the market's current personality. This movement is known as *volatility*. If a market has had wide swings over the past few days, its volatility is considered high. If a market is calm, it exhibits low volatility. In the Dynamic Breakout system, we used volatility as the indicator of current market conditions. We used standard deviation as the volatility measure. Standard deviation increases when the range of price swings are increasing, and decreases when price variability slows.

Deriving a formula that reflects a certain aspect of a market is the first step in making a parameter dynamic. The second step is the actual application of the formula that converts a static parameter into one that changes. Through observations and analysis, we discovered that channel breakout systems were chopped to pieces during times of high volatility, whereas on the other hand, these systems traded well during times of low volatility. We concluded that the channel length (the number of days in the highest high and lowest low calculations) should be increased during times of high volatility and decreased during times of low volatility. The end result of the formula and its application is known as an *adaptive engine*. An adaptive engine can be modified and plugged into different types of trading systems.

The Dynamic Breakout system starts out looking to buy/sell when the highest high/lowest low price for the past 20 days is penetrated. The channel lengths are changed based on market volatility. The volatility

TABLE 10.6   Performance Results of Nonadaptive System with Benefit of Hindsight

ONE CONTRACT PER TRADE
TEST PERIOD 1/1/83–12/31/89
$75 ALLOWED FOR COMMISSION AND SLIPPAGE

Individual Market	Total PL ($)	Avg PL/ Yr ($)	Max DrawDn ($)	Trds/ Yr	Win (%)	W:L	Gain/Mr +DD (%)
US Bonds	39,670	5,667	13,650	14	43.9	1.5	34.7
British Pd.	51,569	7,367	18,356	7	52.2	1.8	37.1
Deutsche Mark	31,875	4,554	9,350	13	46.2	1.6	42.6
Japanese Yen	56,263	8,038	11,488	6	52.4	2.8	57.2
Swiss Franc	44,713	6,388	14,038	7	51.1	2	40.5
Treasury Note	30,570	4,367	9,370	14	45.8	1.5	40.2
Euro $	13,575	1,939	8,675	15	36.8	1.4	21.2
Crude Oil	23,500	3,711	5,780	13	48.2	1.8	47.5
Cotton	24,020	3,431	15,550	8	52.7	1.8	20.7
Gold	5,410	773	16,190	14	39.8	1.1	4.4
Soybeans	21,340	3,049	13,475	18	45	1.3	20.6

Summary Performance

Net Profit ($):	285,799
Maximum Drawdown ($):	65,243

TABLE 10.7   Performance Results of Nonadaptive System without the Benefit of Hindsight

ONE CONTRACT PER TRADE
TEST PERIOD 1/1/90–8/31/99
$75 ALLOWED FOR COMMISSION AND SLIPPAGE

Individual Market	Total PL ($)	Avg PL/ Yr ($)	Max DrawDn ($)	Trds/ Yr	Win (%)	W:L	Gain/Mr +DD (%)
US Bonds	−18,850	−1,950	35,880	15	38.9	0.9	−5.1
British Pd.	11,438	1,183	37,688	7	33.3	1.1	3
Deutsche Mark	−463	−48	38,363	14	40.4	1	−0.1
Japanese Yen	92,063	9,524	22,025	6	55	2.4	38.7
Swiss Franc	50,413	5,215	24,750	7	56.5	1.6	19.7
Treasury Note	−8,970	−928	24,020	14	37.1	0.9	−3.6
Euro $	9,600	993	5,600	13	41	1.5	16.3
Crude Oil	28,380	2,936	12,670	14	39.4	1.4	20
Cotton	35,360	3,658	33,630	8	46.8	1.4	10.6
Gold	−5,240	−542	11,010	14	38.5	0.9	−4.4
Soybeans	−13,080	−1,353	22,235	19	37.8	0.9	−5.7

Summary Performance

Net Profit ($):	180,645
Maximum Drawdown ($):	79,080

measure is defined as the standard deviation for the past 30 days' closing prices. The channel lengths change in the same proportion as does the daily volatility. If yesterday's channel length was 20 and today's volatility increases by 5%, then today's channel length becomes 21. If today's volatility decreases, the channel lengths contract. Because dynamic parameters are a reflection of the markets, there are some instances when the markets go completely crazy and cause the parameters to get astronomically large or infinitesimally small. In these situations there must be some overriding rule to keep the parameters within an acceptable range. We use a ceiling value of 60 days and a floor value of 20. The parameters cannot exceed 60 or fall below 20.

To verify the validity of dynamic parameters, we tested a basket of commodities over nine plus years on the Dynamic Breakout system. We also tested the same commodities on a similar system with non-adaptive parameters over the same time period. We first optimized the non-adaptive parameters from 1983 through 1989 and used the best in the walk forward test that commenced on January 1990. Table 10.6 on page 217 shows the optimized performance numbers for the non-adaptive system from January 1983 through December 1989.

TABLE 10.8   Performance Results of Adaptive System

One Contract Per Trade
Test Period 1/1/90–8/31/99
$75 Allowed for Commission and Slippage

Individual Market	Total PL ($)	Avg PL/ Yr ($)	Max DrawDn ($)	Trds/ Yr	Win (%)	W:L	Gain/Mr +DD (%)
US Bonds	37,160	3,844	27,760	13	39.3	1.4	12.6
British Pd.	18,638	1,928	46,475	14	35.6	1.2	4
Deutsche Mark	−5,063	−524	37,138	13	39.8	1	−1.4
Japanese Yen	134,438	13,907	24,688	12	53.6	2.8	51
Swiss Franc	56,375	5,832	13,300	13	45.5	1.5	38.8
Treasury Note	34,650	3,584	11,380	11	43.5	1.6	27.9
Euro $	8,775	908	7,025	11	42.9	1.5	12.1
Crude Oil	25,200	2,607	13,070	15	37.8	1.4	17.3
Cotton	30,855	3,192	24,530	16	33.8	1.3	12.5
Gold	−12,870	−1,331	20,370	16	31.8	0.8	−6.1
Soybeans	−15,120	−1,564	23,180	15	32.2	0.8	−6.4

Summary Performance

Net Profit ($):	313,033
Maximum Drawdown ($):	38,683

Table 10.7 on page 218 shows the walk-forward test of those optimized parameters from January 1990 through August of 1999. Table 10.8 shows the performance of the Dynamic Breakout system with dynamic parameters on the same portfolio over the same time period covered by the walk-forward test of the system with optimized nonadaptive parameters. Adaptivity won this test hands down.

YOU DESIGN THE TRADING SYSTEM, NOT YOUR COMPUTER

With all the data and testing software and super computers that are available today, we are seeing more and more systems designed by computers and not by humans. Trading ideas that should be placed in the trash are being revitalized by computers and overoptimization. Just because a computer can infinitely optimize parameters until it finds different parameter sets that work on different markets, does not mean it has uncovered a trading principle. Many system testers/traders start with an idea that fits into their trading psychology, but after many nights of testing and optimizing and curve fitting, they usually end up with something that is completely alien to them.

Everybody starts a trading system out with a core idea. They then initially test the idea and if the results look somewhat promising, they usually will cultivate the idea further. This cultivation usually comes in two distinct forms: addition of logic and optimization. Either form can lead to the road of enlightenment or the road of destruction, if they are not universal to all markets and all market conditions. We have already spoke about overoptimization and curve fitting, but there are other dangers lurking out there when developing trading systems. For example, let's say you have developed and tested a multimarket system and through performance analysis you discovered that soybeans shouldn't be traded on Tuesdays and pork bellies shouldn't be traded on Fridays. The rest of the markets are okay throughout the week. This is a form of curve fitting through the addition of logic that is not universal through all markets and market conditions. Now, if you had discovered that trades should be eliminated across the board if yesterday's volatility was too high, then that would be a valid addition of logic. It is universal to all markets and market conditions.

HOW TO EVALUATE TRADING SYSTEM PERFORMANCE

Trading system evaluation goes well beyond just looking at the bottom line—profit. There are other key statistics one should look at when evaluating performance. In addition to profit, we like to look at these other statistics:

- *Maximum draw down:* The highest point in equity to the subsequent lowest point in equity. The largest amount of money the system lost before it recovered.
- *Longest flat time:* The amount of time the system went without making money. This could occur right off the bat or at the end of a string of winners.
- *Average draw down:* Maximum draw down is a one time occurrence, but average draw down takes all of the yearly draw downs into consideration.
- *Profit to loss ratio:* This statistic represents the magnitude of winning trade dollars to the magnitude of losing trade dollars. The higher the ratio the better. Beginning traders are always stuck on the percentage of wins. This statistic is so much more informative, because it tells you the ratio of wins to losses. Systems that have a high percentage of wins do not necessarily have a high profit to loss ratio. Quick profit taking systems can have up to 90% wins but average only a small profit per trade. Would you

rather have a system with 90% wins and makes $50 on winning trades and loses $25 on losing trades or would you prefer a system that had 33% wins and made $2000 on each win and lost $200 on each loss?

- *Average trade:* The amount of profit or loss you can expect on any given trade. This is another statistic that is more important than percent wins.

- *Profit to draw down ratio:* Most traders are risk averse; they look at the risk before they look at the reward. Risk in this statistic comes in the form of draw down, whereas reward is in the form of profit. Of the following, which scenario would you choose? For $100 you have a 10% chance of making $1000 or for $1000 you have a 10% chance of making $10,000. Most traders, due to their limited capital, choose the scenario with the less risk. Even though the risk to reward ratio is exactly the same.

- *Outlier adjusted profit:* With any trading system, you are going to have one or two monstrous wins and/or monstrous losses. The probability of these trades reoccurring are extremely slim and should not be included in an overall track record. We have seen profitable S&P systems make all of their money on a small handful of trades and lose on almost all others.

- *Most consecutive losses:* The total number of losses that occurred consecutively. This statistic gives the user an idea of how many losing trades one may have to go through before a winner occurs.

- *Sharpe ratio:* Indicates the smoothness of the equity curve. The higher the ratio, the more smooth the equity growth or decline. This ratio is calculated by dividing the average monthly or yearly return by the standard deviation of those returns.

- *Long and short net profit:* In most markets, a robust system will split the profits between the long trades and the short trades. You probably wouldn't want to trade a system that made all of its money on one side of the trades. There are exceptions to this and markets that have had a bullish bias, such as the S&P futures and most stocks, usually have a propensity to long trades.

- *Percent winning months:* A system that averages only one winning month out of twelve is probably undesirable. You would want a system that wins at least five months out of the year.

- *Visual representation of equity:* A picture is worth a thousand words. An equity curve expresses more to the eye than any tabular reports. We have seen systems that look decent in reports, but look horrible as an equity curve. It is easier to interpret draw down, longest flat period, equity curve volatility, and equity growth in a visual medium.

For demonstration purposes, let's analyze a system from the last chapter and apply the performance statistics that we just discussed. Let's take a look at the pattern system that we closed the last chapter out with. Table 10.9 includes the overall performance statistics of our system tested on the U.S. bonds from January 1983 through August 1999. Seventy five dollars was levied against each round turn trade for commission and slippage.

The maximum draw down in this case was $13,330. A very respectable number and one that could probably work in to the budget of most traders. A lot of beginner traders see this amount and can't believe that on this one market this system lost $13,300 at one point. Typical draw down figures are a wake up call to most under capitalized traders.

TABLE 10.9   Performance Numbers of the Pattern System on U.S. Bonds

ONE CONTRACT PER TRADE
TEST PERIOD 1/1/90–8/31/99
$75 ALLOWED FOR COMMISSION AND SLIPPAGE

Total Net P/L ($)	103,330	Avg. Net/Year ($)	6,200
Winning Months (%)	62	Avg. Ret. MaxDD/Yr (%)	39
Max DrawDn ClsTrd ($)	12,410		
Max DrawDn w/OTE ($)	13,330		
Best Trade ($)	7,155	Worst Trade ($)	−3,705
Average Trade ($)	126	Net Prof:Loss Ratio	1.4
Average Win ($)	933	Average Loss ($)	−594
Long Net P/L ($)	89,970	Short Net P/L ($)	13,360
No. of Trades	1,231	Avg. Trades/Year	49
No. of Winning Trades	488	Percent Winners (%)	47.20
No. of Losing Trades	743	Most Cons. Losses	7
Avg. Days Per Trade	0.5	Longest Flat Time (Days)	486
Time in the Market (%)	25	Sharpe Ratio	0.25

	Net P/L ($)	Max ClsTrd ($)	No. of Trades	Win (%)	Avg Win	Cons Loss	Flat No. of Days
Last 6 months	1,700	3,730	30	50.0	703	5	70
Last 12 months	10,290	3,730	50	48.0	978	5	70
This year	2,180	3,730	37	45.9	781	5	70
Last year	17,700	1,290	46	58.7	923	4	46
Total	103,330	12,410	818	47.2	933	7	486

Over a sixteen plus year track record, this system on this market went close to two years without making a penny. This could have occurred at the beginning, the middle or the end of the test period and therefore this could happen again at any time after someone starts to trade it. Traders must understand the mentality of their system, so they can prepare for such occurrences in the future. A flat time of this length would not be that significant if it occurred after many years of profitability, but would be devastating if it occurred right off the bat.

In many cases, the average draw down figure is a better determining factor for minimum required capital than maximum draw down, due to the fact that maximum draw down is a look at the worst case scenario. However, many traders like to be ultra conservative when allocating money to trading and like to use the worst case scenario. The net profits for this system outnumbered the net losses by a 1.4 to 1 ratio and the average trade was $131. The profit to maximum draw down ratio was 7.71, a highly respectable showing. The overall equity is not affected greatly by eliminating the best winning and worst losing trade, which indicates an even distribution through out all the trades; a few large trades did not make this system profitable. At one time, this system suffered through

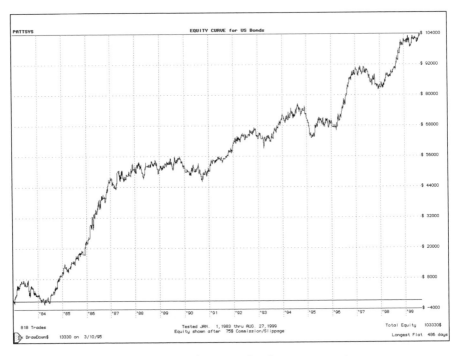

FIGURE 10.4   Equity curve for the pattern system.

seven consecutive losses. This is good information to know before actual trading commences. A high Sharpe Ratio indicates smoothness, and this system had that with a 12.2 ratio. There was only one statistic that worried us about the performance of this system and that was the long profit to short profit comparison. This system made nearly 90% of its profit on the long side. What would happen to future performance if the U.S. bonds entered into an extended bear market? In addition, this system had 60% winning months. Remember, know your system inside and out and hopefully you will be prepared for situations like seven consecutive losers in a row. The historical equity curve shown in Figure 10.4 on page 223 indicates smooth and consistent equity growth and illustrates a high Sharpe Ratio. This is the type of equity curve that you want to see in the past and hope to see in the future.

HOW TO EVALUATE TRADING SYSTEM
PORTFOLIO PERFORMANCE

All of these performance statistics should be used to determine a system's future viability. However, we must keep in mind that we are looking at a system on a market-to-market basis. Long-term success in trading can only be achieved by diversification. In addition to a microscopic market-to-market analysis, we must add a macroscopic portfolio analysis so that we can determine system and portfolio viability. It is easy to see how one market will perform on a system, but it is more difficult to see how two or more markets, traded simultaneously by the same system, interact with each other and affect the end results. We know if you trade two markets with one system, the total end profit is a simple summation of the individual profits. However, the overall maximum draw down figure of the two markets, in most cases, is not the simple summation of the individual draw downs. Here lies the beauty of diversification; profit increases more in proportion than maximum draw down. If two very different markets are traded on the same system, the probability of them drawing down at the same time is extremely low.

Figure 10.5 illustrates the goal of trading more than one market. When one market is losing, we hope the other market is making more than enough to cover the loss. This is why it is so important to analyze a system through two dimensions: individual market (microscopic) and portfolio analysis(macroscopic). Both forms of analysis don't always agree with portfolio inclusion. Referring back to our pattern system, we came up with a portfolio of two different markets. Table 10.10 shows a summary of the market by market analysis. In this analysis, it is plain to see that a portfolio of just these two markets would be antiproductive from a draw down standpoint.

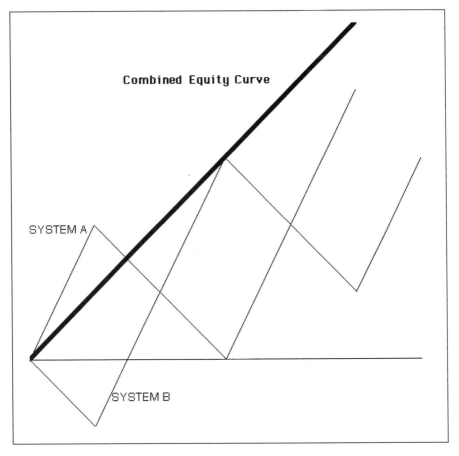

FIGURE 10.5   The goal of diversification (vertical = profit; horizontal = time).

TABLE 10.10   Individual Performance of the British Pound and Swiss Franc

ONE CONTRACT PER TRADE
TEST PERIOD 1/1/83–8/31/99
$75 ALLOWED FOR COMMISSION AND SLIPPAGE

Individual Market	Total PL ($)	Avg PL/ Yr ($)	Max DrawDn ($)	Trds/ Yr	Win (%)	W:L	Gain/Mr +DD (%)
British Pd.	44,200	2,652	24,688	44	40.5	1.2	10.1
Swiss Franc	46,438	2,786	22,900	45	40	1.2	11.3

Summary Performance

Net Profit ($):	90,368
Maximum Drawdown ($):	45,531

TABLE 10.11 Portfolio Performance Increased by Adding Less Than Desirable Markets

ONE CONTRACT PER TRADE
TEST PERIOD 1/1/83–8/31/99
$75 ALLOWED FOR COMMISSION AND SLIPPAGE

Individual Market	Total PL ($)	Avg PL/ Yr ($)	Max DrawDn ($)	Trds/ Yr	Win (%)	W:L	Gain/Mr +DD (%)
British Pd.	44,200	2,652	24,688	44	40.5	1.2	10.1
Swiss Franc	46,438	2,786	22,900	45	40	1.2	11.3
Pork Bellies	36,376	2,183	19,788	42	44.9	1.2	9.8
Wheat	−338	−20	10,538	47	38.9	1	−0.2

Summary Performance

Net Profit ($):	125,978
Maximum Drawdown ($):	42,998

Sometimes adding markets that seem to be underachievers on a market by market basis can help the overall performance. Table 10.11 demonstrates improved portfolio performance. By manipulating and adding anti-correlated markets the overall profit increased by 39% while overall maximum draw down decreased by 5%. Some markets that are ruled out due to their individual performance sometimes adds value at the portfolio level. Portfolio analysis is a must when it comes to building a successful trading plan. A trading system cannot be considered good unless it can trade a basket of different and somewhat anti-correlated markets.

CONCLUSION

Hopefully, this chapter shed some light on the problems of interpreting historical system performance data. A curve fitted track record is as worthless as the paper it is printed on and can bolster false confidence in a nonrobust system. Optimization and/or reoptimization is not the answer to the ever-changing markets. There has been promising research on adaptive parameters, which could eliminate curve fitting altogether. If you develop a trading system and most of the design was contributed by your computer and hindsight, then you should know that your design will only work in the past. Once curve fitting has been ruled out of a track record, in depth analysis of the track record is necessary to determine system viability. In addition to determining a system's viability, one must analyze the track record to determine compatibility between the system and the trader's psychology. You can't simply look at individual market performance to develop a trading plan. The interaction of trading individual markets simultaneously on a system plays a big role in portfolio composition. Success in trading futures or stocks can only be attained by diversification, therefore one must look beyond individual market performance and look at the entire picture.

11

MONEY MANAGEMENT

Money management is the most important tool to successful trading, but only about 10% of individual traders incorporate it into their trading plan. Just because a trader has a small amount of capital doesn't mean he can't apply the ideas of money management. Many traders feel that these concepts can only be utilized by large CTAs and institutions. This chapter argues the opposite and illustrates how money management concepts can be utilized at any capital level.

Money management involves examining the concepts of risk and return in reference to investor preference. The objective is to choose a desired rate of return and then minimize the risk associated with that rate of return. In general, there are four decisions involved in the trading process:

1. Buy/sell (system or strategy).
2. Which commodity or stock to trade.
3. How many contracts of each commodity to trade.
4. How much equity to risk at any given time.

The first decision involves the mechanics of trading itself without reference to money management. The last three decisions apply directly to the maximization of profit and the minimization of risk. Since 75% of the decision process deals with the management of risk and reward, 75% of research time should be spent on money management and portfolio composition. Principles dealing with risk and reward should be considered from the outset of system development and made an integral part of the system.

STATISTICS—A NECESSARY TOOL

Statistics is a branch of mathematics used to measure the probability of possible outcomes. We can use statistics to measure the risk and return of trading an individual commodity or stock or a portfolio of different markets. Most traders use net profit as their measure of return and maximum draw down figure as their measure of risk, but with statistics we can measure risk/return in terms of all events, not just two. In the money management world, risk is defined as the standard deviation of returns that represents the volatility of the equity curve. The higher the standard deviation, the less smooth the returns and curve. The deviation amount represents how much one can make or lose on a monthly basis. The overall objective of using statistics in money management is to minimize the standard deviation of returns with respect to the mean return. We plan to keep things simple in this chapter, so the only statistical tools that we will use will be mean and standard deviation.

Formulas

x = Variables or events (could be anything from widgets to monthly returns)

n = Number of variables or events (a minimum of thirty)

Mean = Summation of all x / Number of x

Standard deviation = Square root (Summation$((x - Mean)^2) / n - 1$)

Examples for calculating the mean and standard deviation of numerical series:

$$x1 = 400$$
$$x2 = -90$$
$$x3 = 200$$
$$n = 3$$
$$x1 + x2 + x3 = 510$$
$$Mean = (x1 + x2 + x3) / n = 510 / 3 = 170$$
$$x1 - Mean = 400 - 170 = 230$$
$$x2 - Mean = -90 - 170 = -260$$
$$x3 - Mean = 200 - 170 = 30$$
$$(x1 - Mean)^2 = (230)^2 = 52900$$
$$(x2 - Mean)^2 = (-260)^2 = 67600$$
$$(x3 - Mean)^2 = (30)^2 = 900$$
$$Summation((x - Mean)^2) / n - 1 = (52900 + 67600 + 900) / 2 = 60700$$
$$Standard\ deviation = Square\ root(60700) = 264.4$$

A value will fall within one standard deviation above and below the mean 68% of the time. With respect to our example, there is a 68% chance that future events (x) will fall between the values of –94.4 and 434.4. There is a 95% probability that future events will fall within two standard deviations above and below the mean. In addition to the overall goal of maximizing profit while minimizing risk, money management also tries to reduce the probability of total meltdown also known as the risk of ruin.

RISK OF RUIN

This statistical term is used to describe the probability of a trader losing all of his or her trading capital. Risk of ruin is a basically a function of three different variables: amount of capital risked per trade, percentage of wins, and the win to loss ratio of the trading system. The amount of money that is risked per trade is governed by money management, whereas the other two variables are quantified by the trading system you wish to trade. The risk of ruin is heavily concentrated in the early stages of trading a system. The higher the bet or (risk) per trade the higher the risk of ruin. If you start out with $20,000 and bet $5,000 on each trade, you are ruined if your first four trades are losers. The probability of this occurring is a function of the bet size and the probability of success of the trading system (for simplification we assume that the amount that we win or lose is the same and constant). If the chance of losing on the first trade is 45%, then the probability of having four losing trades in a row is $(45\%)^4$ (We raised our chance of loss by the number of losing trades necessary to cause ruin right off the bat.) or approximately 4%. If you bet less, than the probability of ruin decreases. Instead of betting $5,000 per trade, you bet $2,500 then the probability of ruin right of the bat is $(45\%)^8$ or .17%.

If a trader is profitable in the early stages of trading and has increased his initial capital, then four losses (consecutive or net) can no longer ruin him (if his bet size remains constant). Even though the number of consecutive losses needed to cause ruin increases over time, so does the probability of more consecutive losses. The following formula gives the probability of eventual ruin (PR) over the long run:

$$PR = (1 - TA / 1 + TA)^{IU}$$

where TA is the trader's advantage (percent wins – percent losses) and IU is the initial trading units. If a trader's initial capital is $20,000 and the bet size is $5,000 then IU = four. The probability of eventual ruin for the following scenarios is:

Total capital:	$20,000	Total capital:	$20,000
Bet size:	$ 5,000	Bet size:	$ 2,500
Trading advantage:	10%	Trading advantage:	10%
Probability of ruin:	44.8%	Probability of ruin:	20.1%

Total capital:	$20,000	Total capital:	$20,000
Bet size:	$ 2,000	Bet size:	$ 1,000
Trading advantage:	10%	Trading advantage:	10%
Probability of ruin:	13.4%	Probability of ruin:	1.8%

These numbers are only valid if you are trading on a one contract basis. The risk of ruin changes dramatically if the number of contracts vary. In addition, these equations assume that the amount won when you win is always the same and always equal to the amount lost when you lose. As we had stated previously, risk of ruin is a function of percent wins, win to loss ratio, and bet size. So far we have ignored the win to loss ratio. In the real world, most profitable trading systems have less than 50% wins and win:loss ratios greater than 1.2; therefore, leading to the fact that wins and losses are not always of the same magnitude. Ralph Vince, in his book *Portfolio Management Formulas* (New York, 1990), offers risk of ruin equations that take this fact and others into account.

Risk of ruin is an interesting figure, but does not provide much insight in how to manage or trade one's account effectively. What have we learned from risk of ruin and the examples? Self-preservation is best achieved by not betting the farm. If you bet (risk a percentage of equity) sensibly and trade a system with positive expectation, then the probability of ruin is quite small.

CAPITAL ALLOCATION MODEL

You now have the tools necessary to understand our Capital Allocation Model. First we will demonstrate how to allocate capital across a single market portfolio using a small sample of data and then we will use the same approach on a portfolio of two markets. At the end of the chapter, we will demonstrate the effectiveness of the capital allocation model on a real system on medium- and small-sized accounts.

Remember our goal is to maximize profit while minimizing risk. This goal must be attained without going outside the barriers of acceptable risk. To attain this goal, we must know how much money to allocate to each market and the number of contracts that we should trade. In the model, capital is a function of equity, mean monthly returns, and market risk. Equity is simply the initial capital that we have to start trading. In these examples, returns are not compounded; we use the initial total capital for all calculations. Mean monthly returns is the amount of money that we can expect from our system on a monthly basis. Market risk is the amount of money that can be lost on a trade on a daily basis. Money managers use several different measures to monitor market risk:

- *Mean range:* Find the mean of the ranges over a previous 3 to 50 days. Convert the mean to a dollar value. For example, if the mean range in the Swiss Franc of the previous 10 days is 40 points and the Swiss Francs are worth $12.50 a point, the dollar value of risk in equal to $500. The probable amount that the market will move is equal to the average range for the past x days. This isn't always the case, but you need probabilities to build your allocation model upon.

- *Mean change in closes:* The mean change in closes over a previous 3 to 50 days will be more representative of the risk since this value will give the expected risk for holding a position.

- *Mean change in closes down vs. mean change in closes up:* The mean change in down closes over a previous time period represents the risk associated with holding a long position.

- *Standard deviation of closes:* The standard deviation of closes gives a more accurate picture of risk because it shows the amount of daily variability within a 68% confidence interval. This is a more involved calculation, but with today's computers this should not pose a problem.

However measured, risk is the most important variable to track and is the main component of the capital allocation model.

Single Market Portfolio

The first step in the model is to come up with a system that has a positive expectation of returns. This system can trade stocks or futures, it really doesn't matter. Before allocating capital we need to measure mean monthly return and market risk on a one contract basis. In addition, we need to know how much of our equity we want to risk on each trade. At this point, we don't know how much equity to risk because that is what we are searching for. However, we do know the boundaries of acceptability.

$$C = f(E, m, r)$$

where C = Amount of capital to risk to achieve an acceptable risk/ Reward ratio

E = Iterative amounts of equity to risk on each trade

r = Current market risk

m = Mean monthly return

In this example, we will allocate capital to only one market and then later move to two markets. After we have tested our system on a one contract basis, we need to measure E, m, and r at the beginning of a period (month, week, day). Let's say that our bond system made $6000 over the past six months, therefore our mean monthly return would be $1000 ($6000 / 6 months):

January	$2000
February	–$1000
March	–$1500
April	$3000
May	$2000
June	$1500
Total	$6000
	m = $1000

We will use the 30-day average true range as our measure of market risk. For demonstration purposes, let's assume that the average true range for the past 30 days is 36 points. Thirty-six bond points is the equivalent of $1125.

$$r = \$1125$$

Let's pretend that we are a money manager and we have $100,000 to play with and we would like to achieve 20% return on this capital, but we don't want to have an end-of-month draw down greater than 3%. We know the bounds of acceptability, but we have no idea of how much money to risk on each individual trade. By looking at historical performance of our system and current risk in the market, we can create several different portfolios (or what if scenarios) by allocating different levels of equity to be risked on an individual trade basis. We will optimize our risk parameter to achieve an acceptable risk/reward ratio. In this example, our portfolio will simply consist of different lot sizes (number of contracts) of bonds.

TC = $100,000 (total capital)

E = Varying amounts of acceptable individual trade risk

E = (TC * allowed risk per trade)

$5000 at 5% ($100,000 * 5%)

$4000 at 4%

$3000 at 3%

NUMC = Number of contracts

NUMC = E / r

Portfolio 1	E = (TC*5%) = $5000	r = $1125
	NUMC = $5000 / $1125 = 4	
	(can't have fractional parts)	
Portfolio 2	E = (TC*4%) = $4000	r = $1125
	NUMC = $4000 / $1125 = 3	
Portfolio 3	E = (TC*3%) = $3000	r = $1125
	NUMC = $3000 / $1125 = 2	

Next measure the return on all available portfolios:

ROR = rate of return

ROR = (mean monthly return * NUMC) / Total Capital

ROR = (m * NUMC) / TC

Portfolio 1   ROR = ($1000 * 4) / $100,000 = 4% = 48% yearly

Portfolio 2   ROR = ($1000 * 3) / $100,000 = 3% = 36% yearly

Portfolio 3   ROR = ($1000 * 2) / $100,000 = 2% = 24% yearly

Next measure the risk on all available portfolios by referring back to our monthly return values:

	Return
January	$2000
February	−$1000
March	−$1500
April	$3000
May	$2000
June	$1500
July 1st	we are here at this point in time

Portfolio 1   **NUMC** = 4   **ROR** = 48%

	Return	Four Contract Basis
January	$8000	Attained by multiplying Jan's performance by NUMC
February	−$4000	
March	−$6000	
April	$12000	
May	$8000	
June	$6000	

Mean montly return = 4% standard deviation 7.26%

68% of time: monthly returns will be between −3.26% and 11.26%

Portfolio 2   **NUMC** = 3   **ROR** = 36%

	Return	Three Contract Basis
January	$6000	
February	−$3000	
March	−$4500	
April	$9000	
May	$6000	
June	$4500	

Mean montly return = 3% standard deviation 5.5%

68% of time: monthly returns will be between −2.5% and 8.5%

Portfolio 3   **NUMC** = 2   **ROR** = 24%

	Return	Two Contract Basis
January	$4000	
February	−$2000	
March	−$3000	
April	$6000	
May	$4000	
June	$3000	

Mean montly return = 2% standard deviation 3.6%

68% of time: monthly returns will be between −1.6% and 5.6%

If you, as a money manager, had informed your clients that your goal was to achieve 20% per year with at most a 3% end-of-month draw down, then Portfolio 2 would be your choice:

$C = f(E, m, r)$

C = 4% of $100,000 or $4000 to risk on each trade.

Two-Market Portfolio

We will use the same allocation model and apply it to the same system, but this time we will trade the bonds and soybeans. Table 11.1 shows the performance of the bonds and beans for the past six months.

First step is to measure the current market volatility. We will use the same measure of volatility as we did in the first example of our capital allocation model (thirty-day average true range). The current volatility for the bonds is $1125 and $400 for the beans. The next step is to create a range of different portfolios that reflect different levels of equity risk.

Before we do this step, we should discuss the concept of normalization. The manner in which we calculate the number of contracts of a certain market incorporates the notion of normalization. Due to the fact that we are using a constant amount of equity to risk on each trade and that we measure the amount of risk for each market, we trade more contracts of a less risky commodity than we do for one that involves more risk. If we are risking $1000 per trade and the market risk for the bonds is $500, then we would trade two contracts of bonds. Now if we risk the same amount of money in the beans and the market risk for this commodity is $250, then we would trade four contracts. We have normalized the number of contracts from one market to another based on risk. The normalization process allows us to compare apples to apples and oranges to oranges. We are trading the same units of risk for the soybeans as we are for the bonds.

Table 11.2 shows the different portfolios and their returns based on different amounts of risk. Table 11.3 shows the risk in terms of standard

TABLE 11.1   Performance of Bonds and Beans

Monthly Returns	Bonds ($)	Beans ($)
January	2,000	(200)
February	(1,000)	200
March	(1,500)	300
April	3,000	(450)
May	2,000	700
June	1,500	200
Mean monthly return (one contract basis)	1,000	125

TABLE 11.2   Return for Different Portfolios

Total Capital ($)				100,000				
Mean monthly returns for bonds ($)				1,000				
Mean monthly returns for beans ($)				125				

	Risk Amount (%)	Bonds Market Risk ($)	Beans Market Risk ($)	Amount of Risk per Trade ($)	Number of Bond Contracts	Number of Bean Contracts	ROR Yearly Bonds (%)	ROR Yearly Beans (%)	Total Yearly (%)
Portfolio 1	3	1,125	400	3,000	2	7	24.0	10.5	34.5
Portfolio 2	4	1,125	400	4,000	3	10	36.0	15.0	51.0
Portfolio 3	5	1,125	400	5,000	4	12	48.0	18.0	66.0

deviation of trading the different portfolios. Portfolio 1 would probably be the choice of most money managers, due to its low standard deviation and decent return.

Now let's test a real system with this same capital allocation model. In this test, we will measure market risk on a daily basis and allocate contracts for the following trade in the same manner as we demonstrated in the previous examples. We will wait until the next trade and change the number of contracts if necessary. Reallocation time frames are up to the preference of the trader/manager. We haven't seen an advantage of reallocating on a smaller time frame than on a trade-by-trade basis. In our previous examples, we reallocated on a monthly basis to make things easier for demonstration purposes. As in our previous examples, we will create three separate portfolios reflecting three different levels of individual trade risk. We tested the Donchian system that was explained in Chapter 9 on the Japanese Yen and U.S. bonds with our capital allocation model and $100,000 initial capital. Table 11.4 shows the portfolios of bond and yen with their respective monthly returns and standard deviations. The optimal portfolio is the one that fits within the trader's or money manager's realm of acceptability. A risky money manager would have a different portfolio than one that is more conservative. Which portfolio would you choose?

A hundred thousand dollars is a lot of money, what if a trader only had $20,000? Could a small trader apply these concepts to his trading. Definitely! That is the beauty of the capital allocation model—it thinks first in terms of risk and then in terms of reward. Let's test the same system on the same portfolio, but this time let's utilize $20,000 as our total capital parameter. We could optimize risk parameters and create a range of different portfolios, but at this level of equity if we don't use at least 5% of risk per trade, we won't get any trades. In addition, we will incorporate the old adage, "If you can't stand the heat, get out of the kitchen." If the market risk exceeds $1000, we will not take on any new trades until the market cools down. This is another important reason to

TABLE 11.3 Risk for Different Portfolios

	1 Contract Bonds ($)	1 Contract Beans ($)	Total ($)	Return (%)
January	2,000	(200)	1,800	1.8
February	(1,000)	200	(800)	−0.8
March	(1,500)	300	(1,200)	−1.2
April	3,000	(450)	2,550	2.6
May	2,000	700	2,700	2.7
June	1,500	200	1,700	1.7
			Average return:	1.1
			Standard deviation:	1.7

Average monthly return range: −0.6% to 2.8%

Portfolio 1	4 Contracts Bonds ($)	10 Contracts Beans ($)	Total ($)	Return (%)
January	4,000	(1,400)	2,600	2.6
February	(2,000)	1,400	(600)	−0.6
March	(3,000)	2,100	(900)	−0.9
April	6,000	(3,150)	2,850	2.9
May	4,000	4,900	8,900	8.9
June	3,000	1,400	4,400	4.4
			Average return:	2.9
			Standard deviation:	3.6

Average monthly return range: −0.7% to 6.5%

Portfolio 2	2 Contracts Bonds ($)	7 Contracts Beans ($)	Total ($)	Return (%)
January	6,000	(2,000)	4,000	4.0
February	(3,000)	2,000	(1,000)	−1.0
March	(4,500)	3,000	(1,500)	−1.5
April	9,000	(4,500)	4,500	4.5
May	6,000	7,000	13,000	13.0
June	4,500	2,000	6,500	6.5
			Average return:	4.3
			Standard deviation:	5.3

Average monthly return range: −1.1% to 9.6%

Portfolio 3	4 Contracts Bonds ($)	12 Contracts Beans ($)	Total ($)	Return (%)
January	8,000	(2,400)	5,600	5.6
February	(4,000)	2,400	(1,600)	−1.6
March	(6,000)	3,600	(2,400)	−2.4
April	12,000	(5,400)	6,600	6.6
May	8,000	8,400	16,400	16.4
June	6,000	2,400	8,400	8.4
			Average return:	5.5
			Standard deviation:	6.9

Average monthly return range: −1.4% to 12.4%

TABLE 11.4 Results of One Allocation Model at Different Levels of Risk

	Capital to Risk on Each Trade (%)	Monthly Average Return (%)	Monthly Standard Deviation (%)
Portfolio 1	3	3.5	13.2
Portfolio 2	4	4.6	17.8
Portfolio 3	5	6.0	22.7

trade as many anticorrelated markets as possible. If one market heats up, then capital can be transferred or redistributed to the markets that are still trading at an acceptable risk level. Table 11.5 shows the performance of trading the bonds and yen on our Donchian system with $20,000 as our initial capital and our "get out of the kitchen" overlay. We also ran the same system on the same markets but on a one-contract basis (Table 11.6).

The capital allocation model increased profits by 49% and decreased overall maximum draw down by 6%. Does this happen to every system that the allocation model is applied to? No. Some systems don't react in a positive manner to this model and this is why it is so important to develop trading systems in concert with money management concepts. Capital allocation models are as numerous as different trading systems.

TABLE 11.5 Performance of Donchian-Based System Utilizing the Capital Allocation Model

VARIABLE NUMBER OF CONTRACTS PER TRADE
TEST PERIOD 1/1/83–8/31/99
$75 ALLOWED FOR COMMISSION AND SLIPPAGE

Individual Market	Total PL ($)	Avg PL/ Yr ($)	Max DrawDn ($)	Trds/ Yr	Win (%)	W:L	Gain/Mr +DD (%)
US Bonds	81,790	4,907	21,340	9	46.7	1.7	20.3
Japanese Yen	131,963	7,918	13,850	11	50.8	2.1	45.2

Summary Performance

Net Profit ($):	213,743
Maximum Drawdown ($):	20,938

TABLE 11.6 Performance of Donchian-Based System without the Capital Allocation Model

ONE CONTRACT PER MARKET PER TRADE
TEST PERIOD 1/1/83–8/31/99
$75 ALLOWED FOR COMMISSION AND SLIPPAGE

Individual Market	Total PL ($)	Avg PL/ Yr ($)	Max DrawDn ($)	Trds/ Yr	Win (%)	W:L	Gain/Mr +DD (%)
US Bonds	45,720	2,743	25,940	10	43.6	1.3	9.6
Japanese Yen	98,188	5,891	20,800	9	49	1.8	25.2

Summary Performance

Net Profit ($):	143,903
Maximum Drawdown ($):	22,317

COMPOUNDING RETURNS

Compounding is the process of allocating capital based on current portfolio (or account) equity. Current portfolio equity takes into consideration past winning and losing trades and initial equity. Compounding is a great concept if there is a lot of money involved; it expands and contracts allocated capital based on current portfolio equity. If a trading plan is successful, more money is allocated to each trade, whereas if a trading plan is in the pits, less money is allocated to each trade. Remember, we said that compounding is a great concept, if there was a lot of money involved. We qualified the concept of compounding, because we feel small accounts should not expand allocation until their initial equity doubles or triples in size. Even good systems can go in the tank after a string of winners and if a small account is not compounded, there is money saved up for a rainy day. We have seen small traders double their exposure after they have had a string of winners, just to lose all their money twice as quick when their trading system experiences a string of consecutive losers. If compounding is of interest to you and it should be if you are trading a good sum of money, you can incorporate it into our capital allocation model with one small change. Instead of using initial capital as the Total Capital (TC) in the formulas, use the current portfolio equity.

PLACEMENT OF PROTECTIVE STOPS AND PROFIT TARGETS

The idea of money management can be built directly into a trading system. Money management at the system level consists of protective stops and profit targets. The Capital Allocation Model extracted money management outside of the system so that it could be used to define different portfolios and scenarios. Many traders use protective stops and profit targets to attain their ideal risk/reward ratios. A protective stop is a way in which the trader has determined his exact risk amount for any given trade. A profit objective is a means by which a trader tries to attain a certain reward based on his risk. The ideas that we discussed earlier in this chapter centered around normalizing the risk of different markets and allocating funds across a portfolio. These same ideas can be used with systems that have money management schemes built directly into the logic. The rest of this chapter shows how profit objectives and protective stops either degrade or improve a systems' overall performance.

Table 11.7 shows the performance of an open range breakout system without a protective stop (simply stop and reverse). Table 11.8 shows the results of the system at different protective stop levels. Notice how the different markets have different optimal protective stops. A $1,500 protective stop in the soybeans does not mean the same thing in the U.S. bonds. Table 11.9 shows the performance of the system utilizing a $1,250 stop. Why don't we use a different stop for each market? The answer is that we don't want to overly curve fit the system by adding a parameter that is different for each market. In addition, a fixed parameter such as the pure dollar stop, does not evolve with market conditions. The overall performance of the system actually degraded with the use of a fixed dollar protective stop. Table 11.10 shows the system with a protective stop that changes with market conditions. Instead of using a fixed dollar value stop, we used a stop that was equivalent to three times the average constant (in this case three) and either added or subtracted the amount from the entry price. This stop outperformed the pure stop and reverse and fixed money management stop. We feel that any system parameter will perform better if it is dynamic and a function of the market.

There is an old saying, "You can't go broke if you take profits." This statement is true if your risk/reward ratios are set up correctly. If you have a profit objective of $50 and a protective stop of $500, I can almost guarantee that you will go broke taking profits. Profit objectives can work, if they are sized or placed correctly. Table 11.11 shows the performance of the same system that we have been testing with different profit objective levels. Most of the markets liked a large profit objective. Table 11.12 shows performance of the system with a

TABLE 11.7　Open Range Breakout System (Stop and Reverse Entry-Exit)

ONE CONTRACT PER MARKET PER TRADE
TEST PERIOD 1/1/83–8/31/99
$75 ALLOWED FOR COMMISSION AND SLIPPAGE

Individual Market	Total PL ($)	Avg PL/ Yr ($)	Max DrawDn ($)	Trds/ Yr	Win (%)	W:L	Gain/Mr +DD (%)
US Bonds	86,540	5,192	24,340	31	43.9	1.3	19.2
Treasury Note	34,100	2,046	23,910	30	44.3	1.2	8.1
Muni Bonds	63,840	4,560	35,460	30	45.4	1.3	12.2
British Pd.	7,313	439	37,438	27	42.3	1	1.1
Deutsche Mark	45,713	2,743	34,250	29	43.2	1.2	7.7
Japanese Yen	54,925	3,296	25,800	25	43	1.2	11.6
Swiss Franc	44,875	2,693	26,225	28	43.9	1.2	9.6
US$ Index	22,100	1,607	34,170	35	40.4	1.1	4.5
Crude Oil	46,100	2,881	9,810	31	45.6	1.4	24.3
Heating Oil	−47,552	−2,853	56,326	31	39.3	0.8	−4.9
Natural Gas	53,660	5,749	12,080	35	44	1.5	35.8
Cotton	−5,320	−319	49,585	34	37.8	1	−0.6
Coffee	168,788	10,127	64,106	35	41.4	1.4	14.7
Sugar	−5,432	−326	28,370	37	37.6	1	−1.1
Soybeans	36,010	2,161	25,025	35	39.6	1.2	8.2
Corn	22,800	1,368	8,663	28	40	1.3	14.9
Wheat	−8,113	−487	21,263	34	39.3	0.9	−2.2
Silver	48,665	2920	33,755	38	39.4	1.2	8.1
Gold	−25,270	−1,516	41,580	35	37.7	0.9	−3.5
Live Cattle	−20,556	−1,233	26,684	38	38.6	0.9	−4.5
Pork Bellies	7,796	468	25,364	35	43.1	1	1.7
Live Hogs	15,940	956	10,752	33	41.4	1.1	8.1

Summary Performance

Net Profit ($):	642,988
Maximum Drawdown ($):	86,311

fixed $1,750 profit objective. We picked $1,750 by simply eyeballing the parameter that seemed to produce the best numbers across all markets. Table 11.13 shows the performance of the system with a protective stop that was a function of the market. In this case, we took profits when the market was in our favor five times the average true range. Again, the dynamic parameter performed better than the static one.

All traders should use some form of protective stop (dynamic stops seem to perform better). Profit objectives can also help system

TABLE 11.8 Open Range Breakout System (Optimized over Several Different Protective Stop Levels)

ONE CONTRACT PER MARKET PER TRADE
TEST PERIOD 1/1/83–8/31/99
$75 ALLOWED FOR COMMISSION AND SLIPPAGE

	Dollar Stop Amount	Total PL ($)	Avg PL/Yr ($)	Max DrawDn ($)	Win (%)	TIM (%)	W:L	Gain/Mr +DD (%)
SF	1,250	50,638	3,038	20,525	39.4	84	1.2	13.7
SF	1,500	55,413	3,325	22,550	40.4	88	1.2	13.7
SF	1,750	57,825	3,470	22,113	41.8	90	1.2	14.6
SF	2,000	54,600	3,276	25,800	42.5	91	1.2	11.9
DX	500	15,370	1,118	33,910	31	71	1.1	3.2
DX	750	2,160	157	40,100	33.3	79	1	0.4
DX	1,000	4,560	332	43,100	34.9	86	1	0.7
DX	1,250	14,800	1,076	36,900	37.3	89	1.1	2.8
DX	1,500	18,970	1,380	33,810	38.3	93	1.1	3.9
DX	1,750	19,550	1,422	33,200	38.8	95	1.1	4.1
DX	2,000	17,390	1,265	35,630	39.3	95	1.1	3.4
CL	500	25,930	1,621	16,510	38.4	81	1.2	8.7
CL	750	23,240	1,453	13,300	40.7	87	1.2	9.5
CL	1,000	26,660	1,666	12,980	42.7	92	1.2	11.1
CL	1,250	37,230	2,327	10,930	43.6	94	1.3	18
CL	1,500	36,170	2,261	10,470	44.2	96	1.3	18.1
CL	1,750	36,870	2,304	10,430	44.5	97	1.3	18.5
CL	2,000	37,170	2,323	10,960	44.6	98	1.3	17.9
HO	500	−15,166	−910	27,531	32.6	70	0.9	−3.1
HO	750	−23,281	−1,397	32,021	35.2	80	0.9	−4.1
HO	1,000	−30,908	−1,854	37,300	36.3	84	0.9	−4.7
HO	1,250	−42,517	−2,551	46,801	36.5	87	0.8	−5.2
HO	1,500	−36,103	−2,166	47,737	37.9	91	0.8	−4.4
HO	1,750	−43,768	−2,626	54,155	38.1	92	0.8	−4.7
HO	2,000	−42,202	−2,532	51,979	38.2	93	0.8	−4.7
NG	500	47,620	5,102	10,430	38.8	80	1.5	35.4
NG	750	57,180	6,126	10,440	41.8	88	1.5	42.4
NG	1,000	50,430	5,403	12,600	42.5	90	1.5	32.5
NG	1,250	50,170	5,375	11,930	43.4	92	1.4	33.7
NG	1,500	47,200	5,057	16,470	43.6	94	1.4	24.7
NG	1,750	46,590	4,992	15,630	43.6	95	1.4	25.4
NG	2,000	51,250	5,491	11,050	43.8	96	1.4	36.5
US	500	54,520	3,271	18,940	32.8	67	1.2	15.1
US	750	45,610	2,737	24,770	35.8	74	1.2	10
US	1,000	55,110	3,307	26,990	38.1	79	1.2	11.1
US	1,250	59,160	3,550	20,970	39.2	84	1.2	15
US	1,500	64,880	3,893	21,670	40.3	88	1.2	16
US	1,750	79,290	4,757	22,840	41.7	92	1.3	18.6
US	2,000	75,750	4,545	23,800	42.3	93	1.3	17.2

(continued)

TABLE 11.8 *Continued*

	Dollar Stop Amount	Total PL ($)	Avg PL/Yr ($)	Max DrawDn ($)	Win (%)	TIM (%)	W:L	Gain/Mr +DD (%)
TY	500	29,820	1,789	21,470	36.7	73	1.2	7.8
TY	750	37,160	2,230	22,220	39.1	82	1.2	9.4
TY	1,000	39,060	2,344	21,650	41.2	86	1.2	10.1
TY	1,250	25,460	1,528	23,630	41.9	88	1.1	6.1
TY	1,500	20,770	1,246	24,820	42.4	90	1.1	4.7
TY	1,750	38,090	2,285	23,280	43.9	94	1.2	9.2
TY	2,000	38,260	2,296	22,590	44.2	96	1.2	9.5
MB	500	43,010	3,072	19,200	34	72	1.3	14.6
MB	750	53,330	3,809	24,100	38	79	1.3	14.7
MB	1,000	53,770	3,841	27,840	40.1	85	1.3	13
MB	1,250	61,050	4,361	26,010	42.6	89	1.3	15.7
MB	1,500	51,810	3,701	26,980	43	91	1.3	12.9
MB	1,750	62,560	4,469	31,580	44.2	92	1.3	13.4
MB	2,000	66,590	4,756	34,730	44.5	94	1.4	13
BP	500	3,556	213	42,006	25.9	56	1	0.5
BP	750	10,000	600	37,531	30.5	65	1	1.5
BP	1,000	7,931	476	35,606	34.8	72	1	1.3
BP	1,250	−44	−3	41,144	35.9	78	1	0
BP	1,500	−21,525	−1,292	56,850	36	80	0.9	−2.2
BP	1,750	−6,238	−374	48,613	37.4	85	1	−0.7
BP	2,000	8,325	500	39,563	38.7	88	1	1.2
DM	500	45,513	2,731	34,400	34.7	69	1.2	7.6
DM	750	21,113	1,267	39,288	36.5	76	1.1	3.1
DM	1,000	24,875	1,493	35,663	38.8	83	1.1	4
DM	1,250	40,213	2,413	31,188	40.7	88	1.2	7.4
DM	1,500	35,538	2,132	32,775	41.2	91	1.2	6.2
DM	1,750	40,188	2,411	29,988	41.8	93	1.2	7.7
DM	2,000	38,538	2,312	31,525	41.4	95	1.2	7
JY	500	38,050	2,283	23,813	30.3	59	1.2	8.7
JY	750	33,950	2,037	24,850	33.8	67	1.1	7.4
JY	1,000	27,325	1,640	35,263	35.9	74	1.1	4.3
JY	1,250	9,213	553	35,038	36.9	79	1	1.5
JY	1,500	1,275	77	43,388	37.9	83	1	0.2
JY	1,750	27,038	1,622	25,700	40.3	86	1.1	5.7
JY	2,000	13,350	801	33,400	40.3	87	1	2.2
SF	500	45,563	2,734	22,438	31.3	64	1.2	11.3
SF	750	42,025	2,522	27,275	35.1	73	1.2	8.7
SF	1,000	53,488	3,209	25,800	38.1	79	1.2	11.7

TABLE 11.9   Open Range Breakout System (Utilizing a $1,250 Protective Stop)

ONE CONTRACT PER MARKET PER TRADE
TEST PERIOD 1/1/83–8/31/99
$75 ALLOWED FOR COMMISSION AND SLIPPAGE

Individual Market	Total PL ($)	Avg PL/ Yr ($)	Max DrawDn ($)	Trds/ Yr	Win (%)	W:L	Gain/Mr +DD (%)
US Bonds	59,160	3,550	20,970	33	39.2	1.2	15
Treasury Note	25,460	1,528	23,630	31	41.9	1.1	6.1
Muni Bonds	61,050	4,361	26,010	32	42.6	1.3	15.7
British Pd.	−44	−3	41,144	29	35.9	1	0
Deutsche Mark	40,213	2,413	31,188	29	40.7	1.2	7.4
Japanese Yen	9,213	553	35,038	27	36.9	1	1.5
Swiss Franc	50,638	3,038	20,525	30	39.4	1.2	13.7
US$ Index	14,800	1,076	36,900	36	37.3	1.1	2.8
Crude Oil	37,230	2,327	10,930	32	43.6	1.3	18
Heating Oil	−42,365	−2,542	46,675	33	36.5	0.8	−5.2
Natural Gas	50,170	5,375	11,930	36	43.4	1.4	33.7
Cotton	−25,775	−1,547	58,925	36	35.4	0.9	−2.6
Coffee	183,281	10,997	47,250	37	35.6	1.5	21.1
Sugar	−13,339	−800	29,926	38	36.3	0.9	−2.6
Soybeans	22,375	1,343	25,190	36	38.2	1.1	5.1
Corn	19,800	1,188	8,800	28	40	1.3	12.7
Wheat	−6,188	−371	19,900	34	38.9	1	−1.8
Silver	17,745	1,065	45,780	39	36.7	1.1	2.2
Gold	−29,650	−1,779	44,850	36	36.9	0.8	−3.9
Live Cattle	−18,140	−1,088	24,356	38	38.2	0.9	−4.4
Pork Bellies	−13,804	−828	34,100	36	40.3	1	−2.3
Live Hogs	3,620	217	16,488	34	40.7	1	1.2

Summary Performance

Net Profit ($):	441,438
Maximum Drawdown ($):	73,591

performance, if they are used correctly. Overall, we feel that trailing stops offer the best method of taking profits. A trailing stop will follow a market and lock profits in at certain levels. Many times a trending market will retrace a certain percentage before it continues in the initial direction of the trend. Trailing stops give the markets room to gyrate, before taking a profit. These types of stops do not limit the big winners as does the profit objectives.

TABLE 11.10   Open Range Breakout System (Utilizing a Dynamic Protective Stop)

ONE CONTRACT PER MARKET PER TRADE
TEST PERIOD 1/1/83–8/31/99
$75 ALLOWED FOR COMMISSION AND SLIPPAGE

Individual Market	Total PL ($)	Avg PL/ Yr ($)	Max DrawDn ($)	Trds/ Yr	Win (%)	W:L	Gain/Mr +DD (%)
US Bonds	71,890	4,313	23,270	32	43.5	1.2	16.6
Treasury Note	33,640	2,018	23,930	31	43.4	1.2	7.9
Muni Bonds	69,670	4,976	33,940	31	44.5	1.4	13.9
British Pd.	19,669	1,180	33,544	27	41	1.1	3.4
Deutsche Mark	35,188	2,111	36,113	29	41.6	1.2	5.6
Japanese Yen	54,638	3,278	25,813	26	41.9	1.2	11.6
Swiss Franc	53,263	3,196	24,050	29	43.1	1.2	12.4
US$ Index	23,210	1,688	35,860	35	39.8	1.1	4.5
Crude Oil	42,280	2,643	9,590	32	44.1	1.3	22.8
Heating Oil	–46,053	–2,763	52,378	32	37.2	0.8	–5.1
Natural Gas	53,190	5,699	9,840	36	43.2	1.5	41.2
Cotton	–16,140	–968	57,910	36	37.1	0.9	–1.6
Coffee	182,269	10,936	50,925	36	40.3	1.4	19.6
Sugar	–12,522	–751	32,536	38	36.1	0.9	–2.3
Soybeans	32,380	1,943	31,275	35	38.8	1.2	6
Corn	16,138	968	9,463	29	39.1	1.2	9.7
Wheat	–13,063	–784	21,263	35	39.1	0.9	–3.6
Silver	38,265	2,296	39,805	38	38.4	1.2	5.4
Gold	–27,940	–1,676	44,260	36	36.9	0.8	–3.7
Live Cattle	–18,296	–1,098	24,324	38	38.1	0.9	–4.4
Pork Bellies	1,844	111	31,180	36	42.4	1	0.3
Live Hogs	4,784	287	16,816	34	40.7	1	1.6

Summary Performance

Net Profit ($):	594,273
Maximum Drawdown ($):	75,490

TABLE 11.11 Open Range Breakout System (Optimized over Several Different Profit Objectives)

ONE CONTRACT PER MARKET PER TRADE
TEST PERIOD 1/1/83–8/31/99
$75 ALLOWED FOR COMMISSION AND SLIPPAGE

	Dollar Stop Amount	Total PL ($)	Avg PL/Yr ($)	Max DrawDn ($)	Win (%)	TIM (%)	W:L	Gain/Mr +DD (%)
US	250	28,110	1,687	16,290	42	79.7	1.2	8.9
US	500	31,900	1,914	20,900	42	68.1	1.1	8.1
US	750	30,050	1,803	17,740	40	59	1.1	8.8
US	1,000	42,880	2,573	23,420	39	54.8	1.1	9.9
US	1,250	53,150	3,189	19,210	38	51.9	1.2	14.6
US	1,500	77,750	4,665	16,890	36	50.7	1.3	23.8
US	1,750	60,750	3,645	19,800	35	47.1	1.2	16.2
US	2,000	62,660	3,760	23,950	35	45.7	1.2	14.1
TY	250	1,040	62	20,020	40	74.7	1	0.3
TY	500	16,670	1,000	16,250	38	62.7	1.1	5.6
TY	750	16,490	989	18,260	36	52.8	1.1	5
TY	1,000	28,220	1,693	16,890	35	48.9	1.1	9.2
TY	1,250	27,310	1,639	21,370	34	46.3	1.1	7.2
TY	1,500	19,250	1,155	22,130	33	44.3	1.1	4.9
TY	1,750	23,960	1,438	21,610	33	43.8	1.1	6.2
TY	2,000	23,960	1,438	20,940	32	43.5	1.1	6.4
MB	250	28,150	2,011	15,970	41	78.4	1.2	11.3
MB	500	44,920	3,209	22,930	41	67	1.3	13
MB	750	56,150	4,011	29,280	39	58.7	1.3	12.9
MB	1,000	59,640	4,260	26,610	37	53.6	1.3	15
MB	1,250	87,530	6,252	26,910	37	52	1.5	21.8
MB	1,500	91,580	6,541	23,640	36	50.1	1.5	25.7
MB	1,750	83,360	5,954	18,950	34	48.2	1.4	28.7
MB	2,000	97,310	6,951	23,740	34	48.3	1.5	27.2
BP	250	−11,556	−693	24,425	34	75.7	0.9	−2.7
BP	500	13,006	780	21,588	33	67.6	1.1	3.4
BP	750	−319	−19	29,063	32	59.5	1	−0.1
BP	1,000	−15,144	−909	39,494	33	52.6	0.9	−2.2
BP	1,250	4,881	293	29,794	32	48.9	1	0.9
BP	1,500	−10,681	−641	42,331	31	46.2	1	−1.5
BP	1,750	7,294	−438	36,188	31	44.4	1	−1.2
BP	2,000	2,738	164	31,944	30	44.3	1	0.5
DM	250	−3,650	−219	18,638	37	73.3	1	−1.1
DM	500	4,675	281	25,313	36	61.7	1	1.1
DM	750	8,938	536	22,963	35	53.6	1	2.2
DM	1,000	5,113	307	31,738	33	48.7	1	0.9
DM	1,250	1,788	107	33,225	33	45.3	1	0.3
DM	1,500	11,150	669	34,850	32	44.7	1	1.8
DM	1,750	17,975	1,079	40,913	32	44.6	1.1	2.6
DM	2,000	22,813	1,369	39,113	31	43.7	1.1	3.4

(continued)

TABLE 11.11 *Continued*

	Dollar Stop Amount	Total PL ($)	Avg PL/Yr ($)	Max DrawDn ($)	Win (%)	TIM (%)	W:L	Gain/Mr +DD (%)
JY	250	−7,963	−478	20,225	31	72.7	1	−2.1
JY	500	−2,450	−147	26,013	30	64.1	1	−0.5
JY	750	−2,100	−126	34,275	29	56.5	1	−0.3
JY	1,000	5,763	346	34,050	28	52.3	1	0.9
JY	1,250	6,088	365	35,138	28	49.6	1	1
JY	1,500	−1,750	−105	42,938	28	47.1	1	−0.2
JY	1,750	3,275	197	36,888	28	45.8	1	0.5
JY	2,000	8,038	482	33,313	28	45	1	1.3
SF	250	600	36	30,763	38	76.9	1	0.1
SF	500	11,475	689	23,050	36	67.1	1.1	2.8
SF	750	24,513	1,471	28,425	35	59.9	1.1	4.9
SF	1,000	31,850	1,911	33,625	34	53.7	1.1	5.4
SF	1,250	34,938	2,096	30,088	33	51.9	1.1	6.6
SF	1,500	38,025	2,282	26,450	33	49.5	1.1	8.1
SF	1,750	26,300	1,578	29,800	32	48	1.1	5
SF	2,000	54,450	3,267	24,713	32	47.5	1.2	12.4
DX	250	−21,290	−1,548	33,070	45	70.8	0.9	−4.5
DX	500	−19,510	−1,419	42,340	43	58.8	0.9	−3.2
DX	750	−12,690	−923	35,060	42	49.9	0.9	−2.5
DX	1,000	−9,670	−703	36,090	41	45.1	1	−1.9
DX	1,250	5,900	429	35,860	40	43.1	1	1.2
DX	1,500	22,620	1,645	36,270	38	42.6	1.1	4.4
DX	1,750	21,030	1,529	36,350	38	41.7	1.1	4.1
DX	2,000	9,130	664	35,520	37	40.4	1	1.8
CL	250	−13,120	−820	16,080	40	66.9	0.9	−4.5
CL	500	−5,600	−350	10,280	38	52.9	1	−2.8
CL	750	11,220	701	9,090	36	47.1	1.1	6.3
CL	1,000	24,110	1,507	10,710	35	46	1.2	11.8
CL	1,250	30,830	1,927	10,260	34	44.7	1.2	15.7
CL	1,500	33,240	2,078	11,490	34	44.6	1.2	15.4
CL	1,750	36,400	2,275	8,810	33	44.3	1.3	21
CL	2,000	39,360	2,460	8,130	33	44	1.3	24.2
HO	250	−7,959	−478	21,130	39	72.5	0.9	−2.1
HO	500	−17,157	−1,029	23,709	38	56.8	0.9	−4
HO	750	−19,270	−1,156	30,202	36	48.2	0.9	−3.6
HO	1,000	−12,852	−771	27,325	35	45.8	0.9	−2.6
HO	1,250	−33,814	−2,029	39,673	35	41.8	0.9	−4.9
HO	1,500	−38,014	−2,281	44,407	34	40	0.8	−4.9
HO	1,750	−34,121	−2,047	38,900	33	38.7	0.9	−5
HO	2,000	−38,212	−2,293	45,070	33	37.7	0.8	−4.9
NG	250	20,330	2,178	9,050	43	74.6	1.3	16.7
NG	500	15,790	1,692	12,020	42	59.4	1.2	10.6
NG	750	17,510	1,876	11,350	41	51.2	1.2	12.2
NG	1,000	17,780	1,905	10,330	40	47.5	1.2	13.3
NG	1,250	28,310	3,033	9,870	40	46.2	1.2	21.9
NG	1,500	22,170	2,375	8,540	38	44	1.2	18.9
NG	1,750	35,260	3,778	8,100	38	44.2	1.3	31.2
NG	2,000	40,170	4,304	8,110	38	43.5	1.3	35.5

TABLE 11.12   Open Range Breakout System (Utilizing a $1,750 Profit Objective)

ONE CONTRACT PER MARKET PER TRADE
TEST PERIOD 1/1/83–8/31/99
$75 ALLOWED FOR COMMISSION AND SLIPPAGE

Individual Market	Total PL ($)	Avg PL/ Yr ($)	Max DrawDn ($)	Trds/ Yr	Win (%)	W:L	Gain/Mr +DD (%)
US Bonds	60,750	3,645	19,800	35	47.1	1.2	16.2
Treasury Note	23,960	1,438	21,610	33	43.8	1.1	6.2
Muni Bonds	83,360	5,954	18,950	34	48.2	1.4	28.7
British Pd.	−7,294	−438	36,188	31	44.4	1	−1.2
Deutsche Mark	17,975	1,079	40,913	32	44.6	1.1	2.6
Japanese Yen	3,275	197	36,888	28	45.8	1	0.5
Swiss Franc	26,300	1,578	29,800	32	48	1.1	5
US$ Index	21,030	1,529	36,350	38	41.7	1.1	4.1
Crude Oil	36,400	2,275	8,810	33	44.3	1.3	21
Heating Oil	−34,121	−2,047	38,900	33	38.7	0.9	−5
Natural Gas	35,260	3,778	8,100	38	44.2	1.3	31.2
Cotton	−12,290	−737	47,895	38	39.2	0.9	−1.5
Coffee	52,969	3,178	72,300	40	46.4	1.1	4.1
Sugar	−13,126	−788	34,328	39	36.4	0.9	−2.2
Soybeans	9,785	587	25,435	38	39.3	1	2.2
Corn	12,613	757	7,450	29	39.1	1.2	9.5
Wheat	−19,038	−1,142	27,938	35	39.5	0.9	−4
Silver	10,510	631	22,975	41	40.1	1	2.5
Gold	−15,180	−911	28,750	37	38.2	0.9	−3
Live Cattle	−21,312	−1,279	27,756	39	36.8	0.9	−4.5
Pork Bellies	−4,384	−263	36,012	38	44.2	1	−0.7
Live Hogs	−2,688	−161	21,968	36	40	1	−0.7

Summary Performance

Net Profit ($):	260,586
Maximum Drawdown ($):	80,013

TABLE 11.13   Open Range Breakout System (Utilizing a Dynamic Profit Objective)

ONE CONTRACT PER MARKET PER TRADE
TEST PERIOD 1/1/83–8/31/99
$75 ALLOWED FOR COMMISSION AND SLIPPAGE

Individual Market	Total PL ($)	Avg PL/ Yr ($)	Max DrawDn ($)	Trds/ Yr	Win (%)	W:L	Gain/Mr +DD (%)
US Bonds	67,330	4,040	22,080	33	43.3	1.2	16.3
Treasury Note	41,180	2,471	20,620	32	44	1.2	11.2
Muni Bonds	77,120	5,509	33,540	32	44.2	1.4	15.6
British Pd.	11,663	700	35,575	28	41	1	1.9
Deutsche Mark	33,500	2,010	35,950	30	43	1.1	5.4
Japanese Yen	37,575	2,255	19,125	26	43.5	1.1	10.4
Swiss Franc	45,088	2,705	25,488	30	44.1	1.2	9.9
US$ Index	23,140	1,683	33,350	36	40.1	1.1	4.9
Crude Oil	47,180	2,949	9,590	33	43.6	1.3	25.4
Heating Oil	−40,295	−2,418	48,229	33	38	0.8	−4.8
Natural Gas	53,570	5,740	10,780	37	41.5	1.5	38.8
Cotton	−19,815	−1,189	58,705	36	38.1	0.9	−2
Coffee	135,319	8,119	63,019	37	41.8	1.3	12
Sugar	−13,709	−823	34,395	39	36	0.9	−2.3
Soybeans	26,320	1,579	27,965	37	37.9	1.1	5.4
Corn	15,925	956	7,863	29	39.7	1.2	11.4
Wheat	−13,425	−806	26,988	36	39.5	0.9	−2.9
Silver	53,675	3,221	27,575	39	38.7	1.2	10.7
Gold	−21,460	−1,288	37,160	36	37.9	0.9	−3.3
Live Cattle	−16,360	−982	23,672	39	37.3	0.9	−4.1
Pork Bellies	−9,844	−591	40,720	37	42.5	1	−1.4
Live Hogs	2,456	147	19,488	36	41.1	1	0.7

Summary Performance

Net Profit ($):	531,989
Maximum Drawdown ($):	86,311

CONCLUSION

What does money management really do for a trader, especially a small one? The concepts that we discussed here allows traders to customize their trading plans so that their capital is used optimally. At the minimum, these concepts can help a small trader think in the terms of risk and reward and hopefully contribute to self-preservation. We have seen some traders retool their entire trading plans, once they analyzed their trading system with money management concepts. The ideas that we discussed here are just the tip of the iceberg. There are many books devoted to money management that should be read for a more expansive view of different concepts and techniques.

12

TURNKEY SYSTEMS
AND PORTFOLIOS

This chapter presents five different portfolios, ranging from $10,000 initial capital to $300,000, to demonstrate the benefit of diversification. We have created different combinations of systems and/or markets for each portfolio. The systems that we use are the exact systems that we described in Chapter 9, they are:

1. Donchian channel breakout
2. Moving average crossover
3. Short-term open range breakout
4. S&P day trade
5. Pattern Recognition

PORTFOLIO 1 $10,000 INITIAL CAPITAL

At this level, it is difficult to achieve a sufficient level of diversification, but it can be done. We chose the Donchian Channel Breakout system and traded the Swiss Franc and sugar for this small portfolio. A portfolio of this size limits us to what we can trade; there isn't enough money to trade different systems or a lot of different markets. The equity curve for this portfolio is shown in Figure 12.1. The historical maximum draw down exceeded the initial capital of this portfolio, but the average draw down was only around $9,000. Unfortunately, the survival rate for traders with only $10,000 is extremely low. If a trader, at this

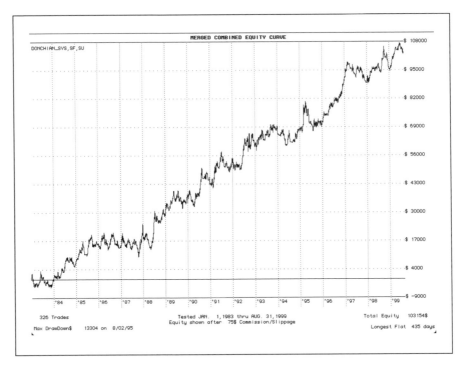

FIGURE 12.1 Portfolio 1—$10,000 (vertical = profit; horizontal = time).

level, hopes to survive for any length of time, he must try to diversify across as many markets as possible.

PORTFOLIO 2 $20,000 INITIAL CAPITAL

The size of this portfolio opens up a lot more potential of diversification than portfolio 1. We feel that this is the minimum account size for anybody wanting to trade futures and individual stocks on a mechanical trading system. Twenty thousand dollars allows room for a system to have a draw down right off the bat and keep the trader in the market for when the system turns around. We chose the same portfolio as portfolio 1, but added the Pattern Recognition system trading the soybeans. The equity curve for this portfolio is shown in Figure 12.2. The two systems meshed well together, because of the different trading frequencies of the two systems. The Donchian system is long-term whereas the Pattern Recognition system is very short-term oriented. The total profit was $145,764 and the total maximum draw down was $14,893.

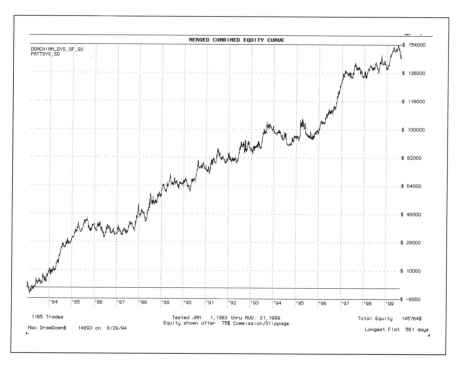

FIGURE 12.2 Portfolio 2—$20,000 (vertical = profit; horizontal = time).

PORTFOLIO 3 $50,000 INITIAL CAPITAL

This portfolio really opens up the doors of what you can achieve through trading futures. At this equity level, several systems and several markets can be traded to increase the level of diversification. We combined the three systems trading a basket of different markets. The three that we combined were the Donchian system, Pattern Recognition system, and the Simple Moving Average system (Figure 12.3). The following list gives the different markets that we traded on the different systems:

Donchian: Swiss Franc, sugar, and crude oil

Pattern recognition: U.S. bonds, natural gas, and soybeans

Simple moving average: Japanese Yen

Again the systems meshed well and we had a total profit of $400,347 and a total maximum draw down of $21,920.

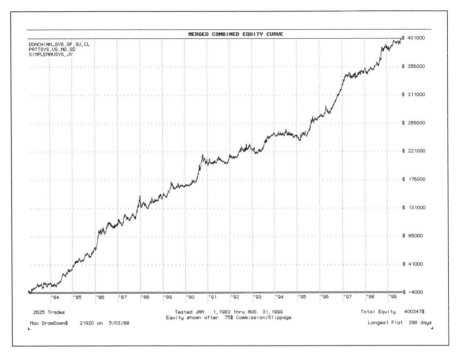

FIGURE 12.3 Portfolio 3—$50,000 (vertical = profit; horizontal = time).

PORTFOLIO 4 $100,000 INITIAL CAPITAL

This account size is usually the minimum that successful CTAs will accept for management. A trader with this type of money has a tremendous opportunity to diversify through many markets and many systems. For this portfolio, we combined the Donchian, Short-Term Open Range Breakout, Pattern Recognition, and the Simple Moving Average systems trading several different markets (Figure 12.4). The following list gives the different markets that we traded on the different systems:

Donchian: Swiss Franc, sugar, and crude oil

Pattern recognition: U.S. bonds, U.S. Treasury Notes, and soybeans

Simple moving average: Japanese Yen and natural gas

Short-term open range breakout: crude oil and corn

This portfolio made $472,602 and experienced a maximum drawdown of $26,165.

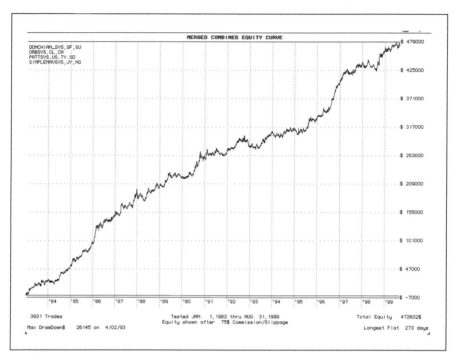

FIGURE 12.4 Portfolio 4—$100,000 (vertical = profit; horizontal = time).

PORTFOLIO 5 $300,000 INITIAL CAPITAL

A portfolio of this size is equivalent to a small institutional sized account. The most successful CTAs will accept only accounts of this size or greater. Many large CTAs won't accept a new account unless it is capitalized by at least $1 million. At this level, we were able to use the full gambit of trading systems that we discussed in Chapter 9 (Figure 12.5). We combined the following systems and markets for this portfolio:

Donchian: Japanese Yen, corn, Swiss Franc and sugar

Pattern recognition: U.S. Bonds, U.S. Treasury Notes, soybeans, and pork bellies

Simple moving average: Japanese Yen and natural gas

Short-term open range breakout: crude oil, corn, live hogs, and U.S Bonds

S&P day trade: S&P500

The synthesis of these systems and markets netted $785,809 and had a draw down of $37,389.

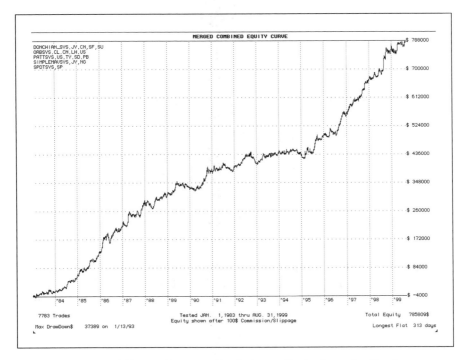

FIGURE 12.5 Portfolio 5—$300,000 (vertical = profit; horizontal = time).

CONCLUSION

One level of diversification is achieved by trading multiple markets on a single system. By trading multiple systems with multiple markets, one can achieve an even higher level of diversification. Even good systems can't trade all markets with equal success. We have shown that different methodologies have success on different markets and sectors of markets. For example, the Pattern Recognition system had much more success trading the soybeans than the Donchian system. Hence, more markets can be added to a portfolio by adding more systems. If System A has success with the U.S. bonds and Japanese Yen, but loses at trading soybeans, and System B has success with beans, then trade all three markets with their respective systems. In addition, diversification can also be achieved by trading the same market on two anticorrelated systems. Again, we can't stress the idea of diversification enough. Your trading success depends on it!

13

TOP TEN SYSTEMS OF ALL TIMES

The question that is perpetually raised at our company is: Of all the systems that Futures Truth tracks, which is the best? Since we are an independent third-party testing facility, we never answer this question. However, we do advise potential system purchasers to search our tables for trading systems that fit their own trading style. While doing so they should keep the following ideas in mind:

1. The length of a real time track record.
2. Consistent performance (not 400% one year and −10% the next).
3. The percentage of maximum drawdown to overall net profit.
4. Data and computer requirements.
5. Open system or black box preference.

Searching our vast tables of trading systems could take a lot of time and effort. In this chapter, we have saved you the time and effort and have come up with the ten systems that we feel are the best. This list changes from time to time and may change in the future. We have listed the top ten systems in order of their general methodology.

Breakout Systems

Aberration by Keith Fitschen

Dynamic Breakout by George Pruitt

Mystery System by Peter Aan

STC Vbased S&P Day Trade by Stafford Trading Company

R-Breaker S&P Day Trade by Richard Saidenberg

Trend Following Systems

Benchmark by Curtis Arnold

DCS II by Peter Aan

Dollar Trader by Dave Fox

Golden SX by Randy Stuckey

Counter Trend Systems

Big Blue by Vilar Kelly

Table 13.1 gives the most pertinent facts about each system.

TABLE 13.1 Top Ten Systems

System	Cost ($)	Number of Historical Days Required	Number of Parameters	Requires Intraday Data	What Type of Markets
Aberration	1,495	80	3	No	Variety
Benchmark	995	100	5	No	Variety
Big Blue	1,000	5	10	No	S&P 500
DCS II	695	56	4	No	Variety
Dollar Trader for Curr.	750	20	10	No	DX, JY, DM
Dynamic Breakout	300	60	4	No	Variety
Golden SX	1,495	30	5	No	Variety
Mystery System	95	50	2	No	Variety
R-Breaker	2,500	5	9	Yes	S&P 500
STC-vbased	1,875	10	9	Yes	S&P 500

Aberration by Keith Fitschen

4241 Pennywood Dr.
Beavercreek, OH 45430
(937) 320-1332

Aberration is a system developed in December 1993 by Keith Fitschen. It performed well since release date and when hypothetically tested back to 1983. We consider his Aberration system among the best in the business. To get the most out of this system, we recommend knowing your drawdown tolerance before you start trading, and trade Aberration with a large, diversified portfolio—as we understand Fitschen does himself. This system also works well with international markets. A computer is necessary for this system (Table 13.2 and Figure 13.1).

TABLE 13.2   Aberration

ONE CONTRACT PER TRADE
TEST PERIOD 1/1/83–8/31/99
$75 ALLOWED FOR COMMISSION AND SLIPPAGE

Individual Market	Total PL ($)	Avg PL/ Yr ($)	Max DrawDn ($)	Trds/ Yr	Win (%)	W:L	Gain/Mr +DD (%)
Coffee	78,638	4,718	76,425	5	42.7	1.5	5.8
Cotton	54,845	3,291	12,835	6	43.4	1.7	23.8
Crude Oil	48,490	3,031	10,800	7	56.4	2	23.6
Swiss Franc	55,600	3,336	16,588	5	51.8	1.6	18.2
Deutsche Mark	42,925	2,576	12,000	5	50	1.6	19.3
British Pd.	26,906	1,614	28,138	5	40	1.2	5.4
Treasury Note	53,970	3,238	16,180	4	52.8	2.2	18.3

Summary Performance

Net Profit ($):	361,374
Maximum Drawdown ($):	73,360

FIGURE 13.1 Abberation system equity curve.

Benchmark by Curtis Arnold

222 S. U.S. Hwy #1
Suite 203
Tequesta, FL 33469

Benchmark is a computerized futures trading system that has performed well since its release date in April 1993. It seems to give the best results when used to trade a basket of commodities, approximately five or more. It is a simple longer term trend following system originally designed by Ted Shen. Curtis Arnold, developer of the Pattern Probability System and author of *Curtis Arnold's PPS Trading System—A Proven Method of Consistently Beating the Market,* purchased the rights to the software in 1995. This system is similar to Aberration in trading time frame, but is considerably different in approach. Benchmark has performed well on portfolios made up of mostly commodities such as soybeans, corn, live cattle, and wheat. A computer is necessary for this system (Table 13.3 and Figure 13.2).

TABLE 13.3   Benchmark

ONE CONTRACT PER TRADE
TEST PERIOD 1/1/83–8/31/99
$75 ALLOWED FOR COMMISSION AND SLIPPAGE

Individual Market	Total PL ($)	Avg PL/ Yr ($)	Max DrawDn ($)	Trds/ Yr	Win (%)	W:L	Gain/Mr +DD (%)
British Pd.	21,344	1,281	63,125	9	38.5	1.1	2.0
Japanese Yen	117,100	7,026	18,950	8	50.0	1.8	32.7
Swiss Franc	60,525	3,632	33,725	8	47.8	1.3	10.2
US Bonds	39,140	2,348	26,610	9	43.1	1.2	8.0
Deutsche Mark	17,063	1,024	29,663	7	45.2	1.1	3.3
Coffee	190,313	11,419	40,856	11	44.4	1.7	25.0
Cotton	60,410	3,625	43,080	8	52.4	1.6	8.2
Orange Juice	42,788	2,567	13,305	8	54.4	1.6	17.9
Soybeans	−10,910	−655	42,335	9	41.5	0.9	−1.5
Silver	−15,955	−957	32,585	8	44.6	0.9	−2.7
Crude Oil	55,330	3,458	13,370	8	53.3	1.8	22.5
Natural Gas	14,130	1,514	24,450	9	48.8	1.2	5.3
Pork Bellies	58,148	3,489	17,308	8	53.5	1.5	17.7
Sugar	11,032	662	7,818	6	50.5	1.2	7.8
Copper	863	52	31,725	8	45.7	1.0	0.2

Summary Performance

Net Profit ($):	660,979
Maximum Drawdown ($):	89,104

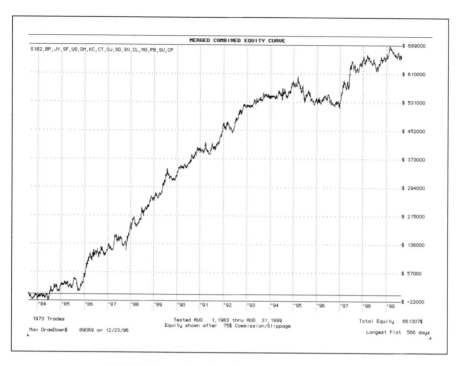

FIGURE 13.2 Benchmark system equity curve.

Big Blue by Vilar Kelly and Mike Barna

11 Pinecrest Dr.　　　　or　　　　140 Old Orchard Drive
Flat Rock, NC 28731　　　　　　　Las Gatos, CA 95032
(828) 697-6502　　　　　　　　　　(408) 356-1800

Mr. Vilar Kelly is a highly respected technician and gives good support to purchasers of his system. He has partnered with Mike Barna, another respected technician and Easy Language expert. He periodically makes slight changes to his methodology which he makes available to his clients at no cost. This is one of the best performing S&P day trade systems that we've seen. Parts of this system were originally released in September 1992. The methodology is unique and might be valuable even if it did not make money based on the unique concepts. Performance has been excellent since release. Back testing also looks excellent. Big Blue is similar to the other S&P day trade systems in this list, but is much more conservative. A computer and intraday data are necessary for this system (Table 13.4 and Figure 13.3).

TABLE 13.4　The Big Blue

ONE CONTRACT PER TRADE
TEST PERIOD 1/1/86–8/31/99
$100 ALLOWED FOR COMMISSION AND SLIPPAGE

Total Net P/L ($)	100,243	Avg. Net/Year ($)	7,335
Winning Months (%)	62	Avg. Ret. MaxDD/Yr (%)	47
		Avg. Ret. with Time (%)	432
Max DrawDn ClsTrd ($)	9,825		
Max DrawDn w/OTE ($)	9,825		
Best Trade ($)	6,588	Worst Trade ($)	−1,700
Average Trade ($)	114	Net Prof:Loss Ratio	1.5
Average Win ($)	689	Average Loss ($)	−461
Long Net P/L ($)	53,470	Short Net P/L ($)	46,773
No. of Trades	878	Avg. Trades/Year	64
No. of Winning Trades	439	Percent Winners (%)	50.00
No. of Losing Trades	439	Most Cons. Losses	10
Avg. Days Per Trade	0.4	Longest Flat Time (Days)	252
Time in the Market (%)	11	Sharpe Ratio	0.32

	Net P/L ($)	Max ClsTrd ($)	No. of Trades	Win (%)	Avg Win	Cons Loss	Flat No. of Days
Last 6 months	4,500	7,758	38	39.5	1,677	7	61
Last 12 months	−2,210	8,158	71	28.2	2,040	10	78
This year	−825	7,758	45	33.3	1,677	7	62
Last year	7,895	9,578	76	35.5	1,878	10	146
Total	100,243	9,825	878	50.0	689	10	252

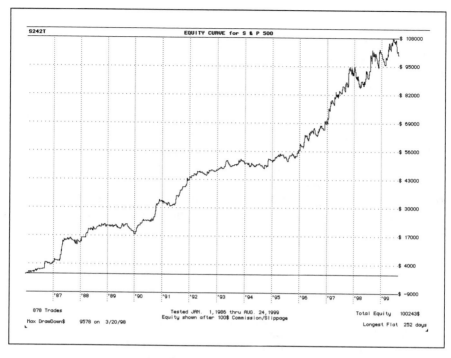

FIGURE 13.3 Big Blue equity curve.

DCS-II by Peter Aan

PWA Futures
2607 Partridge Ave.
Arlington, TX 76017
(972) 386-2901

Peter Aan is a respected technician and is registered with the NFA, thus any information you get from him should be correct. DCS-II is the oldest system in this list. This system also has different parameters for each market, but this doesn't concern us too much due to the fact that the parameters are very similar and they have not been modified since the system was released to the public. DCS-II was released in 1991. A computer is not necessary for this system, but it would make life easier (Table 13.5 and Figure 13.4).

TABLE 13.5   DCS II

ONE CONTRACT PER TRADE
TEST PERIOD 1/1/83–8/31/99
$75 ALLOWED FOR COMMISSION AND SLIPPAGE

Individual Market	Total PL ($)	Avg PL/ Yr ($)	Max DrawDn ($)	Trds/ Yr	Win (%)	W:L	Gain/Mr +DD (%)
Japanese Yen	140,963	8,458	16,375	6	52.3	2.7	44.7
Swiss Franc	71,525	4,292	21,163	7	46.7	1.6	18.8
Pork Bellies	7,916	475	29,532	8	44.5	1.1	1.5
Coffee	103,069	6,184	88,088	8	44.9	1.5	6.7
Sugar	3,718	223	16,341	7	46.3	1.1	1.3

Summary Performance

Net Profit ($):	326,780
Maximum Drawdown ($):	76,095

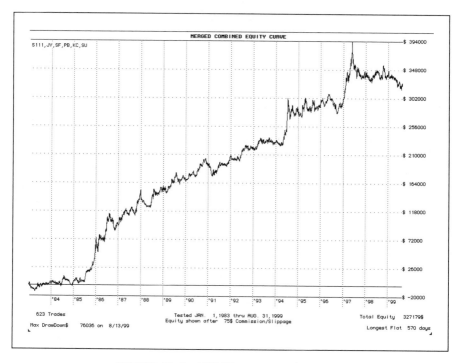

FIGURE 13.4 DCS-II system equity curve.

Dollar Trader for Currencies by Dave Fox

149 Sweet Bay Ave.
New Smyrna Beach, FL 32168
(904) 428-8847

Dave Fox is one of the most honest men we have ever met in this industry. He is a highly respected trader and system developer. He is a long time trader and is registered with the NFA and will trade his system for you. His personal trading style includes the use of options. Dollar Trader is one of the most consistent systems we have seen. The system has 10 parameters which are not optimized and are identical for all markets. You do need a computer and his software to trade the system (Table 13.6 and Figure 13.5).

TABLE 13.6 Dollar Trader for Currencies—Deutsche Mark

ONE CONTRACT PER TRADE
TEST PERIOD 1/1/86–8/31/99
$75 ALLOWED FOR COMMISSION AND SLIPPAGE

Total Net P/L ($)	53,525	Avg. Net/Year ($)	3,916
Winning Months (%)	55	Avg. Ret. MaxDD/Yr (%)	32
		Avg. Ret. with Time (%)	38
Max DrawDn ClsTrd ($)	9,663		
Max DrawDn w/OTE ($)	10,913		
Best Trade ($)	12,350	Worst Trade ($)	−6,313
Average Trade ($)	428	Net Prof:Loss Ratio	1.7
Average Win ($)	2,214	Average Loss ($)	−1,169
Long Net P/L ($)	30,100	Short Net P/L ($)	23,425
No. of Trades	1,231	Avg. Trades/Year	9
No. of Winning Trades	488	Percent Winners (%)	47.20
No. of Losing Trades	743	Most Cons. Losses	4
Avg. Days Per Trade	0.5	Longest Flat Time (Days)	632
Time in the Market (%)	25	Sharpe Ratio	0.15

	Net P/L ($)	Max ClsTrd ($)	No. of Trades	Win (%)	Avg Win	Cons Loss	Flat No. of Days
Last 6 months	1,938	838	4	50.0	1,388	2	36
Last 12 months	5,475	3,025	9	44.4	2,335	3	116
This year	5,913	838	5	60.0	2,250	2	36
Last year	−2,888	3,763	12	33.3	881	4	239
Total	53,525	9,663	125	47.2	2,214	4	632

Dollar Trader for Currencies—Dollar Index

ONE CONTRACT PER TRADE
TEST PERIOD 1/1/86–8/31/99
$75 ALLOWED FOR COMMISSION AND SLIPPAGE

Total Net P/L ($)	71,770	Avg. Net/Year ($)	5,251
Winning Months (%)	56	Avg. Ret. MaxDD/Yr (%)	42
		Avg. Ret. with Time (%)	53
Max DrawDn ClsTrd ($)	10,720		
Max DrawDn w/OTE ($)	11,240		
Best Trade ($)	9,535	Worst Trade ($)	−4,495
Average Trade ($)	588	Net Prof:Loss Ratio	1.9
Average Win ($)	2,721	Average Loss ($)	−1,163
Long Net P/L ($)	20,490	Short Net P/L ($)	51,280
No. of Trades	122	Avg. Trades/Year	9
No. of Winning Trades	55	Percent Winners (%)	45.10
No. of Losing Trades	67	Most Cons. Losses	9
Avg. Days Per Trade	22.3	Longest Flat Time (Days)	592
Time in the Market (%)	79	Sharpe Ratio	0.19

(continued)

TABLE 13.6 *Continued*

	Net P/L ($)	Max ClsTrd ($)	No. of Trades	Win (%)	Avg Win	Cons Loss	Flat No. of Days
Last 6 months	2,950	540	4	75.0	1,163	1	36
Last 12 months	6,910	3,130	9	55.6	2,116	3	128
This year	6,290	540	5	80.0	1,708	1	36
Last year	−5,180	6,330	14	14.3	2,140	9	249
Total	71,770	10,720	122	45.1	2,721	9	592

Dollar Trader for Currencies—Japanese Yen

ONE CONTRACT PER TRADE
TEST PERIOD 1/1/86–8/31/99
$75 ALLOWED FOR COMMISSION AND SLIPPAGE

Total Net P/L ($)	141,663	Avg. Net/Year ($)	10,366
Winning Months (%)	61	Avg. Ret. MaxDD/Yr (%)	53
		Avg. Ret. with Time (%)	67
Max DrawDn ClsTrd ($)	10,700		
Max DrawDn w/OTE ($)	16,975		
Best Trade ($)	17,863	Worst Trade ($)	−8,663
Average Trade ($)	1,336	Net Prof:Loss Ratio	2.7
Average Win ($)	3,684	Average Loss ($)	−1,846
Long Net P/L ($)	69,288	Short Net P/L ($)	72,375
No. of Trades	106	Avg. Trades/Year	8
No. of Winning Trades	61	Percent Winners (%)	57.50
No. of Losing Trades	45	Most Cons. Losses	4
Avg. Days Per Trade	25.9	Longest Flat Time (Days)	487
Time in the Market (%)	79	Sharpe Ratio	0.27

	Net P/L ($)	Max ClsTrd ($)	No. of Trades	Win (%)	Avg Win	Cons Loss	Flat No. of Days
Last 6 months	8,975	863	4	50.0	5,338	1	61
Last 12 months	21,788	1,475	7	57.1	6,031	2	151
This year	11,063	1,475	6	50.0	4,467	2	151
Last year	17,750	4,138	7	57.1	6,100	2	91
Total	141,663	10,700	106	57.5	3,684	4	487

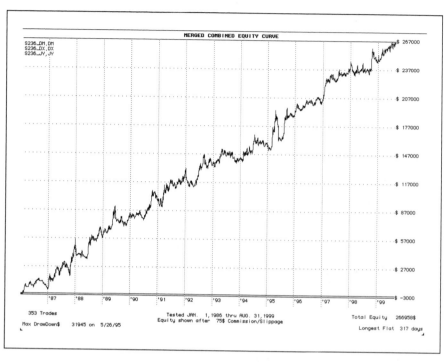

FIGURE 13.5 Dollar trader equity curve.

Dynamic Breakout System by George Pruitt

815 Hillside Rd.
Hendersonville, NC 28791
(828) 697-0273

Dynamic Breakout was developed by George Pruitt at Futures Truth as
a type of Donchian system, where the breakout is calculated dynamically based on volatility. The system uses a $1500 money management
stop. This system was developed in March 1996 and is available for
$300. It can easily be programmed into an Excel spreadsheet (Table
13.7 and Figure 13.6). The Easy Language Code for this system is located in Appendix A.

TABLE 13.7   Dynamic Breakout System

ONE CONTRACT PER TRADE
TEST PERIOD 1/1/83–8/31/99
$75 ALLOWED FOR COMMISSION AND SLIPPAGE

Individual Market	Total PL ($)	Avg PL/ Yr ($)	Max DrawDn ($)	Trds/ Yr	Win (%)	W:L	Gain/Mr +DD (%)
US Bonds	46,560	2,794	23,290	11	38.9	1.3	10.8
Japanese Yen	149,375	8,963	15,138	9	45.3	2.4	50.6
Swiss Franc	88,775	5,327	14,050	9	44.3	1.6	33.8
Live Cattle	532	32	14,892	12	38.2	1	0.2
Cotton	39,750	2,385	28,390	11	38.9	1.3	8.1
Copper	3,550	213	19,588	11	38.8	1	1
Crude Oil	30,270	1,892	20,690	12	43.8	1.3	8.3

Summary Performance

Net Profit ($):	358,598
Maximum Drawdown ($):	29,519

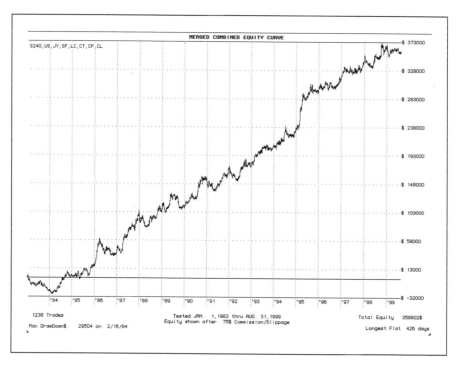

FIGURE 13.6 Dynamic breakout equity curve.

Golden SX by Randy Stuckey

5 Cedar Lane
Crawfordsville, IN 47933
(765) 866-8001

This is a intermediate term system that trades 9 to 12 times per year. It was released in July 1996. The logic is simple and is the same for all futures. Golden SX is an oscillator-based trend following system. There are different parameters for each market. Many times system vendors that have different parameter sets for different markets are criticized that they over-optimized the system. In an attempt to dispel this notion, Randy Stuckey has had us follow a constant version of his Golden SX system. The optimized version has outperformed the constant version and both have been highly successful. Randy Stuckey is a respected technician and his system requires a computer (Table 13.8 and Figure 13.7).

TABLE 13.8   Golden SX

ONE CONTRACT PER TRADE
TEST PERIOD 1/1/83–8/31/99
$75 ALLOWED FOR COMMISSION AND SLIPPAGE

Individual Market	Total PL ($)	Avg PL/ Yr ($)	Max DrawDn ($)	Trds/ Yr	Win (%)	W:L	Gain/Mr +DD (%)
Japanese Yen	135,000	8,100	15,238	7	46.2	2.4	45.5
Coffee	137,494	8,250	30,094	8	51.1	2.3	23.6
Cotton	84,195	5,052	18,740	7	51.2	2.1	25.6
Crude Oil	53,620	3,351	14,500	9	57	1.9	20.3
Treasury Note	74,710	4,483	14,600	8	50	1.9	27.9
Live Cattle	14,540	872	12,224	9	50.3	1.3	6.8

Summary Performance

Net Profit ($):	499,395
Maximum Drawdown ($):	25,267

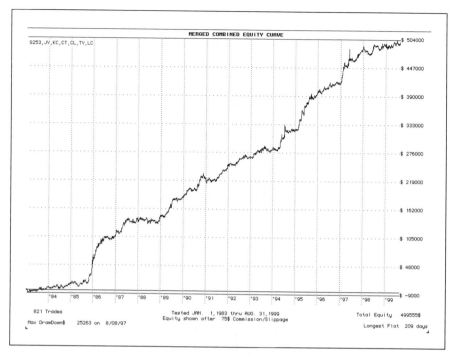

FIGURE 13.7 Golden SX equity curve.

Mystery System by Peter Aan

2607 Partridge Ave.
Arlington, TX 76017
(972) 386-2901

This is a long-term system that has been around for a long time. Peter Aan, recognizing the value, offered this to traders at a very modest price, only $95. We believe this system will continue to show good performance through the years. Don't let the selling price fool you. One thing that we have discovered is that there is no relationship between the price and quality of a trading system. As we stated earlier, Peter Aan is a respected technician and is registered with the NFA (Table 13.9 and Figure 13.8).

TABLE 13.9   Mystery System

ONE CONTRACT PER TRADE
TEST PERIOD 1/1/83–8/31/99
$75 ALLOWED FOR COMMISSION AND SLIPPAGE

Individual Market	Total PL ($)	Avg PL/ Yr ($)	Max DrawDn ($)	Trds/ Yr	Win (%)	W:L	Gain/Mr +DD (%)
British Pd.	87,631	5,258	22,113	20	38.5	1.4	22.3
Deutsche Mark	46,900	2,814	21,675	13	43.8	1.3	12.2
Japanese Yen	164,738	9,884	21,625	7	54.6	2.7	40.9
Swiss Franc	93,313	5,599	19,900	9	51	1.6	25.9
Coffee	180,694	10,842	33,675	18	39.7	1.6	28.1

Summary Performance

Net Profit ($):	573,275
Maximum Drawdown ($):	35,425

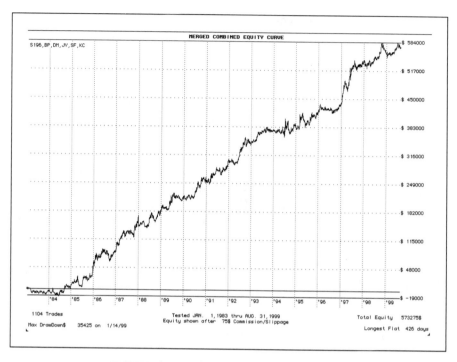

FIGURE 13.8 Mystery system equity curve.

R-Breaker by Richard Saidenberg

35 Tamarack Way
Pleasantville, NY 10570
(914) 741-2147

This system was developed by Rick Saidenberg in July 1993 for S&P day trading. A computer and software makes this system manageable. You do have to follow the market during the day but not closely, approximately every 45 minutes. R-Breaker is a breakout and countertrend system, so in fact there are two systems working simultaneously. One system takes the breakout trades and the other takes the failed breakouts. It is very aggressive and will trade ten plus times a month. A fixed money management stop is incorporated into the logic (Table 13.10 and Figure 13.9).

TABLE 13.10　R-Breaker

ONE CONTRACT PER TRADE
TEST PERIOD 1/1/90–8/31/99
$100 ALLOWED FOR COMMISSION AND SLIPPAGE

Total Net P/L ($)	166,813	Avg. Net/Year ($)	12,206
Winning Months (%)	66	Avg. Ret. MaxDD/Yr (%)	54
		Avg. Ret. with Time (%)	230
Max DrawDn ClsTrd ($)	16,935		
Max DrawDn w/OTE ($)	16,935		
Best Trade ($)	12,250	Worst Trade ($)	−1,468
Average Trade ($)	86	Net Prof:Loss Ratio	1.4
Average Win ($)	703	Average Loss ($)	−449
Long Net P/L ($)	102,975	Short Net P/L ($)	63,838
No. of Trades	1,231	Avg. Trades/Year	142
No. of Winning Trades	488	Percent Winners (%)	46.50
No. of Losing Trades	743	Most Cons. Losses	12
Avg. Days Per Trade	0.5	Longest Flat Time (Days)	432
Time in the Market (%)	25	Sharpe Ratio	0.33

	Net P/L ($)	Max ClsTrd ($)	No. of Trades	Win (%)	Avg Win	Cons Loss	Flat No. of Days
Last 6 months	23,475	7,088	78	37.2	2,391	5	61
Last 12 months	29,608	11,560	152	35.5	2,305	8	76
This year	20,740	9,300	102	35.3	2,296	5	61
Last year	20,045	10,015	150	40.0	1,784	9	113
Total	166,813	16,935	1,939	46.5	703	12	432

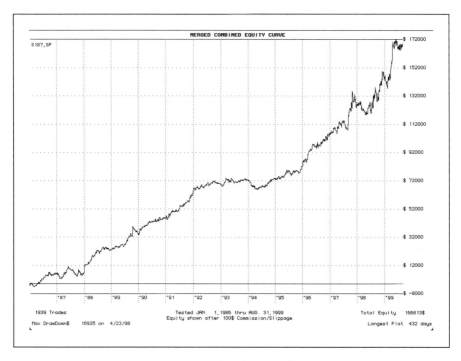

FIGURE 13.9 R-breakout equity curve.

STC-Vbased S&P Day Trade by Stafford Trading

2460 Peachtree Rd NW
Suite 1004
Atlanta, GA 30305
(800) 270-1362
(404) 949-0236

This system was released in June of 1997 and is the youngest system in this list. Rules are simple and you don't need a computer (Trade Station™ Easy Language is available and is highly recommended). This system is a volatility based breakout with a breakout failure overlay (similar to R-Breaker). In addition, there is a filter that eliminates trading during extremely high volatile time periods. This system incorporates money management schemes that are adaptive. This system is more aggressive than Big Blue but less than R-Breaker (Table 13.11 and Figure 13.10).

TABLE 13.11   S&P Day Trade System

ONE CONTRACT PER TRADE
TEST PERIOD 1/1/90–8/31/99
$100 ALLOWED FOR COMMISSION AND SLIPPAGE

Total Net P/L ($)	196,288	Avg. Net/Year ($)	14,363
Winning Months (%)	75	Avg. Ret. MaxDD/Yr (%)	78
		Avg. Ret. with Time (%)	414
Max DrawDn ClsTrd ($)	12,725		
Max DrawDn w/OTE ($)	12,725		
Best Trade ($)	10,810	Worst Trade ($)	−3,463
Average Trade ($)	136	Net Prof:Loss Ratio	1.5
Average Win ($)	792	Average Loss ($)	−485
Long Net P/L ($)	136,100	Short Net P/L ($)	60,188
No. of Trades	1,448	Avg. Trades/Year	106
No. of Winning Trades	704	Percent Winners (%)	48.60
No. of Losing Trades	744	Most Cons. Losses	8
Avg. Days Per Trade	0.4	Longest Flat Time (Days)	248
Time in the Market (%)	19	Sharpe Ratio	0.39

	Net P/L ($)	Max ClsTrd ($)	No. of Trades	Win (%)	Avg Win	Cons Loss	Flat No. of Days
Last 6 months	18,793	10,890	62	45.2	2,087	4	61
Last 12 months	31,273	12,725	120	43.3	2,340	4	115
This year	17,958	10,890	80	43.8	2,160	4	61
Last year	43,855	9,530	122	50.0	1,901	4	41
Total	196,288	12,725	1,448	48.6	792	8	248

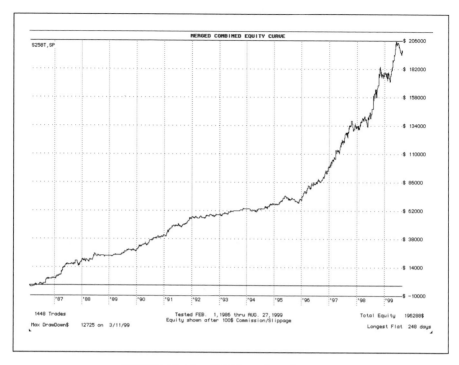

FIGURE 13.10 STC-Vbased equity curve.

BIBLIOGRAPHY

Alexander, Peter. *Beginners Guide to Computer Assisted Trading,* Traders Press Inc., Greenville, SC, 1997.

Chande, Tushar S. *Beyond Technical Analysis,* John Wiley, New York, 1997.

Chande, Tushar S., and Stanley Kroll. *The New Technical Trader,* John Wiley, New York, 1994.

Drummond, Charles. *How to Make Money in the Futures Market . . . and Lots of It!* Drummond Publications, Chicago, 1978.

Drummond, Charles. *Charles Drummond on Advanced P&L,* Drummond Publications, Chicago, 1980.

Drummond, Charles. *The P&L Labs,* Drummond Publications, Chicago, 1981.

Drummond, Charles. *The 1-1 Paper,* Drummond Publications, Chicago, 1985.

Drummond, Charles. *The Energy Paper,* Drummond Publications, Chicago, 1991.

Drummond, Charles. *P&L Accumulation/Distribution: Knowing When to Trade,* Drummond Publications, Chicago, 1993.

Drummond, Charles. *Knowing Where the Energy Is Coming From,* Drummond Publications, Chicago, 1995.

Drummond, Charles. *Pattern Picking,* Drummond Publications, Chicago, 1996.

Drummond, Charles. *Predicting Next Week's Range (and Understanding How the Daily Plays It Out),* Drummond Publications, Chicago, 1996.

Drummond, Charles. *Psycho Paper '96: P&L's Connection with Awareness,* Drummond Publications, Chicago, 1996.

Drummond, Charles, and Ted Hearne. *The Lessons, a Series of 30 Multi-Media Lessons,* Drummond and Hearne Publications, Chicago, 1997–1999.

Gallacher, William R. *Winner Take All,* Probus Publishing Company, Chicago, IL, 1994.

Knight, Sheldon. "How Clean Is Your End-Of-Day Data?" *Futures Magazine, 28:* 9 (September 1999), pp. 64–69.

Krutsinger, Joe. *Trading Systems, Secrets of the Masters,* McGraw Hill, New York, 1997.

Le Beau, Charles, and David W. Lucas. *Technical Traders Guide to Computer Analysis of the Futures Markets,* Business One Irwin, Homewood, IL, 1992.

Rotella, Rober P. *Elements of Successful Trading,* New York Institute of Finance, New York, 1992.

Smith, Gary. *How I Trade for a Living,* John Wiley, New York, 1999.

Tewels, Richard J., C. V. Harlow, and H. L. Stone. *The Commodity Futures Game,* McGraw Hill, New York, 1974.

Vince, Ralph. *Portfolio Management Formulas,* John Wiley, New York, 1990.

Wilder Jr., Welles. *New Concepts in Technical Trading Systems,* Trend Research, Greensboro, NC, 1978.

APPENDIX: EASY LANGUAGE SOURCE CODE

```
{*******************************************}
{ System #1
Program designed and coded by George Pruitt
Donchian Break Out with protective and trailing stops}

vars: daysInTrade(0), lookBack(30), midLevel(0),longLiqPt(0),shortLiqPt(0);

if(marketPosition =1 ) then
begin
        midLevel = entryPrice(0) - (highest(high,30) - lowest(low,30))/2.0;
end;
if(marketPosition =-1 ) then
begin
        midLevel = entryPrice(0) +(highest(high,30) - lowest(low,30))/2.0;
end;

if(marketPosition <> 0 and barsSinceEntry(0)>0 and
(Mod(barsSinceEntry(0),5)=0)) then
begin
    lookBack = lookBack - 2;
    lookBack = maxlist(lookBack,6);
end;

longLiqPt = maxlist(lowest(low,lookBack),midLevel);
shortLiqPt = minlist(highest(high,lookBack),midLevel);

if(barsSinceEntry(0) = 0 and marketPosition <> 0) then
begin
    longLiqPt = midLevel;
    shortLiqPt = midLevel;
end;

if(marketPosition = 1) then exitlong("long exit") at longLiqPt stop;
if(marketPosition = -1)then exitshort("short exit") at shortLiqPt stop;

buy("donchian buy") tomorrow at highest(high,30)stop;
sell("donchian sell") tomorrow at lowest(low,30) stop;

if(marketPosition = 0) then lookBack = 30;
    {*******************************************}


{*******************************************}
```

```
{ System #2
  Program designed and coded by George Pruitt
  Moving Average Cross Over with protective and trailing stops}

vars: daysInTrade(0), atr(0),ptargMult(1),longLiqPt(0),shortLiqPt(999999),
      protLongStop(0),protShortStop(0);

atr = avgtruerange(20);

if(marketposition = 1 and barssinceentry = 0) then protLongStop =
entryPrice(0) - 5*atr[1];
if(marketposition = -1 and barssinceentry = 0) then protShortStop =
entryPrice(0) + 5*atr[1];

if(marketposition <> marketposition(1)) then
begin
      ptargMult = 1;
      longLiqPt = 0;
      shortLiqPt = 999999;
end;

if(marketposition = 1 and high > entryPrice(0) + (5 *atr*ptargMult)) then
begin
      ptargMult = ptargMult + 1;
      longLiqPt = high - 5 * atr;
end;

if(marketposition = -1 and low < entryPrice(0) - (5 *atr*ptargMult)) then
begin
      ptargMult = ptargMult + 1;
      shortLiqPt = low + 5 * atr;
end;

if(marketPosition = 1)then
begin
      exitlong ("long exit") at longLiqPt stop;
      exitlong ("lprot exit") at protLongStop stop;
end;

if(marketPosition = -1)then
begin
      exitshort("short exit") at shortLiqPt stop;
      exitshort("sprot exit") at protShortStop stop;
end;

if(average(close,13)crosses above average(close,39) and close > close[39])
then
begin
      buy("macross buy") tomorrow at open;
end;

if(average(close,13)crosses below average(close,39) and close < close[39])
then
```

```
begin
      sell("macross sell") tomorrow at open;
end;
 {**********************************************}


{**********************************************}
{ System #3
  Program designed and coded by George Pruitt
  Short Term Volatility Based Open Range Break Out}

vars: daysInTrade(0), atr(0),ptargMult(1),longLiqPt(0),shortLiqPt(999999),
       protLongStop(0),protShortStop(0),lowestLow3(0),highestHigh3(0),
       bed(0),sed(0),stb(0),sts(0);

atr = avgtruerange(10);
lowestLow3 = lowest(low,3);
highestHigh3 = highest(high,3);

bed = 0;
sed = 0;

if(close>=close[1]) then sed = 1;
if(close<close[1])  then bed = 1;

if(bed = 1) then
begin
      stb = open of tomorrow + .5*(highestHigh3 - lowestLow3);
      sts = open of tomorrow - (highestHigh3 - lowestLow3);
end;
if(sed = 1) then
begin
      stb = open of tomorrow + (highestHigh3 - lowestLow3);
      sts = open of tomorrow - .5*(highestHigh3 - lowestLow3);
end;

if(marketposition = 1 and barssinceentry = 0) then protLongStop =
entryPrice(0) - 3*atr[1];
if(marketposition = -1 and barssinceentry = 0) then protShortStop =
entryPrice(0) + 3*atr[1];

if(marketposition<>marketposition(1)) then
begin
      ptargMult = 1;
      longLiqPt = 0;
      shortLiqPt = 999999;
end;

if(marketposition = 1 and high[1] > entryPrice(0) + (3 *atr[1])) then
begin
      longLiqPt = entryPrice(0);
end;
```

```
if(marketposition = -1 and low[1] < entryPrice(0) - (3 *atr[1])) then
begin
      shortLiqPt = entryPrice(0);
end;

if(marketPosition = 1)then
begin
      exitlong ("long exit") at longLiqPt stop;
      exitlong ("lprot exit") at protLongStop stop;
end;

if(marketPosition = -1)then
begin
      exitshort("short exit") at shortLiqPt stop;
      exitshort("sprot exit") at protShortStop stop;
end;

buy("stvorbo buy") tomorrow at stb stop;
sell("stvorbo sell") tomorrow at sts stop;


{*******************************************}


{*******************************************}
{ System #4
  Data 1 is a five minute bar ::: Data 2 is a daily bar
  Program designed and coded by George Pruitt
  S&P Day Trade System}

vars:
buyDay(0),sellDay(0),pct1(.30),pct2(.60),raa_days(10),canTrade(0),keyPrice(0),

otcRange(0),retrace_pct(.20),atr(0),stopp(0),hipt(0),lopt(0),retrace(0),
        hi_point(0),lo_point(0),thrust1(0),thrust2(0.0),
        stb(0),sts(0),openofday(999999),sco(0),bco(0),hday(0),lday(0),
        canBuy(0),canSell(0),counter(0),sum(0);

input: openTime(835),strtTime(900),endTime(1430);

if (t =sess1Endtime and date of data2 <> date[1] of data2) then begin
    atr = avgTrueRange(raa_days) of data2;
    value1 = absValue(open of data2 - close of data2);
    sum = 0;
    for counter = 0 to 9 Begin
        sum = sum + absValue(open[counter] of data2 - close[counter] of
    data2);
    end;
    otcRange = sum/10.0;
    canTrade = 1;
    if(otcRange/atr < 0.5) then canTrade=0;

    keyPrice = (high of data2 +low of data2 + close of data2)/3.0;
```

```
    print("keyPrice : ",keyPrice);
    stopp = atr*.30;

    hipt = keyPrice + .25*range of data2;
lopt = keyPrice - .25*range of data2;

retrace = retrace_pct*atr;

hi_point = keyPrice + .75*range of data2;
lo_point = keyPrice - .75*range of data2;

buyDay = buyDay[1];
sellDay = sellDay[1];

if(close of data2 < keyPrice) then begin
    buyDay = 0;
    sellDay = 1;
end;
if(close of data2 > keyPrice) then begin
    buyDay = 1;
    sellDay = 0;
end;

thrust1 =atr *pct1;
thrust2 =atr *pct2;

end;

if (t=openTime) then begin

    hday = 0;
    lday = 999999;
    sco = 0;
    bco = 0;
    canBuy = 1;
    canSell = 1;

    if( buyDay = 1) then begin
      stb = open + thrust1;
      sts = open - thrust2;
    end;

    if(sellDay = 1) then begin
      stb = open + thrust2;
      sts = open - thrust1;
    end;
end;

if(high>hday) then begin
    hday = high;
    if(hday>=hi_point) then sco = 1;
    end;

if(low<lday) then begin
```

```
        lday = low;
        if( lday<=lo_point) then bco = 1;
        end;

if(t>= strtTime and t<= endTime+10) then begin

        if( bco = 1 and canBuy = 1 and canTrade = 1) then begin
          buy("bco buy") tomorrow at lopt stop;
          lday = 0;
        end;

        if(sco = 1 and canSell = 1 and canTrade = 1) then begin
          sell("sco sell") tomorrow at hipt stop;
          hday = 999999;
        end;
          if(marketPosition = 1) then canBuy = 0;
          if(marketposition = -1)then canSell = 0;

          if(canTrade = 1 and canBuy = 1) then buy("buyBreakout") tomorrow at stb
stop;
          if(canTrade = 1 and canSell = 1) then sell("sellBreakout") tomorrow at
sts stop;

end;

if(marketposition=-1) then exitshort(" smmexit") entryprice+3.00 stop;
if(marketposition= 1)then exitlong(" lmmexit") entryprice-3.00 stop;


{*********************************************}

{*********************************************}
{ System # 5
  Program designed and coded by George Pruitt
  Short Term Volatility Based Open Range Break Out with Patttern Recognition}

vars: atr(0),longLiqPt(0),shortLiqPt(999999),
      protLongStop(0),protShortStop(0),lowestClose4(0),highestClose4(0),
      bed(0),sed(0),stb(0),sts(0),canTrade(0);

atr = avgtruerange(30);
lowestClose4 = lowest(close,4);
highestClose4 = highest(close,4);

canTrade = 0;
if( highestClose4 - lowestClose4 < atr) then canTrade = 1;

stb = open of tomorrow + .62*truerange;
sts = open of tomorrow - .62*truerange;

if(canTrade = 1 and entriestoday(date) = 0) then
begin
        buy("pattbuy") tomorrow at stb stop;
        sell("pattsell") tomorrow at sts stop;
```

```
end;
if(canTrade = 0) then
begin
        exitlong("longliq") at sts stop;
        exitshort("shrtliq") at stb stop;
end;
{*********************************************}
```

INDEX

A

Aan, Peter, 259, 266–267
Aberration trading system (by Keith Fitschen), 258, 260–261
Accumulation stage set-up, 12–14
Action/reactions, 88
Adaptive engine, 217
Alpha-beta bands, 178
Arnold, Curtis, 259, 262–263

B

Bar charts of price action, 3, 37–75
  anticipation of pattern completion/reversal, 71–72
  buy zones, 69
  closing price(s), 39, 40–41, 43–55
  closing with non-overlapping bars, 42
  daily range, 47–49
  entry techniques, 43
  four closes in tight range, 45, 46
  gap higher/low openings, 73–75
  hook closing, 60–64
  inside day, 49–51
  narrow range after strong demand/supply, 66
  narrow range bars, 64–68
  outside days or bars, 52
  patterns, short-term (using for profit), 39–43
  pattern gaps, 59–60
  pivot points and swings, 39–40
  profit taking, 71
  reversal day, 52–55
  short-term patterns, short-term (using for profit), 39–43
  stop point, 70 (*see also* Stop points)
  swing charts, 45–46
  three-day equilibrium reverse, 55–59
  time breakout rule, 72
  trend direction, 40, 41–42
  wide ranges, 68–69
Barna, Mike, 264
Benchmark trading system (by Curtis Arnold), 259, 262–263
Big Blue trading system (by Vilar Kelly), 259, 264–265
Big Bullish Candle, 202
Bollinger, John, 120, 178
Bollinger bands, 117, 120, 178–179, 180

Breakout:
  downside Yum-Yum, 108
  open range. *See* Open range
    breakout (BO)
  rule (time), 72
  systems (five in top ten), 258
  tight formation, 128
Bressert, Walt, 36
Bridge/CRB data vendor, 168
Buran, Bob, 103
Buying climax, 14–15
Buy zones, 69

C

Candlestick chart patterns,
  202
Capital Allocation Model,
  231–240, 241
  single market portfolio,
    232–236
  two-market portfolio,
    236–240
Chande, Tushar, 175–176, 177
Channel and trendline trading,
  76–82, 116–121. *See also*
    Trends(s)/trendline trading
  trading the 0–2 line, 78–79
  trend channel system,
    81–82
  trendline and four-close
    system (TL4C), 80–81
Clear out patterns, 114
Closing prices:
  graph, 39
  system development based on,
    43–55
Cole, George, 38
.com stocks, 5
Commodity channel index (CCI),
  174–177
Commodity Futures Trade
  Commission (CFTC), 155
Commodity Systems Inc. (CSI),
  168

Commodity Trading Advisors
  (CTA), 156, 161
Compounding returns, 240
Counter trend systems (one in
  top ten), 259
Crabel, Toby, 102
Curve fitting, 157, 209–217,
  226

D

Daily range, 47–49
Data, 166–171
DCS II trading system (by Peter
  Aan), 259, 266–267
Demand, preliminary, 88–89
DeMark, Tom, 36
Dial/Data division of Tract Data
  Corp., 168
Distribution set-up, 14–17
Diversification, 224–226,
  252–257
Doji Star (candlestick pattern),
  202
Dollar Trader (by Dave Fox),
  259, 268–271
Donchian, Richard, 182–183
Donchian breakout, 3, 117,
  182–185, 187–188, 189, 214,
  252–257, 285
Double tops and bottoms,
  110–111
Drummond, Charles, 139
Drummond geometry and the
  PLdot, 139–152
  factor-of-five rule, 150–151
  formula, 140
  key point in, 141
  multiple time frame approach,
    140, 146–150
  PLdot (Point and Line),
    140
  series of short-term moving
    averages, 140
  short-term trend lines, 140

Dynamic Breakout system (by George Pruitt), 216–219, 258, 259, 272–273
Dynamite triangle, 125–126

E

Easy language source code (Appendix), 285–291
Elliott, R.N., 28
Elliott Wave Theory, 28–36
  A-leg corrections, 32–33
  case study in crude oil, 33–34
  corrective waves or phases, 31
  literature on cycles, 36
  targets for major movements, 30–31
  trading A or ABC corrections to a thrust, 34
  trading plan approach, 35–36
  triangle corrections, 31–32
Entry methods/techniques, 43, 129
Equilibrium reverse, three-day (3DE), 55–59, 134
Equis, 168
Excalibur Testing Software, 2, 171
Exits:
  importance of, 128–133
  types of, 186–187

F

First day in rally, 100
Fitschen, Keith, 120, 258, 260–261
Four closes in tight range, 45, 46
Four-close system, trendline and (TL4C), 80–81
Fox, Dave (Dollar Trader), 259, 268–271
Fundamental *vs.* technical approach, 28
Futures Truth Company, 2–3, 171, 258

G

Gaps:
  gap higher/low openings, 73–75
  pattern gaps, 59–60
General Motors (in case study, July 1998–July 1999), 22–25
Genesis Financial Data Services, 168
Glance Market Data Service, 168
Golden SX trading system (by Randy Stuckey), 259, 274–275

H

Hadady, E., 102
Hammer (candlestick chart pattern), 202
Hardware, 164
Hearne, Ted, 139
High of low bar at a prior pivot point low (HLH), 134
High of low bar for buying and low of high bar for selling, 123–124
Hill, John, 203
Historical testing, 162, 208–227
  adaptive engine, 217
  alternative to optimization (adaptive parameters), 216–219
  curve fitting, 209–217
  Dynamic Breakout system, 216–219
  periodic reoptimization, 214–216
  simulated analysis, 208–209
Hook closing, 60–64
Hurst, J.M., 36

I

Indicators, 171–185
 Bollinger bands, 178–179,
  180
 commodity channel index
  (CCI), 174–177
 Donchian breakout, 182–185
 MACD (moving average
  convergence divergence),
  172–173, 175
 moving average crossover,
  179–182
 relative strength index (RSI),
  172, 174
 stochastics, 172, 173
Inside day, 49–51
Intraday ranges, 103–104
Investing *vs.* trading, 8
Investors Business Daily, 26

K

Kelly, Vilar, 259, 264–265
Keltner channel, 116,
  117–118
 modified, 118–120
Knight, Sheldon, 167, 170
Kroll, Stanley, 175–176, 177

Lambert, Donald, 174
Lane, George, 172
Leslie, Conrad, 7
L formation and reverse L,
  109–110
Low of a high bar at a prior
  pivot point high (LHB),
  134

M

MACD (moving average
  convergence divergence),
  172–173, 175
Mackay, Charles, 26
Margin, 163

Market(s):
 exhaustion, 19
 single market portfolio,
  Capital Allocation Model,
  232–236
 stages of market action,
  10–12
 two-market portfolio, Capital
  Allocation Model,
  236–240
Mechanical trading systems,
  153–163
 benefits of, 155–156
 caveat, 157–158
 cost of, 161
 data vendors, 166–171
 designing (*vs.* computer
  designed), 219–220
 establishing, 164–207
 example of, 154
 hardware, 164
 indicators, 171–185
 myths/facts about, 160–163
 pre-system purchase
  questions, 159–160
 software, 164–165
 vs. trading tool, 154–155
MJK Associates, 168
Money management,
  228–251
 Capital Allocation Model,
  231–240, 241
 compounding returns, 240
 formulas, 229
 placement of protective stops
  and profit targets,
  241–245
 risk of ruin, 230–231
 statistics (a necessary tool),
  229–230
Move ending, 87
Moving average convergence
  divergence (MACD),
  172–173, 175

Moving average crossover,
    179–182, 185, 188–192,
    252–257
Moving markets/stocks,
    finding/trading, 26
Mystery System trading system
    (by Peter Aan), 258, 259,
    276–277

N

Narrow range/wide range,
    64–69, 93–94, 126–127, 134
    narrow-range bars, 68
    narrow-range bars after
        strong demand or supply,
        66
    narrow-range day followed by
        wide-range bar (NRWR),
        134
    wide-range bars, 64–69
    wide-range reversal bar after
        run up, 93–94
Non-overlapping (NOL):
    bar, 134
    closing with non-overlapping
        bars, 42
    overlapping and non-
        overlapping bars, 114–115
    top and bottom, 115

O

Omega Research Inc., 168
Open range breakout (BO),
    102–104, 134, 185, 192–196,
    241–250, 252–257
    short-term, 252–257
    short-term volatility based,
        185, 192–196
Optimization:
    alternative to (adaptive
        parameters), 216–219
    periodic reoptimization,
        214–216

Outside days or bars, 52
Overlapping and non-
    overlapping bars, 114–115

P

Pattern(s), 101–138
    anticipation of pattern
        completion and reversal,
        71–72
    Bollinger bands, 117, 120
    case study, hypothetical,
        130–133
    channel trading systems,
        116–121
    clear out patterns, 114
    Donchian channels or Turtle
        system, 117
    double tops and bottoms,
        110–111
    dynamite triangle, 125–126
    gaps, 59–60
    high of low bar for buying and
        low of high bar for selling,
        123–124
    intraday ranges, 103–104
    Keltner channel, 116, 117–118
        modified, 118–120
    L formation and reverse L,
        109–110
    narrow range/wide range,
        126–127
    non-overlapping top and
        bottom, 115
    opening range breakout,
        102–104
    overlapping and non-
        overlapping bars,
        114–115
    profit protection, 124–125
    pullback, 121–123
    recognition (used in trading
        systems), 185, 201–206,
        252–257

Pattern(s) *(Continued)*
  short-term (using for profit),
    39–43
  small morning tails, 111–114
  spring and upthrust reversal
    action, 107
  spring reversal pattern,
    105–106
  three bars up/down, 124
  tight formation breakout,
    128
  trend up confirmed, 104–105
  two-day flip (2DF), 127
  two-day intersection, 116
  upthrust reversal pattern,
    106–107
  Yum-Yum continuation
    pattern, 108
Pinnacle Data Corp., 168
Pivot points and swings, 39–40
PLdot. *See* Drummond geometry
  and the PLdot
*Popular Delusions and the
  Madness of Crowds*
  (Mackay), 26
Portfolio performance,
  evaluating, 224–226
Prechter, Bob, 36
Price:
  charts of movement of (*see* Bar
    charts of price action)
  closes/closing, 39, 40–41,
    43–55
  function of, 38
  inexorable law of, 37
Profit objective/targets, 21–22,
  134, 187, 241–245
Projections, time/price, 97–99
Prophet Financial Systems, Inc.,
  168
Protective stops. *See* Stop points
Pruitt, George, 258, 259,
  272–273, 285
Psychological makeup, 6–7, 154,
  219

Pullback (PB), 121–123
  buys, 87–88
  after a thrust, 134

R

"Rainbow merchants," 9, 155
Rally:
  first day in, 100
  holding gain and rally from
    support, 91–92
  three-bar, 90–91
R-Breaker S&P Day Trade (by
  Richard Saidenberg), 258,
  259, 278–279
Reaccumulation set-up, 17–18
Relative strength index (RSI),
  172, 174
Reuters DataLink, 168
Reversal:
  day, 52–55
  exit, 186
  spring reversal pattern,
    105–106
  wide-range reversal bar after
    run up, 93–94
Risk of ruin, 230–231
Risk threshold, 5
Rotating day, 113
Rotella, Robert, 153
RSI (relative strength index),
  172, 174
Run up and run down stages,
  18–19

S

Saidenberg, Richard, 258, 259,
  278–279
Selling climax, 12, 14
Set-ups, 8–27, 92–94
  accumulation stage set-up,
    12–14
  case study (General Motors),
    22–25
  distribution set-up, 14–17

end of move, 19
judgment involved, 25–26
market exhaustion, 19
reaccumulation, 17–18
rules, 19–21
run up and run down stages,
18–19
stages of market action,
10–11
stop points, 21
target/profit objective,
21–22
trading moving markets, 26
for trend change, 92–94 (see
also Trend(s)/trendline
trading)
ultimate timing tool, 9
Sharpe ratio, 221, 224
Short-term open range breakout,
252–257
Short-term patterns, 39–43
Short-term volatility based open
range breakout, 185,
192–196
Simulated analysis, 208–209
Small morning tails, 111–114
Software, 164–165
S&P:
day trade system, 185,
196–201, 252–257
use of tools in trading
(hypothetical studies),
134–138
Speculation, 38
Spring (SP), 134
reversal pattern, 105–106
and upthrust reversal action,
107
Stafford Trading Company, 258,
259, 280–281
Stages of market action, 10–11
Statistics:
for evaluating performance,
221–224
as tool, 229–230

STC-Vbased S&P Day Trade by
Stafford Trading Company,
258, 259, 280–281
Steidlmayer, Peter, 112, 113
Stochastics, 172, 173
Stop points, 21, 70, 186–187,
241–245, 246
Stuckey, Randy, 259, 274–275
Support, holding gain and rally
from, 91–92
Support-resistance zones, 95–96
Swings/swing trading, 39–40,
45–46, 83–100
action and reactions, 88
action points for trading the
long side, 83–86
anticipation (key to successful
speculation), 86
charts, 45–46, 83
first day in rally, 100
holding gain and rally from
support, 91–92
move ending, 87
preliminary demand, 88–89
pullback buys, 87–88
sell tops after trend change,
89–90
setups for trend change, 92–94
support-resistance zones,
95–96
three-bar rallies, 90–91
three drives to a bottom, 95
thrust action, 83–86
time/price projections, 97–99
time/space, 89
trend (defining), 99–100
trend continuation, 94
wide-range reversal bar after
run up, 93–94

T

Tails, 41
small morning, 111–114
Taking profits, 71

Target/profit objective, 21–22,
    134, 187, 241–245
Taylor, George, 112
Technical analysis, 3–4, 155
    vs. fundamental approach, 28
Technology revolution, 3, 9–10
Terminal shakeout, 14
Three-bar rallies, 90–91
Three bars up/down, 124
Three-day equilibrium reverse
    (3DE), 55–59, 134
Three drives to a bottom, 95
Thrust/thrust action, 14, 34,
    83–86, 106–107, 134
Tight formation breakout, 128
Time breakout rule, 72
Time/price projections, 97–99
Time/space, and trends/swing
    trading, 89
Timing, 3, 9
Trading:
    channel, 76–82
    charts (*see* Bar charts of price
        action)
    failure rate, 4
    fundamental *vs.* technical
        approach, 28
    vs. investing, 8
    objective of (money), 4–5
    psychological makeup and,
        6–7, 154, 219
    risk, 5
    set-ups ("big picture"),
        8–27
    success and psychological
        makeup, 6–7
    trendline, 76–82
    truths about, 4–7
Trading systems:
    anatomy of, 185–206
    approaches (five) used by the
        best, 185
    Donchian channel, 185,
        187–188

evaluating performance of,
    220–224
exits, types of, 186–187
moving average cross over,
    185, 188–192
pattern recognition, 185,
    201–206
profit objective, 187
protective stop, 186–187
reversal exit, 186
short-term volatility based
    open range breakout, 185,
    192–196
S&P day trade, 185, 196–201
top ten of all time, 258–281
vs trading tool, 154–155
Trend(s)/trendline trading, 40,
    41–42, 76–82, 89–90,
    92–94, 99–100, 104–105,
    116–121, 140
channel system, 81–82,
    116–121
continuation, 94
counter trend systems (one in
    top ten), 259
defining, 99–100
direction, 40, 41–42
parallel movements, 76–78
sell tops after trend change,
    89–90
setups for trend change,
    92–94
short-term trendlines, 140
time/space, 89
trading the 0–2 line, 78–79
trend-following systems (four
    in top ten), 259
trendline and four-close
    system (TL4C), 80–81
trend up confirmed, 104–105
Turtle system, 117. *See also*
    Donchian breakout
Two-day flip (2DF), 127
Two-day intersection, 116

U

Upthrust (UT), 134
    reversal pattern, 106–107

V

Value Line, 170
Vince, Ralph, 231
Volatility, 216
Volatility based breakout, 204,
    205

W

Wide-range bar, 68–69
Wide-range reversal bar after
    run up, 93–94

Wilder, Welles, 36, 172
Williams, Larry, 102, 192

Y

Yum-Yum continuation pattern,
    108

Z

Zones of support and resistance,
    12–13